T0366225

Socio-Technical
Knowledge Management:
Studies and Initiatives

Meliha Handzic
Sarajevo School of Science and Technology, Sarajevo

IGI PUBLISHING

Hershey • New York

Acquisition Editor:	Kristin Klinger
Senior Managing Editor:	Jennifer Neidig
Managing Editor:	Sara Reed
Assistant Managing Editor:	Sharon Berger
Development Editor:	Kristin Roth
Copy Editor:	Angela Thor
Typesetter:	Elizabeth Duke
Cover Design:	Lisa Tosheff
Printed at:	Yurchak Printing Inc.

Published in the United States of America by
    IGI Publishing (an imprint of IGI Global)
    701 E. Chocolate Avenue
    Hershey PA 17033
    Tel: 717-533-8845
    Fax: 717-533-8661
    E-mail: cust@idea-group.com
    Web site: http://www.idea-group.com

and in the United Kingdom by
    IGI Publishing (an imprint of IGI Global)
    3 Henrietta Street
    Covent Garden
    London WC2E 8LU
    Tel: 44 20 7240 0856
    Fax: 44 20 7379 0609
    Web site: http://www.eurospanonline.com

   Library of Congress Cataloging-in-Publication Data

Handzic, Meliha.
  Socio-technical knowledge management : studies and initiatives / Meliha Handzic, Author.
    p. cm.
  Summary: "This book connects knowledge management theory to knowledge management practice, allow-ing the empirical research presented to resolve challenges. It provides a better understanding of the benefits and limitations of various socio-technical knowledge management initiatives, especially in the realm of social-oriented knowledge culture, communities, initiatives and rewards, measurement, technology-oriented knowledge repositories, modeling, rating, alerting, and discovery systems"--Provided by publisher.
  Includes bibliographical references and index.
  ISBN 978-1-59904-549-8 (hardcover) -- ISBN 978-1-59904-551-1 (ebook)
  1. Knowledge management. 2. Decision making. 3. Critical thinking. I. Title.
  HD30.2.H3644 2007
  658.4'038--dc22
                     2006034514

British Cataloguing in Publication Data
A Cataloguing in Publication record for this book is available from the British Library.

Dedicated with love to Nihad, Nedim, and Namik

Socio-Technical Knowledge Management:

Studies and Initiatives

Table of Contents

Preface xi

Section I:
Theoretical Foundations of Knowledge Management

Chapter I
Memory, Learning, and Management:
Introducing Basic Knowledge Concepts 1
Abstract 1
Introduction 2
What is This Thing Corporate Memory? 3
Linking Corporate Memory with Organisational Learning 5
Mobilising Corporate Memory via Knowledge Management 7
Anatomy of an Integrated Knowledge Management Model 11
Conclusion 13
References 13
Appendix 16

Chapter II
Inquiry Systems:
Understanding How People Gain Knowledge 18
Abstract 18
Introduction 19
Review of Inquiry Systems 20
Empirical Study 22

Research Design and Subjects 23

Results 24

Conclusion 27

References 27

Appendix 28

Chapter III
Knowledge Space:
Building Foundations for Advancing Knowledge **32**

Abstract 32

Introduction 33

Review of Existing Models and Frameworks 33

Construction Knowledge Spaces in Organisations 36

Case Study 41

Conclusion 43

References 44

Section II:
Studies of Technology-Based Knowledge Management Initiatives

Chapter IV
Electronic Brainstorming:
Stimulating Creative Idea Generation **47**

Abstract 47

Introduction 48

System Description 49

Empirical Evaluation 52

Results 53

Discussion 54

Conclusion 56

References 56

Chapter V
Groupware:
Enabling Knowledge Sharing Across Time and Space **58**

Abstract 58

Introduction 59

Technologies for Knowledge Sharing 60

Empirical Study 61

Results 62

Discussion 64

Conclusion 66

References 67

Chapter VI
Electronic Memory:
Increasing Knowledge Availability 69
Abstract 69
Introduction 70
Knowledge Availablility and Decision Making 71
Empirical Study 74
Results 76
Discussion 78
Conclusion 80
References 81

Chapter VII
Visualisation System:
Facilitation Knowledge Interpretation 84
Abstract 84
Introduction 85
Visualisation System 86
Empirical Study 89
Results and Discussion 90
Conclusion 93
References 93

Chapter VIII
Knowledge Miner:
Assiting in Pattern Discovvery and Prediction 96
Abstract 96
Introduction 97
Knowledge Discovery Approaches and Technologies 98
Data-Mining-Tool Description 99
Empirical Study 100
Results 101
Discussion 102
Conclusion 104
References 104

Chapter IX
E-Learning Portal:
Enhancing User Experience 107
Abstract 107
Introduction 108
E-Learning Portal 109

Empirical Study..110
Results and Discussion 111
Conclusion 117
References 118

Chapter X
Quality Monitor:
Assessing Knowledge Credibility...**119**
Abstract..119
Introduction...120
Concept of Quality 121
Empirical Study...122
Results and Discussion 126
Conclusion 129
References 129

Chapter XI
Neural Network:
Automating Knowledge Application **132**
Abstract..132
Introduction...133
Literature Review...134
Empirical Study...137
Experimental Results 142
Conclusion 147
References 148

Section III:
Studies of Socially-Oriented Knowledge Management Initiatives

Chapter XII
Exercising Space:
Facilitating Learning Through Experimentation **151**
Abstract..151
Introduction...152
Experiential Learining...152
Empirical Study...155
Results 157
Discussion..157
Conclusion 160
References 160

Chapter XIII
Social Environment:
Promoting Knowledge Sharing Through Personal Interaction **164**
Abstract 164
Introduction 165
Empirical Study 167
Results 171
Discussion 173
Conclusion 176
References 176

Chapter XIV
Task Contingencies:
Examining if Two Heads are Always Better Than One **179**
Abstract 179
Introduction 180
Task Complexity 181
Empirical Study 182
Results 185
Discussion 185
Conclusion 189
References 189

Chapter XV
Communities of Practice:
Enhancing Collective Effectiveness **193**
Abstract 193
Introduction 194
Social Aspects of Communities of Practice 195
IT Community Description 198
Empirical Study 199
Results 201
Discussion 201
Conclusion 203
References 204
Appendix 207

Chapter XVI
Mode of Socialisation:
Comparing Effects of Informal and Formal Socialisation on
Organisational Performance **208**
Abstract 208
Introduction 209

Socialisation, Creativity, and Organisational Competitive Performance...... 210
Empirical Study.. 212
Results 214
Discussion... 215
Conclusion 216
References 217
Appendix 219

Chapter XVII
Organisational Culture:
Determining Knowledge-Sharing Attitudes **221**
Abstract.. 221
Introduction... 222
Organisational Culture 223
Empirical Study.. 225
Results 226
Discussion... 228
Limitations and Directions for Future Research 229
Conclusion 229
References 230
Appendix 231

Chapter XVIII
Incentives and Rewards:
Motivating Knowledge Sharing **233**
Abstract.. 233
Introduction... 234
Incentives and Rewards 235
Empirical Study.. 236
Results and Discussion 238
Conclusion 240
References 240
Appendix 242

Chapter XIX
Specialist Training:
Cultivation Knowledge Management Professionals **245**
Abstract.. 245
Introduction... 246
Converging Disciplines... 247
Knowledge Management Curriculum Development............................. 249
Innovative Teaching and Learning 250
Cross-Cultural Teaching and Learning 254

Conclusion 256
References 257
Appendix 258

Section IV:
Issues and Challenges for Knowledge Management Practice and Research

Chapter XX
Theroy vx. Practice:
Finding Out if We Do What We Preach.. 263
Abstract 263
Introduction 264
Adapted Knowledge Management Framework 265
Empirical Study 267
Results 268
Discussion 269
Conclusion 272
References 273
Appendix 277

Chapter XXI
Codification or Personalisation:
Choosing the Right Knowledge Management Strategy 279
Abstract 279
Introduction 280
Review of Knowledge Management Strategies 281
Empirical Study 284
Results 288
Discussion 289
Conclusion 293
References 293

Chapter XXII
Visions and Directions:
Balancing Academic and Practitioner Positions on KM 297
Abstract 297
Introduction 298
Survey of Academics and Practitioners 299
Synthesised Vision an Direction of KM 309
References 311

About the Author 313

Index 314

Preface

Introduction

The book *Socio-Technical Knowledge Management: Studies and Initiatives* has grown out of my research with the knowledge management research group (kmRg) at the University of New South Wales that I founded and led in the period 2000-2004. My particular interest in KM research has concentrated mainly on the significance of knowledge in supporting managerial decision making.

The past 30 years of investigations in behavioural decision making yielded systematic deviations from rational decision making termed "decision biases." Typically, decision biases are described as decision makers' cognitions and mental behaviours that prejudice the quality of their decisions. Most biases tend to have detrimental effects on decision performance.

At the same time, decision support research focused increasingly on application of sophisticated artificial intelligence technologies to support the needs of decision makers. However, despite substantial technical advances, laboratory experiments investigating the influence of decision support systems on decision performance have reported mixed, often disappointing, outcomes.

This led me to investigations of other possible approaches for reducing or eliminating biases from the cognitive strategies of decision makers. Knowledge management (KM) offered a promise. Assuming that the decision maker is the primary source of the biased judgement, my attention started to focus on how to better manage the decision maker's knowledge. This led me to empirical investigations of various social and technical mechanisms whose results could contribute to understanding

Introduction

The book *Socio-Technical Knowledge Management: Studies and Initiatives* has grown out of my research with the knowledge management research group (kmRg) at the University of New South Wales that I founded and led in the period 2000-2004. My particular interest in KM research has concentrated mainly on the significance of knowledge in supporting managerial decision making.

The past 30 years of investigations in behavioural decision making yielded systematic deviations from rational decision making termed "decision biases." Typically, decision biases are described as decision makers' cognitions and mental behaviours that prejudice the quality of their decisions. Most biases tend to have detrimental effects on decision performance.

At the same time, decision support research focused increasingly on application of sophisticated artificial intelligence technologies to support the needs of decision makers. However, despite substantial technical advances, laboratory experiments investigating the influence of decision support systems on decision performance have reported mixed, often disappointing, outcomes.

This led me to investigations of other possible approaches for reducing or eliminating biases from the cognitive strategies of decision makers. Knowledge management (KM) offered a promise. Assuming that the decision maker is the primary source of the biased judgement, my attention started to focus on how to better manage the decision maker's knowledge. This led me to empirical investigations of various social and technical mechanisms whose results could contribute to understanding of key factors that enable and enhance decision-maker knowledge.

While managerial decision support remains my favourite topic of interest in knowledge management, I have recently broadened the scope of research to include other knowledge intensive activities and systems. This book represents a reflection of these efforts in the attempt to "bottle the fog" surrounding the KM phenomena, and to contribute to an improved understanding of the field.

KM Challenges

Although KM is currently highly fashionable and visible, there is a danger that the hype surrounding KM may kill off the field as a fad. This is because KM is relatively immature, prone to misconceptions and misappropriations, and has many unresolved issues that need to be addressed before KM evolves into a mature discipline.

From what we have learnt so far, KM needs to be integrated into the strategic management of the organisation; knowledge context, process, and content all need to be carefully managed in order to preserve or create value for an organisation; and this can only be achieved by applying suitable KM methods, solutions, and tools.

However, the current state of the field reveals competing research paradigms, raging definitional debates, elusive value of knowledge management, evangelism, technology-focused initiatives, early wins difficult to replicate, motherhood status, and foreboding questions beginning to emanate from the ranks of senior executives looking for returns on investments. Moreover, there is a lack of objectivity, as those involved in KM initiatives are often relying on anecdotal evidence emanating from their experience; and a lack of generality, as KM methods are usually context dependent and not easily transferred from one organisation to another.

This book aims to address these concerns by contributing to the following three key issues: the integrated approach to KM; the rigour of research in KM; and the bridge between the theory and practice of KM. The challenging cross-disciplinary KM issues and assumptions can be tackled by seeking the common ground between various individual approaches, by including both theoretical and practical aspects, by mixing the hard (technological) with the soft (social) issues, and by bringing together western and eastern views of the field.

With respect to objectivity, in the research arena, it can be achieved only through a range of rigorous studies that can reliably establish what works, and what does not, and under what circumstances. Once a substantial collection of such studies has been accumulated, general concepts can be identified leading to integrated frameworks and models that can then be tested, leading to proven practical applications. Finally, by covering a variety of research themes from both theoretical and practical aspects of KM, it is possible to close the theory-practice gap and thus contribute to achieving a better understanding of the phenomenon itself.

Book Overview

Socio-Technical Knowledge Management: Studies and Initiatives is a structured compilation of articles founded on experience and research pursued with assistance from many colleagues and students. In recognition, the reference to plural "we" rather than singular "I" is made throughout the chapters. The key features of the book can be summarised as integrated KM approach, research rigour, mix of soft and hard issues, and theory and practice.

Essentially, the book brings together two competing perspectives (social and technical) currently seen in knowledge management research into an integrated sociotechnical framework. Fundamental to the integrated approach is that diverse knowledge elements, activities, and enablers must be in balance and aligned to the organisational context and strategy. However, it often seems that organisations are seeking ways to deal with the rapidly changing environment without really knowing what will work or where they are going. The main purpose of this book is to provide much needed empirical evidence regarding the "true" potential of various sociotechnical knowledge management solutions to enhance and exploit knowledge.

The book appears in times characterised by a great deal of business interest in knowledge management, but with recognition that there is a need for much more formal research in the area. Furthermore, recent knowledge management literature identifies too much theory and too little empirical research in the field. This book seeks to bridge the existing gap between theory and practice by providing a medium for presenting some of the most recent empirical research in the field. It is expected that empirical findings will help students, individuals, and organisations to better understand the benefits/limitations of sociotechnical knowledge management. It is also expected that they will help managers choose more suitable strategies to enhance and exploit their organisational knowledge. Consistent with its objectives, the book identifies and presents a number of traditional and novel social and technical initiatives and situations in which these initiatives can help to improve processes of creation, transfer, and application of knowledge, and thus lead to enhanced performance.

The book starts with an introduction to theoretical foundations of knowledge management concepts, proceeds with a series of empirical studies on the role of technology in knowledge management, followed by studies of socially orientated knowledge management solutions. The book ends with the discussion of major issues and challenges for knowledge management research and practice. With its integrated and systematic approach, the book makes a small but important step in helping individuals and organisations to get an objective and complete picture of the role of social and technical initiatives in knowledge management based on formal and sound empirical research. More importantly, the book shows that the impact of various initiatives is highly contingent upon the context in which the knowledge is generated, transferred, and used. This may help managers to choose more suitable solutions to turn their intangible assets into tangible outcomes.

Book Organisation

The book is organized into four major sections, each containing several chapters. It is designed to permit reading of individual chapters or sections of the book in many different orders, depending on readers' interests. However, readers are advised to first familiarise themselves with chapters in Section I.

Section I: Theoretical Foundations of Knowledge Management

Section I of the book explores theoretical foundations of knowledge management. The section begins with Chapter I presenting basic knowledge management concepts and incorporating them into an integrated KM framework. This framework and its elements are used to provide the structure for the rest of the book. Section I also includes Chapter II, which explores knowledge workers' inquiry systems that deepen our understanding of how people gain knowledge. These systems further provide the justification for building knowledge spaces as foundations for advancing knowledge in Chapter III. The chapter illustrates the concept of knowledge space using most recent knowledge management innovations and applications.

Section II: Studies of Technology-Based Knowledge Management Initiatives

Section II of the book focuses on the role of a variety of information and communication technologies and systems in knowledge management processes. The eight chapters in the second section of the book examine both traditional and novel technologies that support knowledge creation, transfer, and utilisation of knowledge. The first article is concerned with the development of new knowledge. Chapter IV examines the role of innovative technology in supporting creative idea generation. The next article is devoted to knowledge sharing. In Chapter V the main emphasis is on user perceptions of effectiveness and use of knowledge sharing technologies in different time and place application contexts.

The next two chapters in Section II examine systems and technologies that support knowledge storing and organisation. In Chapter VI the focus is on the benefits and limitations of electronic memory systems in providing required knowledge for decision support. Chapter VII discusses the use of a knowledge visualisation system as an effective tool for representing knowledge for human interpretation and assimilation. The next chapter addresses the question of discovering hidden patterns embedded in codified knowledge artefacts. Chapter VIII examines the role of a specific knowledge-mining system based on statistical analysis and graphical visualisation in supporting trend analysis and prediction.

Chapter IX is devoted to an integrated e-learning solution. This chapter describes the anatomy of a corporate e-learning portal and evaluates it from the employee trainees' perspective. The next chapter addresses the issue of knowledge measurement. Chapter X explores the effectiveness of a knowledge-rating system in assessing knowledge credibility. Finally, Chapter XI considers the process of knowledge application. In this chapter the focus is on the emerging trends involving the use of intelligent systems, such as neural networks, in solving complex decision problems such as granting loans.

Section III: Studies of Socially Orientated Knowledge Management Initiatives

Section III of the book is devoted to social contingencies that influence the effectiveness of knowledge processes. The eight chapters in the third section of the book examine the role of a variety of contextual and organisational factors in knowledge management including organisational culture, structure, leadership, rewards and incentives, and measurement.

The first two chapters examine the role of the organisational environment in knowledge management. Chapter XII focuses on the role of exercising space in stimulating individual learning, while Chapter XIII emphases the facilitating role of interactive environment in knowledge transfer, and its positive effect on performance. Chapter XIV highlights the difference in relative performance impacts of formal and informal modes of socialisation to creative performance, while Chapter XV identifies major task contingencies as moderators of knowledge-sharing effects on decision performance.

The next two chapters focus on structural and cultural factors. Chapter XVI examines the impact of communities of practice on building organisational social capital and enhancing its collective effectiveness through greater commitment, friendship, satisfaction, and trust among community members. The next Chapter, XVII, identifies organisational culture as a major facilitating or inhibiting factor that affects knowledge sharing, while Chapter XVIII reveals that intrinsic rewards may be as powerful a motivator of knowledge sharing as extrinsic ones.

Recognising that there is a growing demand for managerial and professional knowledge workers, the final Chapter, XIX, in this section, looks at the issue of cultivating knowledge management professionals. It addresses specialised knowledge management education providing skills and capabilities needed to take the lead for knowledge management initiatives to improve enterprise competitiveness in an ever-changing global environment.

Section IV: Issues and Challenges for Knowledge Management Practice and Research

The final Section, IV, of the book addresses major issues and challenges for knowledge management research and practice. The first of three chapters in this section of the book looks at the level of understanding and uptake of knowledge management in practice. Chapter XX surveys academics from two IT schools to find out if "we do what we preach." The chapter examines people's perceptions of the importance of, and their satisfaction with, main social and technical aspects of their knowledge management system. The next Chapter, XXI, deals with knowledge management strategies. It compares the effectiveness of codification and personalisation strategies in order to provide some guidance for practice on how to choose the appropriate strategy for the specific context. The final Chapter, XXII, of this section, and of the whole book, as is appropriate, looks at the future of knowledge management. The chapter presents visions and directions for a knowledge management future based on a small survey of academics and practitioners interested in knowledge management.

Value to Community

With the increasing number of academics and practitioners who see themselves as knowledge management (KM) specialists, there was clearly a growing need for a authoritarian and rigorous source for KM theory and empirical work. This book represents a small but important step in that direction. It serves as a source of emerging ideas and rigorous research required to direct future research efforts and to take the field into the future. Although it is recommended for readers that have a basic background in knowledge management, the book offers new insights for both novices and experienced professionals.

The book is of value to both the academic and the practitioner communities in the field of KM, as the goals of the book are to present an objective picture of the field, based on both formal and sound research, as well as seeking to integrate the many diverse perspectives held on KM by researchers and practitioners. It is also hoped that the book will become a useful reference for postgraduate students undertaking research in knowledge management.

Moreover, by drawing upon lessons from empirical studies presented in the book, it will be possible to devise a practical guide for managers to direct their decisions in terms of why and how they need to support knowledge enabling within their organisations. By identifying "proven" critical steps, key factors, and possible alternative paths, the book will put a practical tool into the hands of managers that can help them unleash the power of knowledge within their organisations.

Meliha Handzic, Author
Sarajevo School of Science and Technology
(The University of Buckingham Partner)
Sarajevo, Bosnia, and Herzegovina

Acknowledgment

There are many people whom I would like to thank for their help and support in the process of writing this book. I owe a great deal of gratitude to my colleagues and students from the knowledge management research group (kmRg), at the University of New South Wales, for helping me realise a comprehensive research program that forms a basis for this book. I am especially grateful to Peter Parkin and Christine van Toorn for their valuable input and assistance whenever necessary. I am also indebted to three anonymous manuscript reviewers for their helpful insights, critiques, and suggestions. I thank Kristin Roth of IGI Global for her enthusiasm about the book and her professional advice during the publishing process. Finally, I would like to thank my family for always being there for me. I could not have done this without their patience, encouragement, and support throughout the duration of this project.

Section I

Theoretical Foundations of Knowledge Management

Chapter I

Memory, Learning, and Management:
Introducing Basic Knowledge Concepts

Abstract

The importance of mobilising corporate knowledge for organisational success has been widely recognised. Accordingly, the aim of this first chapter of the current volume is to provide an overall introduction to the topic and set the scene for the remaining chapters of the book. In particular, the chapter examines current understanding of the concept of corporate memory, its relationship to organisational learning, and the potential role of knowledge management initiatives in mobilising corporate memory. The challenge is to enhance a firm's learning capability and thus contribute to its competitiveness.

Introduction

The world economy is currently experiencing a major transition from industrial to knowledge-based economy. In the emerging new economy, knowledge, rather than financial capital, land, or labour, is seen as the main source of competitive advantage of a business organisation (Drucker, 1993; Stewart, 1997). In such an economy, knowledge resources of an organisation not only enable its products and services to be provided, but knowledge itself is for sale as a product, thus ensuring that the organisation has a viable economic life within industry and market context.

The knowledge-based perspective of the firm suggests that an organisation's knowledge resources can predict its performance in a dynamic competitive environment. Currently, knowledge intensive organisations are at the forefront of organisational performance (Teleos, 2003). However, it is important to note that the basis for achieving competitive advantage from knowledge-based assets is not so much the existence of knowledge per se, but rather the organisation's ability to effectively apply the existing knowledge to create new knowledge and to take action.

To capitalise on knowledge and maintain competitive advantage, organisations need to mobilise the collective assemblage of all intelligences (referred to as *corporate memory*) that can contribute towards building a shared vision, renewal process, and direction for the organisation (Liebowitz, 2000). Yet, recent surveys show that most organizations either suffer setbacks from losing key knowledge through employee departures, or believe that much of their needed knowledge exists inside the organisation, but find problematic identifying it, finding it, and leveraging it (Alavi & Leidner, 2001). The often-quoted phrase "if only we knew what we know" catches the regret for missed opportunities to profit and improve from knowledge.

The knowledge problem framework (Sambamurthy & Subramani, 2005) suggests that knowledge problems in organisations can be viewed as a combination of the problems of knowledge coordination, knowledge transfer and knowledge reuse. These knowledge problems reflect the difficulty of identifying and locating knowledge sources required to solve specific problems, the complexity of transferring or obtaining the knowledge required to solve specific problems, and the difficulty of ensuring the application of preexisting knowledge rather than the development of new knowledge when advisable. Such knowledge problems have led to systematic attempts to improve the management of organisational knowledge. However, harnessing knowledge for corporate advantage is not an easy task and many knowledge management initiatives fail. The focus of this book is on identifying those knowledge management solutions that make a real difference to the performance in the context of decision making.

The main objective of this introductory chapter is to explore the concept of corporate memory and present some preliminary thoughts on how it should be managed to maximally contribute to the competitiveness of an organization. First, the chapter reviews various existing conceptualisations of corporate memory. Then, it discusses the relationship between corporate memory and organisational learning. This is followed by the examination of the role of knowledge management initiatives in mobilising a firm's corporate memory and influencing its learning capability. The chapter ends with a summary of conclusions and pointers to research issues addressed in the remaining chapters of the book.

What is This Thing Corporate Memory?

The knowledge management (KM) literature holds many varying definitions of corporate memory and its related concepts. In practice, corporate memory (CM) is often equated with organisational memory, knowledge base, memory bank, or corporate intellectual assets. Walsh and Ungson (1991) define corporate memory as stored knowledge from an organisation's history that can be brought to bear on present decisions. Stein and Zwass (1995) also view it as a means of bringing knowledge from the past to bear on present activities and influencing organisational performance. This view is further reinforced by Jennex and Olfman (2003), who define corporate memory as the retention of experiences, knowledge, information, and data about events in an organisation that are then applied to future events to support decision making.

The comprehensive review of definitions by Stein (1995) reveals that most proposed definitions focus on the persistence of knowledge in an organisation. Any knowledge that contributes to the performance of an organisation (e.g., knowledge about products, processes, customers, etc.) could be stored in the corporate memory and made available to enhance the efficiency and effectiveness of knowledge-intensive work processes. According to Alavi and Leidner (2001), corporate memory includes knowledge residing in various component forms, including written documentation, structured information stored in electronic databases, codified human knowledge stored in expert systems, documented organisational procedures and processes, and tacit knowledge acquired by individuals and networks of individuals. Becerra-Fernandez et al. (Becerra-Fernandez, Gonzales, & Sabherwal, 2004) also view corporate memory as the aggregate intellectual assets of an organisation, a combination of both explicit and tacit knowledge that is crucial to the operation and competitiveness of the organisation.

A distinction is made in literature between technical and humanistic approaches to corporate memory. From the technical perspective, a corporate memory is interpreted as an explicit, disembodied, representation of the knowledge in an organisation (Van Heijst, van der Spek, & Kruizinga, 1996). This concrete CM comprises of concepts and information represented by physical memory aids such as computerised files and databases (Jennex & Olfman, 2003). Its main function is presentation of knowledge for a given context. It incorporates a variety of knowledge forms ranging from data- and text-based documents and models, to digital images, video, and audio recordings. From the humanistic perspective, CM is viewed as an abstract form comprising unstructured concepts and tacit knowledge that exists in the organisation's culture and in the minds of its members. It serves the function of interpretation, providing the frames of reference that promote adaptation and learning (Jennex & Olfman, 2003).

The literature also distinguishes between individual and collective memory. Individual memory is developed based on a person's observations, experiences, and actions. Collective memory includes other components such as organisational culture, transformations, structure, ecology, and information archives (Alavi & Leidner, 2001). While individual memory represents a vital component of the organisational knowledge base, it is considered insufficient to the success of organisational actions. Many organisational processes depend on collective elements of knowledge that are being developed through interactions among many participants (Probst, Raub, & Romhardt, 2000).

The relative importance of various forms of corporate memory depends upon the nature of the organisation. Typically, organisations that adopt a codification knowledge strategy place greater emphasis on building computer-based knowledge repositories, while those who adopt personalisation strategy rely more on individual memories of their employees (Hansen, Nohria, & Tierney, 1999). Some researchers warn that when a significant portion of a company's knowledge is stored in the minds of its employees, there is an increased danger of knowledge loss from employee turnover. They also warn that such knowledge gaps are extremely difficult to fill (Probst et al., 2000). The emerging integrated approaches recognise that different forms of corporate memory are woven together to form a whole (Handzic & Hasan, 2003).

From this discussion, it can be seen that corporate memory has two principle goals: (1) to control current activities in order to avoid past mistakes, and (2) to integrate knowledge across organisational boundaries (Jennex & Olfman, 2003). In another words, its main function is to enhance the learning capability of an organisation and subsequently, improve its effectiveness. However, this may or may not happen. The tomb/attic metaphor is often being used to describe a type of corporate memory where knowledge is deposited to "rest in peace" never to be accessed again. In contrast, the wellspring/pump type ensures that knowledge is fully exploited to improve organisational performance (Fayyad & Uthursamy, 2002; Stewart, 1997; Van Heijst et al., 1996). The challenge for knowledge management is to find ways to turn corporate memories from tombs to wellsprings of knowledge (Handzic & Bewsell, 2005). To do so requires a good understanding of the issues and factors influencing the development of corporate memories. It also requires understanding of the relationship between corporate memory and organisational learning, and of the means and tools available to mobilise corporate memory for learning, and thus, performance.

Linking Corporate Memory with Organisational Learning

Nowadays, it is essential for organisations to develop the ability to learn, that is, to gain knowledge necessary to act in response to changing environmental conditions, and then to use that knowledge to modify the organisation's potential actions. In literature, this ability is often referred to as "organisational learning." Garvin (1998) provides a small sample of definitions of organisational learning. To some scholars it means a process of improving actions through better knowledge and understanding, to others behavioural change through information processing, or process of detecting and correcting errors.

In order to act in accordance with environmental conditions, an organisation's knowledge "stocked" in corporate memory needs to continually "flow" through learning processes. Learning or knowledge flows are processes through which knowledge is created, stored, shared, and applied (Handzic & Zhou, 2005). Various other classifications of knowledge processes found in literature (Alavi & Leidner, 2001; Grover & Davenport, 2001; Wiig, 1999) differ in the number and labelling of knowledge processes, but not the underlying concepts.

The link between learning processes (knowledge flows) and corporate memory (knowledge stocks) can be explained in terms of the tension between exploration and exploitation behaviours (Jashapara, 2004). Through exploration, new knowledge is created that results in the enhancement of corporate memory. Through exploitation, past knowledge already stocked in corporate memory guides individuals and groups to reuse what is already learnt. The efficiency of organizational learning depends on how well knowledge flows provide knowledge stocks to the organization and its members.

The recent knowledge management literature considers three levels of organisational learning: individual, group, and collective (Garud & Kumaraswamy, 2005; Jashapara, 2004; Ryu, Kim, Chaudhury, & Rao, 2005; Van Heijst et al., 1996). Generally, individual learning is defined in terms of increasing one's capacity to take effective action. From the behavioural perspective it is understood as a response to stimuli. The cognitive perspective sees it as a change in states of knowledge. The Lewinian experiential learning model integrates the cognition and action aspects of learning in a four-phase cycle: experience-test-conceptualise-reflect (Jashapara, 2004).

From the activity theory perspective, learning-by-doing is one of three possible types of learning that members of the organization can undergo, the other two being learning-by-investment and learning-from-others. Learning-by-doing assumes that members accumulate knowledge from experience with their work tasks (Ryu et al., 2005). While learning-by-doing can generate expertise in a specific area, it can also lead to a competency trap. Habituation and taken-for-granted attitude can compromise reflection-in-action and thus, inhibit renewal and expansion of knowledge (Garud & Kumaraswamy, 2005). Among important organizational requirements that need to be satisfied before individual learning can take place are getting feedback, that is, knowing effects of their work on the processes that they are involved in, and having freedom in experimenting and deciding how they do their job (Van Heijst et al., 1996).

Communication between organizational members who do similar or different tasks within the organization is an essential prerequisite for learning at a group level. The community of practice perspective on group knowledge draws attention to common identities and beliefs among the community members that are formed through dialogue and discussion. In contrast, the work group perspective emphasises the strength of the ties that members with different epistemologies establish when they work together. In dynamic systems, one type of group knowledge may diverge into another over time. When interdependencies are carefully shaped to avoid conflict, the group's responsiveness to meet complex situational demands can go beyond the capabilities of its individual members (Garud & Kumaraswamy, 2005). Among other important prerequisites for effective learning at a group level are providing a mechanism to discuss experiences and work related issues (a sort of a discussion forum), and having an atmosphere in which communication to others of lessons learned, including failures, is rewarded (Van Heijst, et al., 1996).

The conception of learning at the collective level is explored through the notions of singe-loop and double-loop learning (Argyris, 1998). Single-loop learning involves exploitation behaviours that emphasise efficiency goals. In contrast, double-loop learning involves exploration behaviours where an organisation engages in experimentation, idea generation, and innovation. The organizational requirement for single-loop-learning is that the organizations maintain some kind of digital knowledge repository (Van Heijst et al., 1996). Digital repositories make it easy to accumulate, as well as retrieve and reuse knowledge. However, sometimes the search and reconceptualisation costs may outweigh the potential benefits from reusing the knowledge (Garud & Kumaraswamy, 2005).

In short, different learning strategies have different costs and benefits associated with them, and they can result in different knowledge depth and width. Therefore, the major challenges for knowledge management lie in (1) determining optimal learning strategies and knowledge for different business conditions based on formal and sound research, and (2) providing practical methods and tools to guide managers in making their organizations act as intelligently as possible. The following section examines major KM initiatives suggested to play an important role in organisational learning by enabling and facilitating the processes of knowledge creation, storage, sharing, and application (Handzic & Zhou, 2005).

Mobilising Corporate Memory via Knowledge Management

Knowledge management involves a deliberate and systematic approach to effectively develop a learning capability in organizations. Two major classes of knowledge management initiatives have been proposed to enable and facilitate learning processes and thus mobilize corporate memory: (1) social, including organizational culture, structure, leadership, and measurement; and (2) technological, including a wide range of information and communication technologies and systems. An appreciation of the importance of these sociotechnical factors can aid explicit and deliberate efforts in managing knowledge for the desired outcomes. Therefore, a brief overview of the most important ones, based on Handzic and Zhou (2005), is presented next.

Socially-Oriented Mechanisms

With respect to social influences, organizational culture is recognized as one of, if not the single-most important factor in enabling a productive organisational environment required for sharing knowledge. Therefore, many knowledge management initiatives aim to nurture a knowledge culture by promoting espoused values, systems, structures, and artefacts that will, in effect, entrench a desired mindset in staff members (Handzic & Agahari, 2003). A successful knowledge culture has the vision and leadership that focuses on learning, values knowledge, engenders trust and communication, and tolerates questioning and mistakes. It is established when individuals perceive the process of sharing as a natural way of working, their behaviour is genuine, and it is in their own personal interest to behave as such.

In nurturing a knowledge-conducive culture, organisations can put in place rewards and incentive systems. Such measures are believed necessary to motivate knowledge sharing and knowledge contribution (Evangelou & Karacapilidis, 2005). They can be monetary or nonmonetary, formal or informal, long-term or short-term. Which type of reward or incentive will be used depends on the specific circumstances and requires careful consideration. According to Hauschild et al. (Hauschild, Licht, & Stein, 2001), successful companies reward employees for seeking, sharing, and creating knowledge. In contrast, less-successful companies tend to take a top-down approach, pushing knowledge to where it is needed.

The literature further suggests that the successful adoption of knowledge management in an organisation requires strong leadership to guide it towards managing and using its knowledge resource for maximum benefit (Holsapple, 2003). The distinguishing characteristic of leadership is that of being a catalyst through inspiring, mentoring, setting examples, listening, and engendering trust and respect. Individuals and team leaders with a diverse range of skills, attributes, and capabilities are required to manage and motivate change. These include strong interpersonal, communication and change management skills, an understanding of the business, technological expertise, and the ability to build relationships.

Organisations can make use of a variety of organisational forms to create an environment to support collaboration and knowledge sharing. In general, networked structures, also known as communities of practice (CoPs), are believed to offer the ability for individuals to work together across the organisation, and encourage open communication and learning based on common interests (Wenger, 1998). In contrast, bureaucratic structures that emphasise hierarchies and command and control over individuals discourage innovation (Lesser & Storck, 2001). Communities that regularly engage in sharing and learning may improve business performance by fostering an environment with shared mental models, common understanding, high levels of trust, and mutual obligation.

It has been suggested in the literature that organisations cannot effectively manage knowledge without addressing the measurement issue, and vice versa. The purpose of measurement is to provide metrics and feedback to management. It is argued that organisations need to know what they know and what they must know to be competitive. The outcome of such a measurement exercise is expected to be a more effective knowledge management approach. Historically, the management and measurement of intellectual resources have been pursued separately. The intellectual capital (IC) perspective brings these two streams of thought together. It suggests the need for the alignments of IC with strategic business objectives on one side and learning processes on another (Zhou & Fink, 2003).

Technology-Based Mechanisms

To help better understand the various roles of information technology in managing knowledge, many authors have developed typologies based on the distinction of knowledge processes. Tsui (2003) suggested a framework of KM tools including nine categories: search, meta/Web crawler, process modelling and mind mapping, case-based reasoning, data and text mining, taxonomy/ontological tools, groupware, measurement and reporting, and e-learning. Binney (2001) developed a KM spectrum that consists of six categories: transactional, analytical, asset management, process based, developmental, and innovation/creation. Handzic (2004) suggested four major classes of knowledge management systems: knowledge repositories, search/discovery systems, virtual communication/collaboration tools, and creativity support systems. The first two categories support "codification," and the last two support "personalisation" strategy, as defined by Hansen et al. (1999).

Creating knowledge repositories with the use of knowledge storage tools, such as databases and text bases, is one of the most common KM initiatives (Handzic &

Zhou, 2005). Knowledge contained in a typical knowledge repository includes best practices, lessons learned, competitive intelligence, learning histories, and so forth. This knowledge is usually embedded in documents. Electronic data generated by daily transactions are typically stored in structured database systems. In addition to data and text, multimedia systems organise, and make available to users, their knowledge assets in a variety of other representational forms, such as images, audio, and video forms. Unlike organisational databases that typically store current knowledge, data warehouses and data marts retain historical and cross-functional perspectives. The assumption is that by employing a repository approach to KM, an organisation should enhance corporate memory, provide broader access to relevant knowledge, and increase knowledge sharing and reuse across the organisation. However, the vast amount of codified knowledge stored in repositories may create an excessive cognitive burden for users and hence, discourage people from reusing it.

To improve knowledge access, many organisations employ knowledge-maps. These tools can be viewed as "guides" to knowledge that can help seekers to quickly locate important knowledge already captured and stored in the organisational knowledge repositories and make it readily accessible. Among many benefits suggested from using knowledge maps are enhanced knowledge visibility, improved understanding, and improved decision-making (Wexler, 2001). Knowledge maps may facilitate decision making and problem solving by showing which type of knowledge to use at what stage, and the sources of that knowledge. They can enhance confidence in users, and advance decision makers' understanding of situations at hand. In addition, the use of knowledge maps may facilitate the generation of ideas for knowledge sharing and leveraging. Through IT-based yellow pages, individuals in an organisation may be able to more rapidly locate people who have the needed knowledge.

Data mining and knowledge discovery technologies are suggested to support knowledge development. They look for the hidden patterns in stored knowledge artefacts to discover previously unknown trends or relationships. These applications often use complex and sophisticated algorithms, as well as graphical visualisation to assist people in discovering new knowledge. According to Fayyad, Piatetsky-Shapiro, and Smyth (1996), two main goals of knowledge discovery include description and prediction. Description is concerned with identifying patterns for the purpose of presenting them to the user in an easy-to-understand form. Prediction focuses on mining the patterns for the purpose of predicting future values for the variables in question. In addition to trend and association analysis, clustering, and classification, the current research efforts in these areas also include the use of intelligent agents and the application of competitive intelligence (Blanning, 2000).

Various applications have been developed to support communities of practice and facilitate virtual person-to-person communication and tacit knowledge sharing. Examples include e-mail, electronic discussion forum, bulletin boards, whiteboards, and audio- and videoconferencing, many of which are extremely popular and widely used in practice. E-mail, for instance, is used in many organisations as a primary means of communication among employees (Handzic & Lee, 2005). Electronic discussion forums are another common feature for many corporate intranets and the Internet. Collaborative software, such as groupware, allows members of a group to work together on a task in an anywhere-anytime mode. Some authors (Wasko & Faraj, 2000) argue that virtual communication and collaboration offer extra benefits compared to face-to-face conversation. These include providing a quick way to receive help and valuable knowledge, and enabling a better access to a larger pool of people.

Creative software products, such as virtual reality and mind games, are two groups of technologies focused on fostering creativity and innovative problem solving. Most such systems are designed to stimulate creative thinking based on the principles of associations, memory retrieval, and the use of analogy and metaphor. In multiparticipant settings, it is also assumed that the generation of creative ideas will be stimulated though the participants' interaction where one idea leads to another and the process builds upon itself (Shneiderman, 2000). Furthermore, virtual reality technology enables an individual to become actively immersed in a simulated environment. The assumption is that this enables people to learn more easily through experiential exercise rather than through memorising rules.

Artificial intelligence (AI) systems are starting to appear to assist organisations and individuals in making better decisions and performing at higher levels. Robots and Internet bots, vision systems, natural language processing systems, neural networks, and expert systems are some examples of "smart" knowledge application systems (Becerra-Fernandez et al., 2004). The development of such systems is based mainly on two AI technologies, rule-based and case-based reasoning. Other technologies worth mentioning include constraint-based, model-based, and diagrammatic reasoning. These have very specific applications in solving problems from constrained domains, and from diagrams or drawings.

While these major types of KM technologies are discussed separately, it should be noted that they are often not mutually exclusive (Handzic & Zhou, 2005). There may be situations where a technology does not fall neatly into any of these four categories. In addition, some technologies may be used to support multiple processes and may, therefore, have multiple purposes. Finally, these technologies often do not work in isolation, but are combined to produce a synergic effect. It has been suggested that the availability of such systems should lead to increased organisational learning and result in improved performance.

Anatomy of an Integrated Knowledge Management Model

From the discussion presented in previous sections, one can draw a conclusion that knowledge management requires a multidimensional framework for success. A model of an integrated knowledge management model in Figure 1.1 presents one such holistic and balanced approach to knowledge management adapted from AA (1998). A more complete list of various types of knowledge stocks, processes, and enablers identified in literature is provided in the Appendix to this chapter.

The model emphasises the importance of both social and technological enablers of knowledge processes. Organisational personnel, work processes, structures, and technologies are tightly interconnected and interact closely. When seeking to redesign and change organisations, it is important to find the right balance between these elements. For example, in situations of dispersed geography and increased size and cost of labour, technology may be a vital tool to successful knowledge management. In other cases, increasing the feeling of community and measures of quality may be more important.

Furthermore, the model recognises the dynamic nature of knowledge flows. To be of value to organisational competitive advantage, knowledge needs to constantly flow (Nissen, 2006). However, tensions exist and tradeoffs are needed between knowl-

Figure 1.1. Anatomy of an integrated knowledge management model

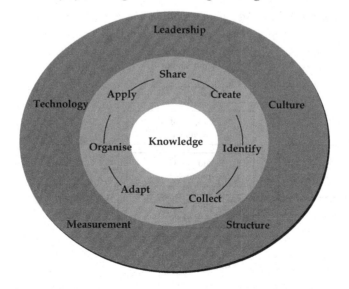

edge sharing and hoarding, as well as learning and doing. Similarly, investing in the exploration of new knowledge needs to be balanced with knowledge exploitation of the existing knowledge. Otherwise, if an organisation focuses solely on exploitation, it can quickly develop competency traps and learn to do wrong things very well. Alternatively, if an organisation focuses solely on exploration, it can prepare itself for a future environment, but fail to survive until such a future arrives.

Finally, the model includes knowledge content in various forms in which it is stocked. Understanding the kind of knowledge that is important in an organisation's particular environment is essential for promoting the most important knowledge flows. Valuable knowledge clumps need to be identified and their flow through the organisations enabled. However, it must be taken into account that tacit knowledge is sticky, slow to move, and hard to imitate, compared to explicit knowledge.

The Handzic (2004) extended KM model, presented in Figure 1.2, further recognises that KM is driven by forces from its surrounding external environment; views KM solutions/initiatives as configurations of sociotechnical knowledge enablers, knowledge processes, and knowledge stocks; and suggests that these create value for the individuals and organisations in the form of learning and performance outcomes. It also proposes a contingency view of KM, which argues that no one solution is best under all circumstances. Instead, individuals and organisations need to choose, among multiple possible paths, the one that fits best their set of circumstances.

Despite the substantial theoretical support for the positive role of various social and technical knowledge management initiatives in enabling and facilitating organisa-

Figure 1.2. Extended knowledge management model

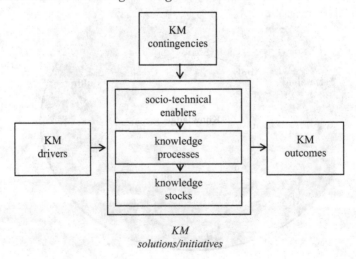

tional learning, little empirical work has been undertaken so far to provide evidence of the actual success of these initiatives in practice. Consequently, there still exists a large gap in the body of knowledge in this area (Alavi & Leidner, 2001). The current volume attempts to fill (to some extent) the existing gap between theory and practice. It reports the results of a series of empirical studies undertaken to address a number of research opportunities of interest to the author. It builds upon and extends the author's earlier work (see Handzic, 2004) focusing mainly on technology. The following chapters address an even mixture of hard technical and soft social aspects of knowledge management.

Conclusion

This chapter presented a discussion on corporate memory, organisational learning, and knowledge management initiatives based on a review, interpretation, and synthesis of a broad range of relevant literature. Several general conclusions may be drawn from this work. First, corporate memory is a complex multidimensional construct comprising both explicit and tacit forms of intellectual material of an organisation that can be found in individuals, groups, and collectives. Second, knowledge stocked in corporate memory can contribute to organisational learning by continually flowing through learning processes of knowledge creation, transfer, and application. Third, knowledge management initiatives drawing on various social and technical tools and capabilities can play a variety of roles in supporting learning processes. The need for empirical research into the impact of these initiatives is identified. It forms the basis for experimental studies presented in the remaining chapters of this book.

References

AA. (1998). *Best practices in knowledge management.* Australia: Arthur Andersen.

Alavi, M., & Leidner, D. E. (2001). Knowledge management and knowledge management systems: Conceptual foundations and research issues. *MIS Quarterly, 25*(1), 107-136.

Becerra-Fernandez, I., Gonzales, A., & Sabherwal, R. (2004). *Knowledge management: Challenges, solutions, and technologies.* Upper Saddle River, NJ: Pearson Education, Inc.

Binney, D. (2001). The knowledge management spectrum: Understanding the KM landscape. *Journal of Knowledge Management, 5*(1), 33-42.

Blanning, R. W. (2000, July 5-7). Knowledge management and electronic commerce. In *Position Papers on Future Directions in Decision Support Research. IFIP WK8.3 Working Conference on DSS*, Stockholm.

Drucker, P. F. (1993). *Post-capitalist society.* New York: Harper Business.

Evangelou, C., & Karacapilidis, N. (2005). On the interaction between humans and knowledge management systems: A framework of knowledge sharing catalysts. *Knowledge Management Research and Practice, 3*(4), 253-261.

Fayyad, U., & Uthurusamy, R. (2002). Evolving into data mining solutions for insight. *Communications of the ACM, 45*(8), 28-31.

Fayyad, U., Piatetsky-Shapiro, G., & Smyth, P. (1996). Knowledge discovery and data mining: Towards a unifying framework. In *Proceedings of the Second International Conference on Knowledge Discovery and Data mining (KDD-96)*, OR.

Garud, R., & Kumaraswamy, A. (2005). Vicious and virtuous circles in the management of knowledge: The case of Infosys Technologies. *MIS Quarterly, 29*(1), 9-33.

Garvin, D. A. (1998). Building a learning organisation. In *Harvard Business Review on Knowledge Management* (pp. 47-80). Boston: HBS Press.

Grover, V., & Davenport, T. H. (2001). General perspectives on knowledge management: Fostering a research agenda. *Journal of Management Information System, 18*(1), 5-21.

Handzic, M. (2004). *Knowledge management: Through the technology glass.* Singapore: World Scientific Publishing.

Handzic, M., & Agahari, D. (2004). Knowledge sharing culture: A case study. *Journal of Information & Knowledge Management, 3*(2), 135-142.

Handzic, M., & Bewsell, G. (2005). Corporate memories: Tombs or wellsprings of knowledge. In B. Montano (Ed.), *Innovations of knowledge management* (pp. 69-85). Hershey, PA: IRM Press.

Handzic, M., & Hasan, H. (2003). The search for an integrated KM framework. In H. Hasan & M. Handzic (Eds.), *Australian Studies in Knowledge Management* (pp. 3-34). Wollongong: UOW Press.

Handzic, M., & Lee, A. (2005, September 8-9). Knowledge sharing via technology. In *Proceedings of the European Conference on Knowledge Management (ECKM 2005)*, Limerick.

Handzic, M., & Zhou, A. Z. (2005). *Knowledge management: An integrative approach.* Oxford, UK: Chandos Publishing.

Hansen, M. T, Nohria, N., & Tierney, T. (1999, March-April). What's your strategy for managing knowledge? *Harvard Business Review*, 106-116.

Hauschild, S., Licht, T., & Stein, W. (2001). Creating a knowledge culture. *The McKinsey Quarterly, 1*, 74-81.

Holsapple, C. W. (2003). *Knowledge management handbook*, Berlin: Springer.

Jashapara, A. (2004). *Knowledge management: An integrated approach.* Harlow, Essex: Prentice Hall.

Jennex, M., & Olfman, L. (2003). Organisational memory. In C. W. Holsapple (Ed.), *Handbook on knowledge management* (Vol. 1, pp. 207-234). Berlin: Springer.

Lesser, E. L., & Storck, J. (2001). Communities of practice and organisational performance. *IBM Systems Journal, 40*(4), 831-841.

Liebowitz, J. (2000). *Building organisational intelligence*, Boca Raton, FL: CRC Press.

Nissen, M. (2006). Knowledge power. In *Harnessing knowledge dynamics: Principled organisational knowing and learning* (pp. 1-14). Hershey, PA: IRM Press.

O'Dell, C., & Grayson, C. J. (1998). *If only we knew what we know.* Free Press.

Probst, G., Raub, S., & Romhardt, K. (2000). *Managing knowledge.* New York: John Wiley & Sons.

Ryu, C., Kim, Y. J., Chaudhury, A., & Rao, H. R. (2005). Knowledge acquisition via three learning processes in enterprise information portals: Learning-by-investment, learning-by-doing and learning-from-others. *MIS Quarterly, 29*(2), 245-278.

Sambamurthy, V., & Subramani, M. (2005). Special issue on information technologies and knowledge management. *MIS Quarterly, 29*(2), 193-195.

Shneiderman, B. (2000). Creating creativity: User interfaces for supporting innovation. *ACM Transactions on Computer-Human Interaction, 7*(1), 114-138.

Stein, E. W. (1995). Organizational memory: Review of concepts and recommendations for management. *International Journal of Information Management, 15*, 17-32.

Stein, E. W., & Zwass, V. (1995). Actualising organisational memory with information systems. *Information Systems Research.* 6(2), 85-117.

Stewart, T. A. (1997). *Intellectual capital: The new wealth of organisations.* New York: Doubleday.

Teleos. (2003). *2003 global most admired knowledge enterprises: Executive summary.* Retrieved August 15, 2003, from http://www.knowledgebusiness.com

Tsui, E. (2003). Tracking the role and evolution of commercial knowledge management software. In C. W. Holsapple (Ed.), *Handbook on knowledge management*, volume 2 (pp. 5-27). Berlin: Springer.

Van Heijst, G., van der Spek, R., & Kruizinga, E. (1996). Organising corporate memories. In *Proceedings of the KAW'96*, Banff, Canada.

Walsh, J. P., & Ungson, G. R. (1991). Organisational memory. *Academy of Management Review, 16*(1), 57-91.

Wasko, M., & Faraj, S. (2000). It is what one does: Why people participate and help others in electronic communities of practice. *Journal of Strategic Information Systems, 9*, 155-173.

Wenger, E. (1998). *Communities of practice.* Cambridge: Cambridge University Press.

Wexler, M. N. (2001). The who, what and why of knowledge mapping. *Journal of Knowledge Management, 5*(3), 249-263.

Wiig, K. M. (1999). *Successful knowledge management: Does it exist?* Retrieved March 15, 2000, from http://www.krii.com

Zhou, A., & Fink, D. (2003). The intellectual capital Web: A systematic linking of intellectual capital and knowledge management. *Journal of Intellectual Capital, 4*(1), 34-48.

Appendix: List of Major Classes and Examples of KM Components

Knowledge:

Pragmatic (e.g., basic, applied; product, customer, competitor, etc.).

Epistemological (e.g., object, personal; formal, informal, instrumental, contingent, metaknowledge; explicit, tacit; cognitive, technical; embrained, embodied, encultured, encoded, embedded)

Economic (e.g., employee competence, internal structure, external structure; know-what, why, who, when, where, how)

continued on following page

Knowledge processes:

Create knowledge (e.g., develop, acquire, procure, import, collect, experiment, socialise)

Share knowledge (e.g., transfer, distribute, externalise)

Preserve knowledge (e.g., capture, organise, retain, combine, hold, adapt, index, present, filter)

Utilise knowledge (e.g., apply, integrate, use, internalise)

Knowledge enablers (technological):

Digital storage and retrieval technologies (e.g., knowledge repositories, databases, text-bases, data warehouses, data marts; knowledge maps, knowledge directories, yellow pages; search engines)

Communication and collaboration technologies (e.g., e-mail, bulletin boards, whiteboards, e-forums, videoconferencing, groupware)

Data mining and visualisation technologies (e.g., statistical analysis, simulation tools, graphical presentation)

Intelligent technologies (e.g., knowledge-base systems, expert systems, rule induction, decision trees)

Integrated and platform technologies (e.g., Internet, intranets, extranets, portals)

Knowledge enablers (social):

Leadership (e.g., planning, managerial coordination, control)

Culture (e.g., interpersonal behaviours, incentives and rewards, written plans and policies)

Structure (e.g., communities of practice; networks, hierarchies; roles and responsibilities, spaces)

Measures (e.g., financial, nonfinancial; customer, human, process; hard, soft)

Chapter II

Inquiry Systems:
Understanding How
People Gain Knowledge

Abstract

This chapter investigates the inquiry systems of knowledge workers based on Churchman's interpretation of the philosophies of Leibniz, Locke, Kant, Hegel, and Singer. It reports results of a survey of university students from Australia and Europe as representatives of knowledge workers with a great potential to influence future. Data on their approaches to knowledge acquisition, change, relationships to others, and problem solving were gathered by administering a survey questionnaire. The results demonstrate recognizable inquiry archetypes for individuals, and a contingent nature of group approaches upon the cultural context. This leads to important implications for the design of knowledge management support for different individual and collective styles.

Introduction

Knowledge has been widely recognised as a key factor of organisational survival and success in a dynamic and competitive economy (Garvin, 1998; Holsapple & Singh, 2000; Nonaka, 1998; Drucker, 1998). In order for companies to stay competitive in today's uncertain world, they constantly need to pursue new strategies to differentiate themselves from their competition, such as the introduction of new products or the offering of new services (Satzinger, Garfield, & Nagasundaram, 1999). This requires a major shift in their business focus from tangible to intangible (knowledge) assets (Davenport, DeLong, & Breers, 1998; Davenport & Prusak, 1998; Drucker, 1993; Grayson & O'Dell, 1998; Stewart, 1997). In other words, knowledge must evolve and be assimilated at an even faster rate.

To deal with changes, improve services, products, and quality, and also to cut costs and compete in the global market, organizations will need to depend upon the creative and innovative ideas produced by their workforce (Covey, 1989). It is therefore not surprising that organisations place increasing demands for new skills and capabilities for new-age workers. New professionals are expected to be skilled at creating, acquiring, and transferring knowledge (Garvin, 1998; Nonaka, 1998). They need to be capable of continually expanding their capacity to create desired results, nurture new thinking patterns, set free collective aspirations, and learn how to learn together (Senge, 1990).

This chapter suggests that in order for organizations to become productive and efficient learning organisations and to maintain a competitive edge, they can use the ideas developed by Churchman (1971). He developed five archetypical models of inquiring systems based on the theories of knowledge of philosophers Leibniz, Locke, Kant, Hegel, and Singer. These models can be used to make inferences about the design of knowledge spaces in order to support learning in organizations and to discuss how various sociotechnological initiatives/interventions mentioned in Chapter I can be useful in building such spaces.

Given the crucial importance of learning for organizational success in the knowledge economy, the main goal of this chapter is to provide guidance to designing the appropriate knowledge spaces based on our insight into student-knowledge workers' inquiry styles gained in the context of higher IS education. First, the chapter reviews Churchman's descriptions of archetypal inquiry systems. Then, it presents an empirical study into the students' inquiry systems though interrelatedness of their knowledge acquisition, approach to change, relationship to others, and problem-solving behaviour. Next, it discusses implications of these findings for the design of knowledge spaces in order to support different learning styles. Finally, the chapter concludes with a summary of main findings and directions for future research.

Review of Inquiry Systems

Inquiry may be defined as the activity that produces knowledge, and knowledge as the ability to react to and find solutions for the problems we create and encounter. Churchman (1971) looked to the ideas of Locke, Leibniz, Kant, Hegel, and Singer to determine how to design a system of inquiry. Vandenbosch et al. (Vandenbosch, Fay, & Saatciglu, 2001) argued that most theories studied inquiry in terms of individual characteristics, contexts in which knowledge flourishes, or details about processes in which knowledge is developed.

However, in real life, people do not come up with ideas in isolation, and different combinations of contextual and personal characteristics may result in different, but equally effective processes. Taking a broader view of the cognitive styles perspective, Vandenbosch et al. (2001) investigated the interrelatedness of knowledge acquisition, approach to change, relationship to others, and problem-solving approaches to explore the notion of archetypes, based on Churchman's (1971) system of inquiry. The basic features of each archetype are summarized and elaborated in Table 2.1.

The Leibnizian Inquirer

Leibnizian inquirers are seen primarily as the incrementalists, placing a great deal of importance on what they already know. The following is a list of the common indicators of this type: they evaluate new information on the basis of how well it fits with their existing mental models; value experience and skill; like to take small steps, so ideas are usually modest changes; slow to change; they link facts together, using chains of reasoning to arrive at a single, and usually strongly held point of view; uncomfortable with contradiction so always look for a right answer; when

Table 2.1. Five inquiry archetypes

	Leibniz	Locke	Kant	Hegel	Singer
Knowledge acquisition	Searching	Searching	Scanning	Scanning	Scanning
Approach to change	Maintaining	Reacting	Initiating	Initiating	Initiating
Relationship to others	Directing	Mediating	Collaborating	Internalizing	Unpredictable
Problem solving	Retaining	Converging	Diverging	Debating	Unpredictable

information is encountered, it is typically classified according to their preexisting understanding; seek confirmation rather than diverse viewpoints; experienced-based decision makers; make predictions about future events based on their past experience; like to mention the number of years of relevant experience they have. In summary, a Leibnizian inquiring system is a closed system with a set of built-in elementary axioms that are used, along with formal logic, to generate more general fact nets.

The Lockean Inquirer

Lockean inquirers are known as the consensus builders; typically asking others to generate ideas and focusing on agreement. They also have other common characteristics as follows: do not actively attempt to change their environment, unless the change creates harmony and unanimity; suffer excessively from groupthink and unlikely to generate good ideas; lead to good implementation. In summary, inquiring systems based on Lockean reasoning are experimental and consensual.

The Kantian Inquirer

Kantians are viewed as searchers who combine ideas from diverse sources and unusual associations. The following attributes are common to this type of inquirer: very broad in their search; concerned with objectivity; search different points of view and are comfortable with inconsistency and multiple perspectives; easily accept new information into their existing mental models and discard the information when they are no longer appropriate; recognizes changes and opportunities in their environment; engage actively with idea generation and brainstorming strategies; make decisions based on the synthesis of ideas, rather than past experiences or consensus. The most unique feature of Kantian systems is that the theoretical component allows an input to be subjected to different interpretations.

The Hegelian Inquirer

Hegelians are known as the debaters, arguing internally with themselves to develop ideas. They function on the premise that greater enlightenment results from the conflict of ideas. They also have a number of other common characteristics including the following: use values, beliefs, and emotions in addition to logic; care about ethics; theorize and create thought experiments to understand; inquiry takes place through strong internal debate; they like to think beyond the boundaries of standard rules and approaches; harder to come to a conclusion/decision, because of their endless internal debate; more likely to employ lateral thinking.

The Singerian Inquirer

Singerians are considered as most flexible inquirers comfortable with and employing all systems of inquiry. They also exhibit the following common characteristics: frequent, dramatic, and unpredictable change; finding an answer is less important than finding a better question; alternate between making things simpler and making them more complicated; comfortable with myriad information sources; find the optimum mix between commitment to a problem and detachment, between passion for it and decorum or reflection about it, and between deferral and immediacy; constantly assessing, everything is open for inspection at all times, and nothing taken for granted; constantly question and work very hard at remaining bias free.

In summary, using archetypes based on philosophies of Leibniz, Locke, Kant, Hegel, and Singer provides a rationale for knowledge workers' recruitment, as well as the design of knowledge spaces to support their inquiry styles. Leibnizian and Lockean tendencies may be more suited for "get it done" types of tasks, while Kantian, Hegelian, and Singerian tendencies may be more fruitful in "creative" tasks. In general, someone who is a scanner in his or her knowledge acquisition approach is considered to be more creative than someone who is a searcher. On the other hand, someone who is dialectical in knowledge generation is more likely to scan knowledge sources than someone who is a maintainer. Therefore, a debater is more likely to use scanning resources more effectively. The following study was designed to provide insight into archetypes that reflect knowledge workers' dominant inquiry approaches in two different cultural contexts.

Empirical Study

Study Objectives

Given the current infancy of knowledge management theory and practice, there is little empirical research done in the field (Alavi & Leidner, 2001). Therefore, the main objective of this research is to conduct an empirical study to categorise knowledge workers' inquiry systems using the Vandenbosch et al. (2001) classification as a guideline. It is expected that the results of this research will be useful to practitioners in that they may help them to formulate a suitable design for a knowledge space that could accommodate the inquiry styles of different knowledge workers.

If it is clear how knowledge workers approach learning, it will be easier to provide better support systems to encourage knowledge sharing and creativity. This can be helpful for both knowledge managers and workers. Knowledge managers can assist workers more readily if they understand how they learn and acquire knowledge. Knowledge workers can develop better learning skills and understand the importance of managing their knowledge as an asset for their future career paths.

Research Design and Subjects

A survey study, based on the work by Vandenbosh et al. (2001), was conducted to determine knowledge workers' inquiry styles. Voluntary subjects for the study were university students. The study chose to focus on students' inquiry behaviour, as it was felt that students were "knowledge workers" with much potential to influence their future career organisations with their preferred style. Another reason for choosing academic students to study inquiry behaviour and archetypes is the belief that results may have some important implications for tertiary education. Students' preferred inquiry style may trigger more suitable ways of teaching them. Convenience sampling was used to select the participants.

Two groups of the participating students came from different cultural backgrounds (Australia and Europe). Subjects in the first group were 72 students enrolled in the Knowledge Management Systems and Technology course at the University of New South Wales (UNSW). The second group of subjects was 55 students enrolled in the Database course at Sarajevo School of Science and Technology (SSST). This offered us an opportunity to examine potential correlations between archetypes and demographic factors such as cultural background.

The survey instrument shown in the Appendix to this chapter was adapted from Vandenbosch et al. (2001). It consists of two types of questions: *closed questions,* where subjects' self-reported their behaviour by selecting one or more inquiry options and indicating percentage time on each; and *open-ended questions* for expressing additional opinions about various aspects of their inquiry behaviour. These were used to gain a deeper insight into knowledge workers' learning needs.

The closed-questions section was divided into four main subsections. Questions were designed to elicit critical incidents regarding students' approach to knowledge acquisition, problem solving, approach to change, and relationship to others. The critical incident technique used has a number of advantages. The questions are set up to follow a structured set of guidelines (coding scheme), so it is easier to analyse and synthesise the results later on. Compared to methods like collecting interview opinions and assessments, results would be more objective as they are based on behaviour responses. Also, using closed-questions in the survey would encourage students to participate in the study due to the reduced time and effort required to fill out the answers to each question.

The first part of the survey required the participants to tick the appropriate method listed in each section and then give an approximate percentage of time spent on each selected method to identify dominant ones. These answers were used to classify students into the appropriate archetypes following the classification scheme presented earlier in Table 2.1. This classification scheme places individuals into specific groups on the basis of their interrelated knowledge acquisition, approach to change, relationship to others, and problem-solving behaviour.

With respect to knowledge acquisition, respondents were assessed in terms of their inclination to *search* for knowledge sources with a predetermined agenda and focus, or *scan* for knowledge sources with a broad agenda and view. With regard to approach to change, the subjects were assessed by their likelihood to *react* to a real or potential problem, *maintain* the status quo, or *initiate* change in order to increase their capacity and influence the environment. Respondents' relationships to others were assessed in terms of their tendency to *direct* others, *mediate* by empowering others, *collaborate* by joining others in generating ideas and making decisions, or *internalise* by attempting to resolve problems individually playing through multiple scenarios. Finally, subjects' problem-solving methods were assessed in terms of *retain* by focusing on ideas that complement and affirm one's own approach, *converge* by closing in upon ideas to find an agreeable solution, *diverge* by considering and expanding upon many ideas to develop a specific solution, and *debate* by dialectic discussions of several ideas in order to develop a specific solution. For example, an individual with a greater percentage of a, b, and c responses to survey questions 1, 2, 3, and 4 would be judged as searching, maintaining, directing, and retaining type, and as such placed into the Leibnizian category.

Results

From the responses obtained for the percentage of time spent on different inquiry methods, we were able to categorise the participants into five archetypes. Comparative results for two groups of subjects (UNSW and SSST) are shown in Figure 2.1.

The participants in the first group (UNSW) clearly reflected four different types. The results revealed the following composition across these types: Leibnizian (57%), Lockean (29%), Kantian (8%), and Hegelian (6%). These results indicate a dominant Leibnitz type, followed by Lockean, Kantian, and Hegelian.

The second group (SSST) presented a somewhat different picture. The results revealed the following composition across all five archetypes: Leibnizian (40%), Lockean (9%), Kantian (33%), Hegelian (14%), and Singerian (4%). These results indicate a dominant Leibnitz type, followed by Kantian and Hegelian, then Lockean.

Figure 2.1. Comparative analysis of respondents' inquiry systems

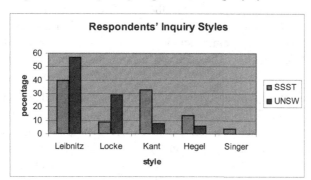

An interesting result is that there were some Singerians found in the second subject group. Singerians are assumed to be very flexible and adaptive and would adopt a variety of different methods for study. However, most of the subjects in this research chose to select a dominant method.

The authors hoped to gain a deeper understanding of the subjects' inquiry systems from responses obtained to the open-ended questions from part 2 of the survey. In this part, subjects were asked to describe in more detail some recent example of their experience in generating ideas. Unfortunately, most of these responses could not be used for a deeper qualitative analysis. About 40% of the subjects did not attempt the second part of the survey at all. Furthermore, most of the responses given were too general and could not provide new insights, but rather add support to the quantitative results. The additional time required to make written comments may have contributed to the poor response rate and quality of subjects' comments. Therefore, our discussion is informed mainly by the descriptive analysis of their quantitative answers.

Discussion of Main Findings

The main findings of this study provide strong support for the extended cognitive style perspective on learning that interrelates knowledge acquisition, approach to change, relationship to others, and problem-solving behaviour of knowledge workers. The current study discovered significant differences among student subjects in their systemic approaches to knowledge based on Churchman's interpretation of philosophies. The study also found that the patterns of dominant approaches at the group level might be contingent upon culture.

As such, these findings have a number of important implications for knowledge managers. More specifically, they suggest the need to design an appropriate knowledge management support system to respond to different individual learners' needs. In addition, knowledge management support systems need to consider the needs of the group as a whole, which will be generally a combination of different archetypes in different cultural contexts.

Firstly, with respect to individual styles, prominent Leibnizian tendencies were found in both UNSW and SSST groups, with 57% and 40% of respondents, respectively. They show that most students believe that knowledge should come from study. They place a great emphasis on facts and they learn using formal logic to make inferences of causes and effects. The Leibnizian type tends to rely heavily on the theory and what they have already learnt. Therefore, providing support in terms of explicit knowledge sources, such as notes and textbooks, would benefit Leibnizians' learning style. A typical Leibnizian response to acquiring knowledge was "reading from documents and reports provided."

Lockean tendencies were discovered in both groups, but were more prominent in the UNSW group (29%) than in the SSST group (9%). Lockeans employ experimental and consensual reasoning. They learn by observing the world, sharing their observations, and creating consensus about what has been observed. To benefit this learning style, group discussions and group assignments could assist students to increase their learning interest and performance, and also for teachers to provide feedback. These are all important sources that help the group to reach consensus. Experimental results of an issue identification study conducted by Aurum et al. (2002) indicate that groups of 4-5 students can identify the majority of relevant issues.

Contrary to Lockeans, a much smaller percentage of subjects were identified as Kantians in the UNSW group (8%) than in the SSST group (33%). These inquirers like to seek knowledge from diverse sources, and are very broad in their search. They tend to scan internal and external environments for purposeful knowledge. Therefore, in order to satisfy Kantians' need in learning, knowledge managers should provide them with many rich resources and readings outside the core texts.

There were some Hegelians found in both groups, although less in the UNSW group (6%) than in the SSST group (14%). Hegelians are the debaters who tend to synthesise opposing models into a new worldview. They rely upon the dialectic process to resolve opposing viewpoints, and they may generate an entirely new idea as a result. Therefore, facilitating the dialectic process would enable the Hegelian to acquire knowledge and encourage them to generate innovative ideas.

Finally, our survey uncovered a small percentage of Singerians in the SSST group (4%), but none in the UNSW group (0%). Singerian inquirers are renaissance people who employ all systems of inquiry. They constantly question and work very hard. In other words, their learning styles are very flexible. Therefore, providing Singerians with all the previously mentioned features and facilities should enable them to gain knowledge and generate new insights in their studies.

At the group level, a comparative analysis of inquiry systems in two cultural contexts reveals a marked difference. A relatively greater percentage of Leibnizian and Lockean archetypes found in the UNSW group reflects the dominant incremental and consensus-based approach to knowledge. In contrast, a relatively larger percentage of Kantian, Hegelian, and Singerian archetypes found in the SSST group suggests a greater inclination towards creative and innovative knowledge.

Designing an appropriate knowledge management support to respond to different individual and group needs presents a major challenge. Various social initiatives and technologies discussed in Chapter I may be able to provide a conducive environment for learning. A knowledge space designed on the principles of knowledge management may provide a necessary place to exchange, share, capture, discover, and obtain knowledge resources for a learner. It also may be a valuable learning community for knowledge workers to share and discuss matters relating to their work. In summary, it can enable or facilitate knowledge processes and enhance learning performance. The knowledge space described in Chapter III is a good example of one such learning tool that can facilitate the needs of different knowledge workers.

Conclusion

This chapter investigated the inquiry systems of university students as knowledge workers, based on Churchman's models. Data on their approaches to information acquisition, change, relationships to others, and problem solving were gathered by administering a survey questionnaire. Our results indicate that recognizable inquiry archetypes emerge for most individuals. They also suggest that the dominant patterns at the group level are contingent upon the cultural context. These results may be used to guide and justify the design of flexible knowledge spaces that can provide support for different individual and group styles and maximize knowledge workers' learning experience.

References

Alavi, M., & Leidner, D. E. (2001). Knowledge management and knowledge management systems: Conceptual foundations and research issues. *MIS Quarterly*, *25*(1), 107-136.

Churchman, C. W. (1971). *The design of inquiring systems: Basic concepts of systems and organisation.* New York: Basic Books, Inc.

Covey, S. R. (1989). *The 7 habits of highly effective people.* New York: Rockfeller Center.

Davenport, T. H., & Prusak, L. (1998). *Working knowledge.* Boston: Harvard Business School Press.

Davenport, T. H., DeLong, D. W., & Breers, M. C. (1998, winter). Successful knowledge management projects. *Sloan Management Review*, 43-57.

Drucker, P. F. (1993). *Post-capitalist society.* New York: Harper Business.

Drucker, P. F. (1998). The coming of the new organisation. In *Harvard Business Review on Knowledge Management.* Boston: Harvard Business School Press.

Garvin, D. A. (1998). Building a learning organisation. In *Harvard Business Review on Knowledge Management.* Boston: Harvard Business School Press.

Grayson, C. J., & O'Dell, C. (1998). Mining your hidden resources. *Across the Board, 35*(4), 23-28.

Holsapple, C. W., & Singh, M. (2000). Electronic commerce: From a definitional taxonomy toward a knowledge-management view. *Journal of Organisational Computing and Electronic Commerce, 10*(3), 149-170.

Nonaka, I. (1998). The knowledge-creating company, In *Harvard Business Review on Knowledge Management.* Boston: Harvard Business School Press.

Satzinger, J. W., Garfield, J. M., & Nagasundaram, M. (1999). The creative process: The effects of group memory on individual idea generation. *Journal of Management Information Systems.*

Senge, P. (1990). *The fifth discipline.* New York: Doubleday.

Stewart, T. A. (1997). *Intellectual capital: The new wealth of organisations.* New York: Doubleday.

Vandenbosch, B., Fay, S., & Saatciglu, A. (2001, fall). Where ideas come from: A systematic view of inquiry. *Sprouts: Working Papers on Information Environments, Systems and Organizations, 1.*

Appendix

Survey of Knowledge Workers' Inquiry Systems

The purpose of this survey is to identify the characteristics of the inquiry approaches of students as knowledge workers. The responses on this survey will be used for the research on managing knowledge. Please answer the following questions by writing in and selecting the option that 'best' describes your approach.

PART I

Q1. Indicate your usual approach to knowledge/information acquisition.

(Please tick one or more of following methods that best describe your approach and also give an approximate percentage (out of 100%) of time on each of them)

		Tick/Percent
a.	seek specific information or information with specific characteristics and content	____/____
b.	look at (evaluates, interprets) information from a prespecified perspective	____/____
c.	seek and/or receive information from similar, stable sources	____/____
d.	seek diverse information or information with diverse characteristics and content	____/____
e.	look at (evaluates, interprets) information from several perspectives	____/____
f.	seek and/or receive information from various, diverse sources	____/____

Q2. Indicate your usual approach to idea generation and problem solving

(Please tick one or more of following methods that best describe your approach and also give an approximate percentage (out of 100%) of time on each of them)

		Tick/Percent
a.	take personal control of idea and solution development efforts	____/____
b.	heavily rely on my own judgments and opinions	____/____
c.	seek consistency and confirmation of personal viewpoint	____/____
d.	highly value and/or rely on past experiences	____/____
e.	seek consensus and agreement among approaches and ideas	____/____
f.	seek synthesis of ideas and information	____/____
g.	clearly define the boundaries and parameters for ideas and solutions	____/____
h.	feel comfortable with inconsistency	____/____

i.   seek diverse experiences and input   ____/____

j.   flexible around the boundaries and parameters for ideas and
solutions   ____/____

k.   challenge and/or like to be challenged by others'
perspectives   ____/____

l.   engage and/or like to be engaged in dialectical debates and
discussions   ____/____

m.   experience difficulty in choosing sides or reaching resolution in
conflicting situations   ____/____

Q3. Indicate your usual approach to change

(Please tick one or more of following methods that best describe your approach and also give an approximate percentage (out of 100%) of time on each of them)

Tick/Percent

a.   am prompted by others about change   ____/____

b.   trigger change in order to adapt to circumstances   ____/____

c.   initiate change only in the face of inevitabilities   ____/____

d.   am slow or hesitant to initiate change   ____/____

e.   trigger change to maintain consistency   ____/____

f.   self-initiate changes   ____/____

g.   am prompted to change by opportunities and/or futuristic
visions   ____/____

h.   trigger change in order to take advantages of, contribute
to, and/or participate in emerging situations or patterns   ____/____

Q4. Indicate your usual approach in relationship to others

(Please tick one or more of following methods that best describe your approach and also give an approximate percentage (out of 100%) of time on each of them)

Tick/Percent

a.   maintain a strong personal point of view   ____/____

b.   consider myself the most knowledgeable in my environment,
and often take the role of educator   ____/____

c.   attempt to convince and/or manipulate others   ____/____

d.   tell people what to do   ____/____

e.   rely on the judgments and opinions of
others   ____/____

f. invite and/or expect others to develop ideas and
    solution   ____/____

g. create and/or enact processes/structures for others
    to develop ideas and solutions   ____/____

h. include judgments and opinion of others   ____/____

i. ask and/or instruct others to develop ideas and
    solutions   ____/____

j. actively involve myself with others in the processes/
    structures of idea and solution development   ____/____

k. assume the role of others when considering the problem   ____/____

l. play through multiple scenarios in my mind   ____/____

m. examine contingencies   ____/____

PART II

Now, please describe in a more detailed way a recent instance when you acquired knowledge, resolved an issue and changed your mind.

Chapter III

Knowledge Space:
Building Foundations for Advancing Knowledge

Abstract

This chapter presents a concept of knowledge space as a physical, virtual, or mental space that serves as a foundation for knowledge development in an organization. Based on the review of previous research, it identifies and describes several different types of knowledge spaces and their roles in supporting processes of knowledge creation, transfer, retention, and application. These are used to provide a practical, generalized approach to constructing organizational knowledge space for advancing individual and collective knowledge.

Introduction

In essence, the development of an organisation's knowledge stock or capital is the result of the dynamic organisational knowledge processes. The effectiveness of these processes is impacted by a number of social and technological factors, as discussed in Chapter I.

Managers are responsible for developing and implementing an optimal mix of socio-technical knowledge management initiatives to support knowledge workers' needs and processes of an organization, as discussed in Chapter II. Hence, it is important that they have a good understanding of the dynamism of knowledge processes and awareness of the different conditions that can facilitate successful support of these processes. To this end, in this chapter, we introduce the concept of "knowledge space" as a platform for advancing individual and/or collective knowledge.

According to Nonaka and Konno (1998), knowledge space can be thought of as a shared space for emerging relationships. It can be physical (e.g., office), virtual (e.g., e-mail), or mental (e.g., shared ideals), or any combinations of them. Different knowledge spaces support different knowledge processes and thereby impact knowledge development. Awareness of the different characteristics of knowledge spaces can facilitate successful support of knowledge development.

Researchers have, for some time, been investigating fundamental conditions for knowledge development from different perspectives (Becerra-Fernandez & Sabherwal, 2001; Nonaka & Konno, 1998; Snowden, 2002). The most recent knowledge-management literature suggests that we are entering the third generation of knowledge management. The new generation of thoughts is beginning to replace our current focus on Nonaka's (1998) tacit explicit knowledge conversion (SECI model) and our earlier emphasis on Hammer and Stanton's (1995) efficient provision of knowledge through business process reengineering (BPR initiatives). In particular, the third age of knowledge management recognises the need to manage the content, the narrative, and the context of knowledge (Snowden, 2002). Presented in the following section is an overview of major existing models and frameworks.

Review of Existing Models and Frameworks

The Concept of "ba"

Perhaps the most frequently quoted and used category in the knowledge-management literature is that which distinguishes tacit from explicit knowledge, based on

Polanyi's (1966) original concepts. This has led to the knowledge creation spiral of Nonaka and Takeuchi (1995), which views organisational knowledge creation as a process involving a continual interplay between explicit and tacit dimensions of knowledge. Four levels of carriers of knowledge in organisations are assumed, namely individual, group, organisational, and interorganisational.

The model presented in Figure 3.1 describes a dynamic process in which explicit and tacit knowledge are exchanged and transformed through four modes. *Socialisation* enables tacit knowledge to be transferred from one individual to another. *Externalisation* converts tacit knowledge into explicit knowledge in the forms of concepts and models. *Combination* allows the existing explicit knowledge to be restructured, systemised, and combined into new explicit forms. *Internalisation* allows individuals to absorb explicit knowledge and broaden their tacit knowledge so that new knowledge and skills could be developed.

Subsequently, Nonaka and Konno (1998) introduced the concept of "ba," a Japanese word with a special meaning of the concept of "place," to address the question of fundamental conditions for knowledge creation. They suggested that four types of "ba" (originating, interacting, cyber, and exercising) act as promoters of processes of socialisation, externalisation, combination, and internalisation, and so enable knowledge creation.

In particular, "*originating* ba" promotes the *socialisation* mode and is the place from which the knowledge creation process begins. Such a common space is needed so that people can share knowledge and experiences through face-to-face conversations. "*Interacting* ba" represents the *externalisation* mode, and is the place where tacit knowledge is converted into explicit knowledge. In interacting ba, people share knowledge through dialogue and collaboration. "*Cyber* ba" represents the *combination* mode and is the virtual place of interaction. In cyber ba, people interact

Figure 3.1. Four types of ba and processes of knowledge conversion

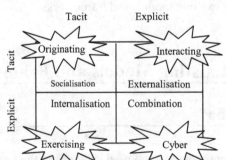

and communicate virtually, utilising modern network technologies. "*Exercising* ba" represents the *internalisation* mode, and is the place where explicit knowledge is converted to tacit knowledge. "Exercising ba" provides a common space for continuous individual learning and reflection.

The "cynefin" Model

The term "cynefin" is a Welsh word for habitat or place. It should be understood as the place of our multiple cultural, religious, geographic, trial, and other belongings and experiences. Snowden (2002) used the idea of cynefin in order to explain the complex acts of knowing and interrelatedness of content, narrative, and context management.

Snowden classifies knowledge content into known, knowable, complex, and chaos. The known content should only include evidence-based, proven best practices. Business processes can be used as a basis for knowledge modelling. Knowable is the domain of good practice where shared community expertise can be developed, given the resources, capability, and time. Complex content can be best understood in terms of patterns. The patterns are defined as emergent properties of the interaction of the various agents. Chaos represents the realm of the completely unknown and uncharted. Creativity and innovative ideas are of utmost importance in such circumstances.

The nature of knowledge content is key to understanding the narrative management. The choice of the most suitable narrative (process, strategy, or activity) to deliver knowledge content is highly contingent upon the nature of that content. Cataloguing and describing legitimate best practices is the best way of conveying what is known. Case studies have been suggested as a highly useful and relevant means of knowledge transfer when a complicated situation or process is being explained (Remenyi, Money, Price, & Bannister, 2002). As a general rule, the less abstract and the more illustrative the description of complexity, the greater the audience's understanding. With respect to knowable, organisations usually need to study past events to learn which components of various complicated systems and their relationships are important, and use what they discover to create predictive and prescriptive models for future. Knowledge management initiatives presented in the book can help people find the nature of various phenomena of interest and discover their interrelationships more easily and better.

While the issues of conveyance surrounding complicated, but known and knowable content, are reasonably well understood, this is not true for the domains of complex and chaos. Most humans make decisions on the basis of perceived patterns, so perceiving and understanding patterns is the key for managing complexity. Visualisation appears to be a useful vehicle to explore emerging patterns. However, in the realm of chaos, the only way to learn is to create, to break down old patterns, and form new ones. The creative stimulus of chaos can, through brainstorming, produce new capabilities in the ecology.

Snowden's (2002) research departs from much of the earlier held universalistic perspective of knowledge management by suggesting that the effectiveness of a knowledge narrative (process, strategy, or activity) depends on the knowledge context. His position is that a bureaucratic context is good as a training environment, communities of practice encourage knowledge exchange through socialisation, informal contexts use stories and symbols to provide shared understanding, while innovative contexts require action and risk taking to impose order on chaos.

Constructing Knowledge Spaces in Organisations

To enhance organisational knowledge creation, it is important to understand the characteristics of different knowledge spaces and their relationship with the corresponding mode of knowledge conversion (Alavi & Leidner, 2001).

Conditions for Knowledge Creation

Handzic and Zhou (2005) suggest that particular attention should be paid to the conditions that form part of an organisational environment conducive to knowledge creation. These include, among others, giving people the freedom to have new ideas, giving people time to think, letting people pursue their own projects, and providing creative zones spatially separated from the normal working environment. Tolerance for mistakes is also an important factor, as is the congruence of individual interests with the collective goals.

Aids to innovation also include methods for planning and guiding the innovation process. These vary from techniques for stimulating creativity and rewarding employee suggestions, to formalising a systematic approach to problem solving, to using metaphors for expressing tacit knowledge. Stimulating techniques can be classified into three basic categories: free association, structured relationships, and group techniques (Marakas, 1999). In the category of structured relationship techniques, the focus is on the generation of new ideas via forced combinations of diverse ideas or concepts. However, the most widely used techniques involve using brainstorming techniques with groups to generate ideas. The end result is a map that contains a set of ideas that can be evaluated, organised, and prioritised.

Conditions for Knowledge Transfer

With respect to knowledge transfer, Handzic and Zhou (2005) note that this is not a simple process, as organisations often do not know what they know, and have weak systems for locating and retrieving knowledge that resides within the organisation. Organisations must nurture a supportive organisational environment and establish a technical infrastructure to facilitate knowledge sharing and transfer. These include (1) making knowledge visible; (2) developing knowledge networks, and (3) providing organisational support, most of which are discussed in Part II and III of this book.

1. **Making knowledge visible:** If the existing individual and organisational assets can be visualised, retrieved, and located, then the conditions for the sharing and distribution of knowledge are in place. Directories of experts, or yellow pages, can be used to raise the visibility of specialist knowledge. For example, the directory can list problem areas that occur frequently, together with names of potential problem solvers. Knowledge maps of various kinds may also be used to locate expertise.

2. **Developing knowledge networks:** for organisations operating on a global scale, computer-supported knowledge networks are useful. The modern technical infrastructure for knowledge distribution includes two main categories of technologies, company-wide data networks, such as intranets and groupware or computer-supported cooperative networks. Intranets offer a high level of security, and permit knowledge assets to be used without delay owing to internal administration. Compared to communication networks (e.g., e-mail), groupware offers an extra functionality (e.g., group scheduler) that coordinates knowledge distribution and helps to ensure consistency.

3   **Organisational support:** While technical infrastructure is needed for efficient distribution of knowledge, it is not sufficient to ensure effective knowledge transfer in an organisation. There must also be sufficient willingness among employees to communicate knowledge. At an individual level, this willingness may be influenced by factors such as pride in one's knowledge, availability of time, and fear of endangering one's own position. Company culture can also affect the scope and content of knowledge transfer. The use of power, an atmosphere of trust, and management attitudes all play a part in creating the right culture for effective knowledge transfer.

Conditions for Knowledge Storage

According to Handzic and Zhou (2005), organisational knowledge storage and retention is also not as simple and straightforward a process as some might expect. Like any other information system, if a repository ignores or cannot meet the needs of its users, it would be of little use. To address the issue of how to develop successful knowledge repositories, in addition to the authorship of entries mentioned above, Markus (2001) suggests that careful attention should be paid to three additional factors: (1) the costs involved in creating and using good repository records, (2) how to motivate high quality contributions, and (3) the role of human and technical intermediaries in knowledge documenting and reuse.

1.   **Providing adequate time and resources:** The task of making good documentation can be very time-consuming and resource demanding. However, most knowledge workers are busy professionals, and documentation may not be their first priority. The potentially high costs can act as a disincentive for knowledge workers to produce and use quality documentation.

2.   Hence, appropriate incentives are needed to encourage quality submissions and contributions. These may include explicit reward systems and an open, sharing organisation culture.

3.   Intermediates or facilitators can play an important role in building good knowledge repositories. They abstract, index, author (re-author), translate, synthesise, and sanitise a variety of raw materials to create knowledge records for reuse. Markus (2001) observes that much of the documenting work is done most effectively by human intermediaries, and their roles in knowledge reuse are currently underappreciated. Nonetheless, technology is taking an increasing role in knowledge documenting and reuse.

Conditions for Knowledge Application

Companies that have world-class processes for developing new knowledge may still fail. This is because the possession of knowledge does not automatically guarantee its successful application in daily work. There are a number of factors that hinder the effective use of knowledge in everyday activities of an organisation. They may arise from organisational blindness, fear of revealing one's own weaknesses, or a general mistrust of outside knowledge. Therefore, appropriate measures must be taken to ensure that valuable skills and knowledge assets are effectively utilised. These are briefly discussed next.

1.   **Meeting the needs of users:** When information systems are left unused or project reports unread, it is often because they do not meet the needs of the users. Many studies show that individuals usually make use of knowledge based

on convenience and ease of use. A good way to encourage use is to make the knowledge infrastructure user-friendly. Some of the features that make systems user-friendly are simplicity, timelines, and compatibility. This means that the required knowledge should be localised and transferred simply and quickly, and should be made available in the form that permits prompt application and continued use.

In general, the organisational knowledge base can be used with greater effectiveness if it offers ready access to interesting information and knowledge, gives guidelines on how it can be obtained, and is current and of high quality. A software program that offers little noticeable improvement will often be ignored, as will a scientific memo on an irrelevant topic. The key issue is finding the right balance between the cost of obtaining and the benefit of using the knowledge.

2. **Fostering a supportive working environment:** User-friendly workspaces can encourage the use of knowledge. Proximity to the required knowledge can be achieved by positioning of workstations and sections to allow easier communication or exchange between individuals or sections. Open and flexible layouts with fewer offices and more shared work and conference spaces that can be used by many people at different times are also useful. Making individual offices and workshops more attractive are other simple ways of creating an atmosphere that encourages use of knowledge. New knowledge will be applied more readily in a context of collective problem solving.

Some organisations use designated physical spaces, usually located at the central points of the office building, to serve as centres to encourage knowledge exchange and utilisation. Such centres provide opportunities for the graphical presentation of material in the form of wall, video, or interactive displays. The contents can include news and messages from different projects and people, and provide a type of "ideas market." This makes these places inviting, and enables employees to identify and access the knowledge they need, thus encouraging and fostering its application.

The Handzic "k-space" Model

Knowledge spaces can be created by organizational effort. However, how exactly will companies create knowledge spaces and assure the continuous transformation of knowledge within the organization depends on what kind of knowledge is concentrated in it, and on the situation and strategy of a company. Different approaches to creating knowledge spaces are possible coming from cognitive psychology, philosophy, education, science, finance, and information technology.

Chapter I of this book has identified two broad groups of sociotechnological factors that can act as major knowledge catalysts and enable or facilitate knowledge processes, and thus, contribute to knowledge output. The primary role of interventions with respect to organisational structure, culture, and leadership, is seen in creating an organisational environment conducive to knowledge development. Technological solutions are perceived as a facilitating tool for knowledge sharing, representation, and transformation, as well as improving people's ability to acquire knowledge.

Davenport and Prusak (1998) maintain that it is only possible to realise full power of knowledge by taking a holistic ecological approach to knowledge management. Following their recommendations, this section presents the author's own conceptualisation of knowledge space, or "k-space," for advancing individual and collective knowledge in an organisation.

The proposed model, shown in Figure 3.2, is essentially a 2×2 matrix with "explicit" and "tacit" knowledge as columns, and "know-what" and "know-how" types of knowledge as rows of the matrix. Individual cells contain instances of specific knowledge types and their related sources and processes. For example, explicit know-what comprises facts and figures that may be stored in databases or documents.

Figure 3.2. Conceptual model of "k-space"

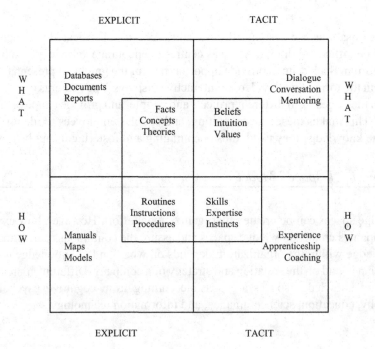

Explicit know-how includes rules and methods that can be found in models or in organisational procedures. Tacit know-what consists of shared ideas and beliefs of knowledge workers, while tacit know-how represents their instincts and expertise gained through long-term personal experience.

Case Study: Virtual k-space for a Graduate Course

A conceptual model, presented in Figure 3.2, was used to develop a specific virtual k-space for a graduate course learning/teaching. In the context of graduate education, the *explicit know-what* quadrant consists of the resources that can be used by students to acquire explicit knowledge. For example, all the students can obtain lecture notes, relevant readings, and access to databases. The *explicit know-how* quadrant contains search facilities, and rules and patterns discovered by individual students while mining data. The *tacit know-what* section consists of areas, such as discussion forums and announcements, that enable students and educators to share information. Finally, the *tacit know-how* quadrant supports the individual's tacit knowledge learning that can be gained through personal experience and activities such as assignments/tutorials etc.

The model suggests that students' course knowledge can be enhanced by enabling and facilitating availability, sharing, and finding of relevant information, as well as learning by doing. In order to minimize information overload, it is also suggested by the framework that students should be supported by intelligent search and mining facilities. The model also recognizes the importance of tacit knowledge. Past researchers show that students may benefit from sharing knowledge with others as well as from interaction with their peers (Handzic & Low, 2001; Handzic & Tolhurst, 2001). Self-directed learning, such as assignments, and a self-paced online learning session with continuous guidance and feedback would respond to the need for cultivation of students' skills for problem solving and decision making, as well as creativity.

The main objective of the course k-space was to provide students with a one-stop point of interaction for all their study needs; a portal that students could go to and obtain lecture notes, assignments, reference materials, discussions, surveys, search facilities, links, and many other useful tools. The idea of each section in the course k-space was to implement one or more facilities from a quadrant of the conceptual matrix. In addition, each section supported different idea-generation/learning styles. Chapter II found that different students have preferences for different inquiry methods, and if their preferred method is provided, the productivity and enjoyment of the course will be increased.

The design of course k-space presented here is the work of students attending the Knowledge Management Systems and Technology course at UNSW (for more details see Chong, Johson, & Chan, 2001). It consists of several parts, as follows:

- *Home section* contains announcements, quotes, and news, as well as evaluation forms, polls with results, and search facilities.

- **Contact details** incorporates contact person, consultation hours, class and lab venues, additional help, and comments.

- **Course details** includes recommended text, lecture notes, recommended readings, assignments, and course outline. It is expected to be of particular value to Leibnizians, who rely heavily on theory, and typically acquire knowledge by studying documents and reports provided.

- **Discussion forum** has assignment discussions, lecture comments, additional users posting, and search/posting tools. It represents an ideal support for Lockeans, who like to share their observations and create consensus.

- **Resources** section contains university links, research papers, field-related Web sites, and search engines. It provides an ideal learning support for Kantians, who typically seek knowledge by scanning a wide variety of external sources.

- **Solution finder** provides questions and answers, as well as simulation games. It is envisaged as a learning space for Hegelians, who tend to construct and internally debate different viewpoints and generate new solutions.

Figure 3.3. Course Details section of course k-space

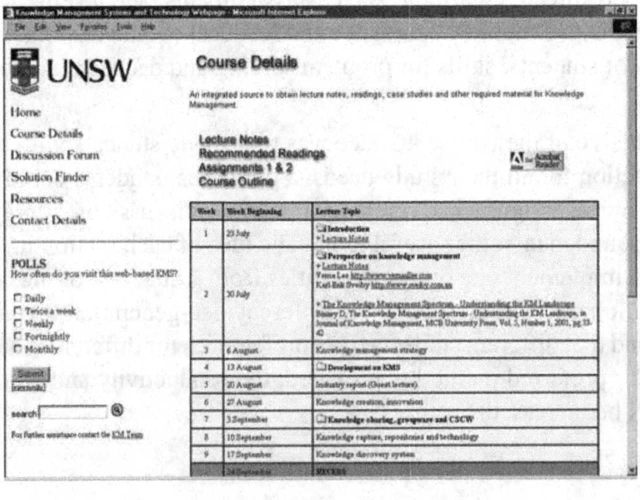

As an example, the *Course Details* section of the proposed course k-space can be seen in Figure 3.3. The purpose of the *Course Details* section is to allow users to obtain information necessary to assist them with the course. *Course Details* provides an overview of the course schedule over the 14 weeks. This page outlines the week number, week beginning date, and the lecture topics. The first two headings of the course outline are self-explanatory. Under the lecture topics heading, it contains folders for each of the 14 weeks. Furthermore, Acrobat reader software is available for download, as all the files are saved in PDF format, and users can easily gain access to these notes.

In summary, the course k-space supports individual learning by facilitating knowledge processes that foster the development of relevant knowledge of different types of students. It allows for taking small steps and incremental learning (Leibnizian), as well as building consensus (Lockean). More importantly, the course k-site encourages higher forms of inquiry involving forming associations and combining information from diverse places (Kantian), and constructing ideas through internal debate of all the factors (Hegelian). Finally, it allows for flexibility by considering all forms of inquiry (Singerian), if any such students exist. Other benefits of the proposed course k-space for students include enabling global access, ease of use, self-service, and collaboration. For educators, it provides a means to reduce paper work, and to publish and maintain useful and dynamic information in a variety of forms. For interested readers, Chapter IX of this book provides empirical evaluation of a specific course k-space from the user perspective.

Conclusion

The main objective of this chapter was to introduce the concept of knowledge space and explain its role in advancing individual and/or collective knowledge of an organization. It is important that organizations can propose, select, and design appropriate KM interventions to support knowledge processes, and thus enhance their knowledge capital. Managers need to be able to identify and appraise those conditions that will enable and facilitate different steps and phases in the knowledge development spiral. This chapter identifies and describes major characteristics of spaces that support knowledge creation, transfer, retention, and application. It is hoped that the awareness of different characteristics of different knowledge spaces should help these managers in constructing more a knowledge-conducive environment in their organizations.

References

Alavi, M., & Leidner, D. E. (2001). Knowledge management and knowledge management systems: Conceptual foundations and research issues. *MIS Quarterly*, *25*(1), 107-136.

Becerra-Fernandez, I., Gonzales, A., & Sabherwal, R. (2004). *Knowledge management: Challenges, solutions, and technologies.* Upper Saddle River, NJ: Pearson Education, Inc.

Chong, R., Jonson, C., & Chan, M. (2001). *Knowledge Website project report* (Knowledge Management Systems and Technology Course Assignment). October, UNSW.

Davenport, T. H., & Prusak, L. (1998). *Working knowledge.* Boston: Harvard Business School Press.

Handzic, M., & Low, G. (2002). The impact of social interaction on performance of decision tasks of varying complexity. *OR Insight*, *15*(1), 15-22.

Handzic, M., & Tolhurst, D. (2002). Evaluating an interactive learning environment in management education. *Educational Technology & Society*, *5*(3), 113-122.

Hammer, M., & Stanton, S. (1995). *The reengineering revolution: A handbook.* New York: HarperCollins.

Handzic, M., & Zhou, A. Z. (2005). *Knowledge management: An integrative approach.* Oxford, UK: Chandos Publishing.

Marakas, G. M. (1999). *Decision support systems in the 21st century.* NJ: Prentice-Hall.

Markus, A. (2001). Towards a theory of knowledge reuse: Types of knowledge reuse situations and factors in reuse success. *Journal of Management Information Systems, 18*(1), 57-93.

Nonaka, I. (1998). The knowledge-creating company. In *Harvard Business Review on Knowledge Management* (pp. 21-45). Boston: Harvard Business School Press.

Nonaka, I., & Konno, N. (1998). The concept of ba: Building a foundation for knowledge creation. *California Management Review, 40*(3), 40-54.

Nonaka, I., & Takeuchi, H. (1995). *The knowledge creating company: How Japanese companies create the dynamics of innovation.* New York: Oxford University Press Inc.

Polanyi, M. (1966). The logic of tacit inference. *Philosophy, 41*(1), 1-18.

Remenyi, D., Money, A., Price, D., & Bannister, F. (2002, September). The creation of knowledge through case study research. In *Proceedings of the European Conference on Knowledge Management (ECKM 2002),* Dublin.

Snowden, D. (2002). Complex acts of knowing: Paradox and descriptive self awareness, *Journal of Knowledge Management, 6*(2), 110-111.

Section II

Studies of Technology-Based Knowledge Management Initiatives

Chapter IV

Electronic Brainstorming:
Stimulating Creative
Idea Generation

Abstract

This chapter describes and empirically tests a specific electronic brainstorming system aimed at stimulating creative and innovative performance of software developers in the context of innovative product design. The system is based on a solo brainstorming method that provides users with external stimuli and exposes them to a large number of inputs over a short period of time. An empirical test was conducted using 45 volunteer student subjects. It reveals a beneficial effect of the system on the participants' ability to produce the requirements model for a new software product. In particular, interaction with the system resulted in a significant increase in the total number of ideas generated by the participants, but within similar categories of ideas. The findings suggest that the system may be useful in facilitating performance in working contexts involving creative thinking and problem solving

Introduction

There is a widespread recognition in business literature that creativity and innovation are major sources of the economic growth and competitive advantage of today's organisations (Drucker, 1985; Satzinger, Garfield, & Nagasundaram, 1999; Tomas, 1999). It is, therefore, not surprising that surveys show that these two issues are among the top priorities for senior executives in industry today (BW, 1998). There is also an acknowledgement that software has emerged as central to all sophisticated innovations (Quinn, Baruch, & Zien, 1997). In many cases, software is the end product itself, or it is the highest value component in the end product. This is true for most of the fastest growing industries including IT, entertainment, communications, advertising, logistics, and financial services. In other cases, software facilitates most stages of value creation and innovation processes.

The changing economic landscape, particularly the growing importance of software-based innovations, suggests the need for better management of the professional knowledge of software developers. There is a growing need to develop relevant creative and innovative capabilities to enable these employees to work more productively and contribute to economic growth. The purpose of this study is to address the issue of creativity and innovation by describing and testing a specific computer-based system aimed at stimulating the creative thinking and idea generation of software developers represented by students of software courses.

Creativity can be defined as the production of novel and appropriate ideas, solutions, and work processes (Shalley & Perry-Smith, 2001). While newness and novelty are the key dimensions of creative expressions, appropriateness is also an essential requirement in the context of problem solving and innovation. Generally, the education sector should nurture creativity, so that students can be successful in their future roles as innovative professionals and business people. More specifically, it is of utmost importance that informatics students be given an opportunity to develop and apply creative and innovative skills to software processes and products.

Some theorists believe that creativity is reserved only for the gifted, while others see it as a skill that can be learned (Ford, 1996; Marakas, 1998). The author of this book sees creativity as a property of a thought process that can be acquired through instruction and practice. A variety of factors have been suggested to influence creative thinking. Handzic and Cule (2002) grouped them into two broad categories: social and technological. The focus here is on information technology. The role of technology is seen primarily in terms of facilitating the creative process, including generation, exploration, communication, and dissemination of ideas (Shneiderman, 2000; Sridhar, 2001).

The main objectives of this study are to (1) describe a specific electronic brainstorming system based on a solo brainstorming method as a potentially suitable tool for stimulating software developers' creative thinking and idea generation, and (2) empirically test the effectiveness of the system in enhancing software developers' creative performance in the context of innovative software product design.

System Description

Based on Shneiderman's (2000) framework, an integrated and interactive "idea generator" system to support creative performance has been proposed by Handzic and Loy (2004). The genex framework stands for "generator of excellence" and describes what user interface features are needed in developing effective personal computer software tools that will make people more creative, more frequently. It consists of four fundamental activities (phases) that embody the process of producing creative works: collect, relate, create, and donate; and eight proposed tasks that, if repeated, can help people become more creative more often and allow the user to accomplish the four phases.

The four activities or phases of the process are not a linear path, and users should be able to conduct the activities in any order. In doing so, the software tool will

Figure 4.1. Idea generator system

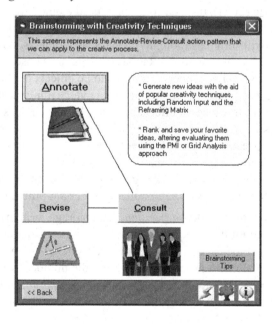

support the users' common desire to iteratively improve their creative works. The framework was constructed on various principles, including the belief that "new knowledge is built on previous knowledge," "powerful tools can support creativity," "refinement is a social process," and that the production of "creative work is not complete until it is disseminated."

The eight specific tasks that a creative support tool should implement include the following: searching and browsing digital libraries, the Web, and other resources; visualizing data and processes to understand and discover relationships; consulting with peers and mentors for intellectual and emotional support; thinking by free associations to make new combinations of ideas; exploring solutions, such as "what if" tools and simulation models; composing artefacts and performances; reviewing and replaying session histories to support reflection; disseminating results to gain recognition and add to the searchable resources.

The proposed idea generator system can be viewed as a personal knowledge management tool that primarily aims to support the individual in the daily exercise of creative thinking. Essentially, the system shown in Figure 4.1 supports the activities of searching and browsing digital libraries for sources of stimulating material; consulting with peers and mentors for intellectual and emotional support; thinking by free association to generate new ideas; composing artefacts and performances; reviewing and replaying session histories to support reflection; disseminating results to gain recognition and add to the searchable resources.

To support the activity of thinking by free association, a brainstorming session was incorporated based on the "random input" creativity technique (De Bono, 1992). According to Handzic (2004), this is a commonly used method for generating new ideas, particularly in situations such as developing new products. The assumption is that a random word will stimulate thoughts on associated objects, related concepts, and functions suggested by the word. Random words are chosen from concrete nouns and manipulative verbs. Concrete nouns can be objects that can be touched or seen, for example, cat, plane, stereo. Manipulative verbs imply an action that can be applied to an object to cause an effect, for example, minimise, solidify, rotate, stretch. These types of words are suggested to be more effective than adjectives or abstract concepts because they can be vividly imagined. The random-input tool shown in Figure 4.2 allows users to generate and record ideas that surface while using the random words. A random word is generated by the tool whenever the user clicks the Random Word button, or automatically at certain time intervals.

Furthermore, the system included a personal idea storage system for managing ideas, a pop-up search utility to explore prior ideas to reconsider and elaborate, a mechanism to allow incidental ideas to be registered quickly and modified or classified later on, and evaluation procedures to assess the number of ideas and their quality. These features were suggested as necessary to support the long-term and nonintentional idea generation as they allow users to record useful ideas that may

Figure 4.2. Random input tool

surface accidentally outside the brainstorming sessions (Shibata & Hori, 2002). They also allow users to confidently evaluate competing ideas and compare them in a deliberate, systematic, and transparent process (Asensio, 2001).

The idea evaluation tool included in the system was based on a grid analysis approach (Gabora, 2002). It involves producing a table that lists and scores various ideas or options to choose from, and specifies various factors that need to be taken into consideration, together with their relative importance. Thus, the tool allows the users to verify that an acceptable selection and number of useful creative solutions have been presented. The option with the highest overall score is considered to be the best choice. The grid analysis tool shown in Figure 4.3 illustrates how users enter the criteria in which to judge the list of favourite ideas against, and specify how important each criterion is by assigning relative weights.

This system was built primarily with the intention of empowering the process of creative knowledge generation and performance. The following empirical test was carried out by Handzic and Loy (2006) to evaluate the system from the user's point of view. The test is limited to the brainstorming component of the system only.

Figure 4.3. Grid analysis tool

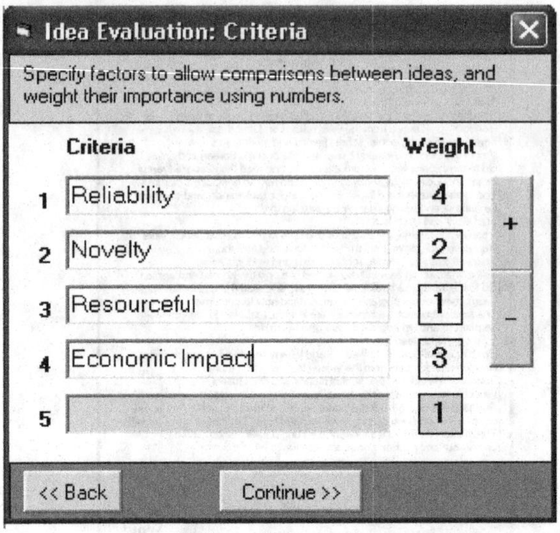

Empirical Evaluation

The system was empirically tested in a simulated software product design situation. It involved a fictitious organisation, The CyberToys, whose intention was to develop an innovative software toy, the "alien" cyber friend. Subjects adopted the role of a software developer working for the firm. Their task was to generate ideas with respect to the anticipated software-based toy using an object-think approach. This approach assumes that an object named "alien" knows "things" (e.g., attributes such as colour and shape), and it knows "how to do" things (e.g., how to move and sing). During the task performance, the subjects were required to produce two sets of documents, one before and one after interacting with the system provided to aid their task. Before interaction, subjects were asked to generate and record a range of ideas based solely on their past knowledge and experience. Then, they were asked to interact with the system and produce a second written document, identifying additional ideas.

A total of 45 subjects participated in the study on a voluntary basis. The participants were drawn from a pool of students attending a course in computer graphics at a small European university. They received no monetary incentive for their participation, but were motivated by their intrinsic interest in the subject matter. The experimental session lasted about 30 minutes. At the beginning, the subjects received instructions regarding the case study and task requirements.

The subjects' accomplishment in the task was evaluated in terms of the total number of relevant ideas they generated (denoted "ideas"), and the percentage of ideas belonging to two categories of ideas (denoted "know things" and "know how to do things"), as assessed by an expert judge. The judge was a software developer with over 30 years of experience. The judge examined the students' ideas for relevance and assigned them to appropriate categories. The classification scheme enabled examination of the changes in the quantity, as well as the quality of ideas generated by the students due to system use.

Results

Two sets of results of the analysis of the collected survey data are presented in this section. The first examines the respondents' demographics. The second presents aspects of respondents' creative performance.

With respect to demographics, the profile of the sample was examined in terms of the respondents' age, gender, and cultural background. The average respondent can be described as being a young person (aged between 19 and 21), either male or female (23 vs. 22) and coming from the southeastern region of Europe.

In order to understand the effects of the system on individual participants' creative performance, we statistically analysed the changes in the number and categories of ideas generated "after" the interaction with the system compared to those "before." The paired T-test was selected as the most suitable method for the analysis (Huck, Cormier, & Bounds, 1974). The results are presented in Table 4.1.

The results of the analysis performed indicate a significant positive impact of the system on the quantitative, but not qualitative aspects of the participants' creative performance. Table 4.1 shows significant results for the variable ideas but not the categories.

With respect to the quantitative aspect of performance, the results indicate a highly significant positive impact of the system on the total number of relevant ideas generated by the participants. As shown in Table 4.1, there was a significant increase in the number of relevant ideas generated due to using the system. More specifically, the mean value for total ideas increased by 4.93; from 6.69 before, to 11.62 after the interaction ($p<0.001$).

However, the results indicate no significant impact of the system on the qualitative aspect of participants' performance. Table 4.1 shows that there was no significant increase in the relative composition of relevant categories addressed by the par-

Table 4.1. Participants' creative performance

Dependent Variable	Before Interaction	After Interaction	Nature of Change
Ideas (number)	6.69	11.62	+4.93*
Categories (percentage) • know things • know how to do things	 63% 37%	 62% 38%	 -1% +1%

Note: *p<0.001

ticipants as a result of their use of the system. The mean percentage of the two different categories addressed by the subjects (know things vs. know how to do things) was similar before (63% vs. 37%) and after (62% vs. 38%) the interaction with the system.

Deeper analysis of the generated ideas revealed that the most common responses in the "know things" category reflected the desired attributes of the alien friend, such as colourful and funny. Typical responses found in the "know how to do things" were sing and dance. Few had ideas of a multilimbed friend who would act as a reminder, wake-up service, and obey orders such as turn lights on/off. Given the respondents' demographics, these ideas may reflect some sampling bias.

Discussion

The experimental results indicate that a solo brainstorming-based system had a significant effect on some aspects of students' creative performance in the context of an innovative software design. The effect was evident in the quantitative, but not the qualitative aspects of the performance evaluated. Users were found to generate a significantly greater number of relevant ideas, but of similar nature as the result of their interaction with the system.

The results of this study provide substantial support for the view that creative performance can be enhanced by appropriate instruction, as suggested by some theorists (Ford, 1996; Marakas, 1998). The stimulating system studied here was found to contribute to a significant improvement in the quantity of ideas generated by the participating students. These results also agree with some of our earlier findings from empirical studies conducted in natural disaster and business planning contexts (Aurum, Cross, Handzic, & VanToorn, 2001; Handzic, 2004). Essentially, the results support the idea that thinking applications can be developed, learnt, practiced, and used to generate ideas. Thus, they can enable an individual to think, provided that the principles are clearly understood.

It has also been suggested in the literature (Satzinger et al., 1999) that the idea generation method is one of the most important sources of encouraging creativity. The results of our study indicate that the brainstorming technique underlying our proposed system was a highly appropriate method for stimulating creative thinking and idea generation in a software development task. Students were found to generate a significantly greater number of relevant ideas when supported by the system. Essentially, the session helped students to uncover ideas without being constrained, to stimulate their own thinking by external influences, and to capture all of their thoughts.

The findings of the study also support the proposition that an electronic tool following a specific creativity technique can assist the creative process (Sridhar, 2001). One of the main advantages of such a tool is the speed at which ideas can be produced. Furthermore, the ideas can be stored and revisited at a later time. The tool can also provide a variety of stimuli that enhance imagination. The electronic system implemented in this study provided all of this, plus a written protocol that brought a formal structure to the idea generation process.

Our findings may have some important implications for innovative business sectors. Generally, they suggest the need to acknowledge the importance of teaching knowledge workers how to think creatively. There is also a need to implement technologies whose purpose is to help prepare the workforce for the knowledge-based economy. It appears that some governments and institutions are starting to emphasise the significance of promoting the creative thinking of the young (Sunderland, 2000), and educational institutions are beginning to implement changes in courses taught in business schools (Sangran, 2001).

The results of this study suggest that the system tested here may be a useful teaching tool in a variety of courses involving creative thinking and problem solving. They also suggest that it is likely to be most valuable in situations where the problem is unstructured, goals indistinct, and the outcome of an action cannot always be clearly identified. The tool is a rather generic one, since it uses a technique that can be applied to a variety of scenarios, and can help people process relevant documents whilst identifying issues. These documents act as a "trigger" to stimulate domain specific ideas from users.

While the current study provides a number of interesting findings, some caution is necessary regarding their generalisability due to a number of limiting factors. The application of laboratory conditions with students as participants is a limitation of this study. We believe that in fieldwork, and with real-world software professionals, the users' individual achievements would improve even further. The emphasis of the present study was on individuals. It would be interesting to examine the effect of the system on the creative performance of groups. Future research may address some of these issues.

Conclusion

This chapter reported a study of knowledge-creation technology. The study proposed and empirically tested a specific computer-based system for stimulating creative problem solving in the context of innovative software design. The system was designed on the basis of a solo brainstorming technique. The essence of the tool was to provide users with external stimuli, and expose them to a large number of inputs over a short period of time. The brainstorming component of the system was tested in this study. The results of the test indicated that the tool was quite helpful. Users were able to improve their creative performance and generate a greater number of relevant ideas, although within similar categories. These findings have important implications for knowledge management practice, as they suggest that the system can be useful in a variety of unstructured problem situations. Future research is recommended to address current study limitations.

References

Asensio, A. (2002, May). The process of idea management. *Executive Update.*

Aurum, A., Cross J., Handzic, M., & VanToorn, C. (2001). Software support for creative problem solving. In *Proceedings of the IEEE International Conference on Advanced Learning Technologies (ICALT 2001).*

B. W. (1998, December 14). *Business Wire.*

Collins, P., Kleeman, D., Martin, E., Richard-Smith, A., & Walker, D. (1997). Heritage information: A behavioural simulation for teaching information systems design. In H. Rehersar (Ed.), *Proceedings of the 2nd NSW Symposium on Information Technology and Information Systems (SITIS '97).* Australia: The School of Information Systems, UNSW.

DeBono, E. (1992). *Serious creativity.* UK: Advanced Practical Thinking Publ.

Drucker, P. F. (1985). *Innovation and entrepreneurship: Practices and principles,* New York: Harper & Row.

Ford, C. M. (1996). Theory of individual creative action in multiple social domains. *Academy of Management Review, 21*(4), 1112-1142.

Gabora, L. (2002, October). Cognitive mechanisms underlying the creative process. In *Proceedings of the Creativity and Cognition Conference.*

Handzic, M. (2004). *Knowledge management: Through the technology glass* (pp. 109-124). Singapore: World Scientific Publishing.

Handzic, M., & Cule, M. (2002, July). Creative decision making: Review, analysis and recommendations. In *Proceedings of the conference Decision Making in Internet Age, DSIage 2002,* Cork, Ireland (p. 443-452).

Handzic, M., & Loy, A. (2004). *Electronic brainstorming technology evaluation* (Working paper). Australia: University of New South Wales.

Handzic, M., & Loy, A. (2006, June 29-July 1). Creative decision support system: An empirical evaluation. In *Proceedings of the International Conference on Creativity and Innovation in Decision Making and Decision Support (CIDMDS 2006),* London.

Huck, S. W., Cormier, W. H., &Bounds, W. G. Jr. (1974). *Reading statistics and research.* New York: Harper and Row Publishers.

Marakas, G. M. (1998). *Decision support systems in the twenty-first century.* Upper Saddle River, NJ: Prentice Hall.

Quinn, J. B., Baruch, L. J., & Zien, K. A. (1997). *Innovation explosion: Using intellect and software to revolutionize growth strategies,* New York: The Free Press.

Sangran, S. (2001, February). Preparing students to be k-professionals. *Computimes Malaysia, 22,* 1-2.

Satzinger, J. W., Garfield, J. M., & Nagasundaram, M. (1999). The creative process: The effects of group memory on individual idea generation. *14*(4), 143-160.

Shalley, C. E., & Perry-Smith, J. E. (2001). Effects of social-psychological factors on creative performance: The role of informational and controlling expected evaluation and modelling experience. *Organisational Behaviour and Human Decision Processes, 84*(1), 1-22.

Shibata, H., & Hori, K. (2002, October). A system to support long-term creative thinking in daily life and its evaluation. In *Proceedings of the Creativity and Cognition Conference.*

Shneiderman, B. (2000). Creating creativity: User interfaces for supporting innovation. *ACM Transactions on Computer-Human Interaction, 7*(1), 114-138.

Sridhar, R. (2001, February). India: Software for breaking mental blocks! *Business Line, India, 22,* 1-3.

Sunderland, K. (2000, July). The power of a silly idea. *Charter, 71*(6), 49-51.

Tomas, S. (1999). Creative problem solving: An approach to generating ideas. *Hospital Material Management Quarterly, 20*(4), 33-45.

Chapter V

Groupware:
Enabling Knowledge Sharing
Across Time and Space

Abstract

This chapter reports on usage and effectiveness of various technologies available for knowledge sharing among employees in a global organisation. Clearly, different types of technologies were preferred in different application contexts. E-mail was preferred in different-time-same-place and different-time-different-place, presentation software in same-time-same-place, and voice conferencing in same-time-different-place contexts. Jointly, technologies used in same-time contexts were perceived as more effective than those in different-time contexts irrespective of place.

Introduction

A great deal of knowledge within organisations resides in the minds of its employees. To capitalise on individual knowledge, organisations need to turn it into organisational knowledge through "sharing." Nonaka's (1998) SECI model describes organisational knowledge development as a dynamic process involving a continual interplay between explicit and tacit dimensions of knowledge through processes of socialisation, externalisation, combination, and internalisation. The model identifies socialisation and externalisation as modes that enable tacit and explicit knowledge to be transferred from one individual or group to another within the organisation. These processes correspond to Hansen, Nohria, and Tierney's (1999) personalisation (person-to-person) and codification (person-to-document) strategies for managing knowledge. The concept is also found in many other process-orientated knowledge management frameworks under different names including social learning, knowledge sharing, and knowledge transfer (Alavi & Leidner, 2001).

The assumption is that personalisation (or socialisation) enables tacit knowledge to be transferred between individuals and groups through shared experience, space, and time. Examples include spending time working together or in social meetings. With respect to codification (or externalisation), the notion is that it allows wider dissemination of explicit knowledge within the organisation through shared documents and files. Generally, knowledge sharing is considered as one of the most challenging processes for a knowledge-based enterprise due to employees' possible reluctance to share what they know. It is suggested that in its absence, the gap between individual and organisational knowledge can widen. It is also noted that knowledge sharing is the most susceptible process to the effects of various influencing factors (Ford & Chan, 2003). However, there is a major disagreement within the knowledge management research community regarding the nature and relative importance of various sociotechnological factors to knowledge sharing (Snowden, 2003; Swan, 2003). The focus of this chapter is on technology.

Handzic's (2003) integrated framework places technology among major enablers and facilitators of knowledge processes and thus, sharing. The framework further suggests that context impacts the choice and implementation of knowledge sharing technologies. The contingency perspective warns that no one technology is best under all circumstances (Handzic & Hasan, 2003). Taking the view that technology does have a contingent role to play in knowledge sharing; the main objective of this paper is to explore which technologies are being most used to share knowledge in organisations and how effective they are in different application contexts. In the global economy, of particular interest are different place and time contexts.

Technologies for Knowledge Sharing

From the personalisation perspective (Hansen et al., 1999), the main role of technology is seen in enabling and facilitating interaction among people for the purpose of knowledge sharing. The aim is to create a connected virtual environment for knowledge exchange by allowing knowledge seekers to identify and communicate with knowledge sources (Handzic & Hasan, 2003). From the codification perspective, the main role of technology is to document knowledge processes and store best business practices in shared databases and document management systems. The Interim Australian KM Standard (Standards Australia, 2003) recommends several types of technologies for consideration by organisations when developing knowledge management solutions that support knowledge sharing. These include traditional communication, specialised groupware, and teleconferencing technologies, integrated portals, intranets, and extranets.

Various applications have emerged that use communication networks and facilitate peer-to-peer communication and knowledge sharing. These include e-mail, bulletin boards, chat rooms, white boards, and audio- and video-conferencing. There are also various specialised groupware applications. Groupware is one of the most popular technologies that facilitate connections between people, and transfer of knowledge between knowledge seekers and knowledge providers (Awad & Ghaziri, 2004). It is a type of technology specifically focused on issues related to collaborative processes among people (Marakas, 2003). Groupware comprises a wide range of technologies including telephone, e-mail and messaging systems, newsgroups, work-flow systems, video conferencing, chat rooms, and scheduling systems. People rely on groupware to communicate ideas and experiences, cooperate in problem-solving, coordinate work flow, and negotiate solutions.

Portals, intranets, and extranets use Internet and Web technologies to provide connectivity, and to support knowledge sharing among people, from individuals to small groups to entire organisations. Portals are interfaces that provide a single point of access to multiple sources of knowledge (Awad & Ghaziri, 2004). They provide Web users with a single gateway to communication facilities as well as software applications that consolidate, manage, analyse, and distribute knowledge. Intranets are private, secure spaces on the Web where all members of an organisation can communicate with each other, share information and collaborate on projects (Colmer & O'Brien, 2003). It is a vehicle for inexpensive, easy mass distribution of information. To be a successful enabler of knowledge sharing, an intranet needs to have a directory that structures the site content, a search facility for access to all resources, and a news section that replaces organisation-wide e-mail bulletins (Nielsen, 2002). In addition, it needs to have an open shared space where employees can post messages, questions, ideas, suggestions for improvements, and request help or advice (Arnott, 2000). Extranets extend selected resources of intranets outside the corporate firewall to selected groups of customers, suppliers, business partners, and employees in remote locations.

Various knowledge-sharing tools and applications mentioned can be divided into three main categories based on the level of communication and collaboration support they provide. These categories are: (1) electronic communication tools, (2) electronic conferencing tools and (3) collaborative management tools. Essentially, electronic communication tools send messages, files, data, and documents between people, and thus facilitate the sharing of knowledge. Examples include e-mail, fax, voice mail, and Web publishing. Electronic conferencing tools add a dimension of interactivity to knowledge-sharing activity. Examples include data conferencing via a common whiteboard, voice, and video and audio conferencing. They also include Internet forums (also known as message boards and discussion boards), chat rooms, and electronic meeting systems (EMS). Finally, collaborative management tools include systems, such as electronic calendars, project management systems, and workflow systems, that facilitate and manage group activities.

It is believed that these technologies can provide many benefits. The application of electronic mail, Internet, collaboration technologies, bulletin boards, and newsgroups can support the distribution of knowledge throughout an organisation. Technology can also provide a forum for employees to debate, discuss, and interpret knowledge via multiple perspectives. Most importantly, technology can enhance the sharing of knowledge by reducing the restrictions pertaining to time and distance. However, the vast array of technologies available to support organisations in their quest for effective knowledge sharing can be overwhelming. Therefore, organisations need to identify most favoured forms of technology, and find out in which application contexts these technologies' strengths and weaknesses lie, so that they can determine the appropriate technological infrastructure to support their individual requirements. To answer these questions, the authors conducted a survey study of knowledge workers from a global professional-services organisation to identify different types of technology used in different time and place contexts, and explore their effectiveness in those different contexts.

Empirical Study

This study is a part of the book author's wider research project in knowledge sharing (Handzic & Lee, 2004). The organisation selected for this research is a global company called Quintiles Transnational, which provides a broad range of professional services, information, and partnering solutions to the pharmaceutical, biotechnology, and healthcare industries. With headquarters near Research Triangle Park, North Carolina, Quintiles has about 16,000 employees, and offices in 49 countries. The survey participants involved 49 employees of the Sydney office located in North Sydney, New South Wales.

Due to it being a global company with numerous offices in remote locations, it is imperative that the company implements an effective knowledge-management strategy to endorse successful knowledge sharing between its distributed segments. A preliminary interview with one of the employees revealed that technology is an important factor in facilitating the sharing of knowledge between employees within the organization. It was believed that a research study in such a corporate environment would provide a good indication of the technological contribution to knowledge sharing in different application contexts.

A four-part questionnaire was designed to identify the technologies used in each of the four application contexts of interest (i.e., same/different time/place), and to investigate their effectiveness in these contexts. The same set of statements (see Table 5.2) addressing various aspects of effectiveness was repeated for each context so that their results could be compared later on. The participants were asked first to name the technology most frequently used to share knowledge in each context, and then to evaluate its effectiveness on a scale from 1-strongly disagree to 7-strongly agree.

A total of 70 questionnaires was distributed to the employees of Quintiles in the Sydney office, and 49 were gathered back. The return rate of 70% ensured that the sample was representative of the organisation. The respondents came from different ethnic and cultural backgrounds, gender groups, and had ranging academic histories.

Results

A descriptive analysis of data was performed, as suggested by Miles and Huberman (1994), to identify prevailing patterns and ensure plausibility of findings. The results presented in Table 5.1 indicate that there were 10 different types of technology used in the organisation that were mentioned by the participants for four different place and time contexts.

The frequency scores show that the type of technology most used for knowledge sharing among the organisation's employees in the same place and same time context was *presentation software,* particularly Microsoft's PowerPoint. It was mentioned by 25 (out of 49) participants, which represented 51% of the surveyed population. The next most commonly used technology was *shared documents/files,* mentioned by 14 (29%) participants. *Portals* were the other type of technology used in this application context, indicated by 10 (20%) respondents. The technology most frequently used for knowledge sharing among employees in the same place and different time context

Table 5.1. Technology usage by context

Technology	SPST	SPDT	DPST	DPDT
PowerPoint/Presentation	25	3		
Shared Documents/Files	14			3
Portals	10			
E-mail/Mailbox		43	3	22
Lotus Notes/Groupware		3		3
Bulletin Board				21
Video Conferencing			17	
Voice Conferencing			19	
Instant Messaging			7	
Online Chatting			3	

Note: SPST—same place same time, SPDT—same place different time, DPST—different place same time, DPDT—different place different time

was *e-mail/mailbox*. It was named as the preferred technology by a majority of 43 (88%) respondents. The other two types of technology identified were electronic *presentations* and the *specialised groupware* software Lotus Notes, both of which received 3 (6%) mentions each.

Conferencing was indicated as the preferred technology for sharing knowledge among employees in the different place and same time context. *Voice conferencing* was mentioned by 19 (39%) participants, and *video conferencing* by 17 (35%) participants. Next most common was *instant messaging,* nominated by 7 (14%) participants. *Online chatting* and e-mail/*mailbox* were mentioned only 3 (6%) times each. Finally, the technology most used for knowledge sharing among employees in the different place and different time context was, once again, *e-mail/mailbox*. It was mentioned as the preferred technology by 22 (45%) participants. *Bulletin board* was another frequently used tool, taking up 21 (43%) responses. Other less frequently indicated technologies included the *specialised groupware* Lotus Notes, and *shared documents/file* with 3 (6%) mentions each.

The second part of the survey asked the participants to indicate their level of agreement with each of the survey questions with respect to the effectiveness of the mentioned technology. An average score of participants' responses was calculated for each question in each application context to identify a central tendency. The results are presented in Table 5.2.

Table 5.2. Technology effectiveness by context

Survey Questions	SPST	SPDT	DPST	DPDT
I have trust in technology	5.8	5.9	5.6	5.5
Technology helps achieve common goal	5.9	5.6	5.4	5.3
Technology helps fulfil common responsibility	5.7	4.9	5.5	5.4
Technology improves quality & productivity	5.7	4.9	4.7	4.9
Technology improves communication	5.2	5.3	5.5	5.3
Technology accurately 'voices' my knowledge	4.3	4.4	5.4	4.6
Technology enables shared experiences	5.2	4.7	5.7	4.7
Technology supports open and frank discussions	4.5	3.4	4.3	3.4
Technology delivers understanding of complex situations	4.3	3.8	4.8	3.8
Technology delivers emotional richness of personal interactions	3.2	3.1	3.6	3.1
Technology aids my work operations	6.0	5.5	5.7	5.5

Note: SPST—same place same time, SPDT—same place different time, DPST—different place same time, DPDT—different place different time

Mean scores greater than 4 (out of 7) indicate that participants had trust in technology regardless of the application context. They also considered technology useful in achieving common goals, fulfilling common responsibilities, improving quality and productivity, enabling communication and shared experiences, voicing one's knowledge, and aiding work operations.

In contrast, mean scores less than 4 indicate that participants had unfavourable opinions regarding the ability of technology to support open and frank discussions or convey understanding of complex situations in different time contexts. More significantly, they considered technology unable to convey the emotional richness of personal interactions irrespective of the application context.

Discussion

All respondents indicated that they used some kind of technology to aid knowledge sharing in their organization. Such findings agree with an earlier comprehensive survey of best knowledge management practices (A.A., 1998). This survey revealed that most organisations implement some kind of technology to connect people and enable their interaction and collaboration. However, looking at the nature of technology used, one can clearly see that different types of technology were preferred in different application contexts. Overwhelmingly, *e-mail/mailbox* was the preferred choice for the same-place-different-time and different-place-different-time contexts. *Presentation* software, particularly Microsoft's PowerPoint, was the most widely used technology in the same-place-same-time environment, and *voice conferencing* in different-place-same-time context. On the other end of the spectrum of various technologies mentioned were *online chatting, instant messaging,* and *specialised groupware.*

This high emphasis on *e-mail* reflects similar findings by Zhou and Fink (2003) and Edwards and Shaw (2004). However, the case of specialised groupware is very different. In this study, it was placed lower than in Zhou and Fink's Australian survey, but mentioned a couple of times in two contexts, contrary to no mentions in Edwards and Shaw's UK survey. The overwhelming use of e-mail is an interesting finding, as e-mail is generally not considered to be the most efficient form of knowledge sharing tool available in the market. E-mailing documents around, and creating multiple copies and versions of content across an enterprise wastes both network bandwidth and storage capacity. E-mail is also a technology of exclusion: if you are not on the e-mail address list, you are not collaborating (Rapaport, 2002). Perhaps the reason for its popularity may be found in its usability. E-mail is a highly practical system, as it is easy to use by the least technically minded employees, it is often readily available as soon as they enter the organisation, and there is little training required to use the system.

Our further analysis revealed that overall technologies used for knowledge sharing among employees in same-time contexts were perceived as more effective than those in different-time contexts. However, different patterns were discovered when individual aspects of effectiveness were considered. Question 1 asked the participants if they had trust in the technology they named to be used in the particular application context. In general, the participants had a high level of trust in the technology they have named, irrespective of the application context. When asked about the technology aiding people to achieve common goals, technology was found to be effective in all four contexts. It was also found similarly effective in improving communication of the involved parties.

The next several responses showed no particular pattern. In terms of fulfilling common responsibilities, technology was perceived as less effective in same-place-different-time context than in others. In contrast, technology used in the same-place-same-time context was substantially more effective in improving quality and productivity of the work operations. Interestingly, technology was thought to be more effective in "voicing" the participant's knowledge in the different-place-same-time application context than in any other application contexts.

Most significantly, the next couple of responses indicate that when involving technology, same time may be a more important factor than same place for effective knowledge sharing among people. The study found out that technology-aided col-laboration enabled more effective sharing of experiences in the same-time application contexts than in others. With the aid of technology, people were able to conduct more open and frank discussions during collaboration in the same-time application contexts than in any other. Furthermore, technology delivered the understanding of complex situations better in the same-time than in the different-time application contexts. The potential reason for this may be in that these technologies provide more sophisticated and richer multimedia environments for knowledge sharing. However, their lower usage levels may be attributed to higher cost, lower avail-ability, and greater skill demand.

Overall, it is encouraging that the participants recognized the value of technology as well as its limitations. They agreed that all named technologies aided their work operations regardless of the context. However, in general, they thought that technol-ogy was ineffective in delivering the emotional richness of personal interactions. These results reinforce our earlier findings from the academic environment, which reported a high importance of technology in supporting connectivity, but poor suit-ability for ideas and thoughts exchange (Handzic, 2004). Some other researchers also warn that technologies lack the emotional richness and depth of real, live, in-person interaction (Santosus, 2001), and are unable to fully develop relationships and an understanding of complex situations (Bender & Fish, 2000).

The main findings of this study point to a highly contingent nature of usage and effectiveness of technology in knowledge sharing upon context. As such, they may be useful for both knowledge management practice and research. For practice, they point at strengths and weaknesses of different technologies in different contexts. This knowledge can be useful to organisations in determining the most appropri-ate infrastructure. For research, they reveal that technology can better overcome differences in "place" than "time" factors in enabling effective sharing. However, caution is necessary when trying to generalize these findings due to a number of limitations including single organizational setting, a small number of participants, and self-reported opinions. Future research should address these limitations as well as extend this research further. One possible follow-up study may be a deeper qualitative analysis of participants' preferences to uncover the reasons behind them. This could help in devising better means to overcome current constraints.

Conclusion

This chapter aimed at discovering user preferences for technologies used for knowl-edge sharing among employees of a global organisation. From our analysis, it is evident that their preferences differed depending upon the application (i.e., place and time) context. In summary, *e-mail/mailbox* was the preferred option for different-time (irrespective of place), *presentation* software for same-time-same-place, and *conferencing* for same-time-different-place contexts. With respect to effectiveness, technologies supporting knowledge sharing in same-time contexts were generally perceived as being more effective than in different-time contexts. Among reasons for this may be that these technologies provided a richer medium (eg., audio, video, graphics) for knowledge sharing compared to text-based e-mails. These findings may have important implications and wide applicability in practice. However, methodological limitations of the study need to be taken into account when generalising them. Future research is recommended to address these limitations.

References

A. A. (1998). *Best practices in knowledge management.* Australia: Arthur Andersen.

Alavi, M., & Leidner, D. E. (2001). Knowledge management and knowledge management systems: Conceptual foundations and research issues. *MIS Quarterly, 25*(1), 107-136.

Arnott, D. (2000). *Corporate culture: The insidious lure of the all-consuming organisation.* New York: American Management Association.

Awad, E. M., & Ghaziri, H. M. (2004). *Knowledge management.* Upper Saddle River, NJ: Pearson Education.

Bender, S., & Fish, A. (2000). The transfer of knowledge and the retention of expertise: The continuing need for global assignments. *Journal of Knowledge Management, 4*(2), 125-150.

Colmer, M., & O'Brien, T. (2003). *InfoTrain electronic publishing on the Internet* (Module 3, January). University of South Australia, Australia.

Edwards, J. S., & Shaw, D. (2004, July). Supporting knowledge management with IT. In *Proceedings of the DSS 2004 Conference*, Prato, Italy.

Ford, D. P., & Chan, Y. E. (2003). Knowledge sharing in a multi-cultural setting: A case study. *Knowledge Management Research & Practice, 1*(1), 11-27.

Handzic, M. (2003). An integrated framework of knowledge management. *Journal of Information and Knowledge Management, 2*(3).

Handzic, M. (2004). *Knowledge management: Through the technology glass.* Singapore: World Scientific.

Handzic, M., & Hasan, H. (2003). The search for an integrated framework of KM. In H. Hasan & M. Handzic (Eds.), *Australian Studies in Knowledge Management* (pp. 3-34). Wollongong: UOW Press.

Handzic, M., & Lee, A. (2004). *The role of technology in knowledge sharing* (SISTM Research Information Paper Series No. RIPS2004-A). Sydney, Australia: UNSW, School of Information Systems, Technology and Management.

Hansen, M. T., Nohria, N., & Tierney, T. (1999). What's your strategy for managing knowledge? *Harvard Business Review*, *77*(2), 106-116.

Marakas, G. M. (2003). *Decision support systems in the 21st century* (2nd ed). Englewood Cliffs, NJ: Prentice Hall.

Miles, M. B., & Huberman, M. A. (1994). *Qualitative data analysis*. London: Sage.

Nonaka, I., & Konno, N. (1998). The concept of ba: Building a foundation for knowledge creation. *California Management Review*, *40*(3), 40-54.

Nonaka, I. (1998). The knowledge-creating company. In *Harvard Business Review on Knowledge Management*. Boston: Harvard Business School Press.

Nielsen, J. (2002). *Designing Web usability: The practice of simplicity*. Indianapolis: New Riders Publishing.

Rapaport, L. (2002). *Collaboration: Beyond e-mail*. Retrieved June, 2002, from http://www.transformmag.com

Santosus, M. (2001). KM and human nature. *CIO.com "in the know."* Retrieved December 18, 2001, from http://www.cio.com/knowledge/edit/k121801_nature.html

Snowden, D. (2003). Innovation as an objective of knowledge management (Part I: The landscape of management). *Knowledge Management Research & Practice*, *1*(2), 113-119.

Standards Australia. (2003). *Interim Australian Standard: Knowledge Management* (AS5037 int.). Sydney: Standards Australia International Ltd.

Swan, J. (2003). Knowledge management in action. In C. W. Holsapple (Ed.), *Handbook on Knowledge Management* (Vol. 1, pp. 271-296). Berlin: Springer.

Zhou, A. Z., & Fink, D. (2003). Knowledge management and intellectual capital: An empirical examination of current practice in Australia. *Knowledge Management Research & Practice*, *1*(2), 86-94.

Chapter VI

Electronic Memory:
Increasing Knowledge
Availability

Abstract

Employees in modern organisations have achieved expanded access to corporate knowledge assets via electronic memory systems. Despite their popularity, there is little empirical evidence regarding the impact of these systems on users' job performance. This chapter reports results of an empirical examination of users' knowledge acquisition behaviour and subsequent job performance, in relation to increased amounts of knowledge artefacts provided in electronic memory systems. Results indicate a lack of substantial enhancement in performance as a result of increased amounts of seemingly helpful stored knowledge. Findings suggest this outcome is due to the fact that people tend to use simplifying knowledge acquisition strategies as the amount of stored knowledge artefacts increases.

Introduction

The revolution in the computer industry has brought about multiple ways of capturing and storing knowledge electronically. The main advantage of electronic over traditional storage media is seen in that digital content can be easily edited, repeatedly used, and distributed cheaply via networks. Some analysts predict that there will soon be virtually unlimited digital storage space available at very modest cost (Probst, Raub, & Romhardt, 2000). Thus, companies will be able to put all their knowledge contained in various text documents, graphics, tapes, and films into digital form, and create a comprehensive electronic organisational memory. At the same time, the Internet will offer growing numbers of users easy access to masses of digital materials available in these systems.

Electronic memories have been recognised as the most common type of KM technologies so far, with an objective to capture and store knowledge for later and broader access and reuse (Grover & Davenport, 2001). The Interim Australian KM standard (Standards Australia, 2003) proposes a number of technologies, including databases, textbases, data warehouses, and data marts, as useful technologies in building organisational memories.

The structured part of the organisation's electronic memory typically consists of daily transactions recorded in business documents and notes, or in transaction records stored in structured database systems. In addition to data and text, multimedia systems organise and make available to users the unstructured part of corporate knowledge in a variety of other representational forms, including images, audio, and video formats. Furthermore, data warehouses and data marts retain historical and cross-functional perspectives of organisational knowledge. Data is extracted daily from the business transaction systems, and from any other systems deemed relevant. Compared to data warehouses, which combine databases across an entire enterprise, data marts are usually smaller, and focus on a particular subject or department (Handzic, 2004).

The assumption is that if organised and reused systematically, electronic memory systems can bring competitive advantage to companies that operate in a knowledge intensive environment. In particular, they can serve as a means by which knowledge from the past experience and events may influence present organisational activities (Stein & Zwass, 1995), help to avoid reinventing the wheel by keeping workable solutions, and facilitate change management.

While there is ample evidence to show that organisations do implement various electronic storage technologies as part of their best KM practices (A.A., 1998), there is little empirical evidence regarding the impact of these technologies on users' performance (Alavi & Leidner, 2001). The existing KM research is mainly limited to anecdotal stories and descriptive case studies. Some researchers point out that our ability to accumulate and store knowledge artefacts in electronic memories has, by far, surpassed our ability to process them, and warn of the danger that vast institutional repositories may easily become tombs rather than wellsprings of knowledge (Fayyad & Uthurusamy, 2002).

The main purpose of this chapter is to provide a deeper insight into the potentials and limitations of electronic memory systems in enhancing users' working knowledge and performance in the context of decision making. With the growing abundance of knowledge artefacts enabled by digital storage technology, it is of particular interest to this study to examine whether, and how, knowledge captured in electronic memory systems may assist managerial decision makers in enhancing their working knowledge, and what impact it may have on the quality of their subsequent decisions.

Knowledge Availability and Decision Making

Managerial decision making is regarded as a knowledge-intensive activity. Decision makers' usually obtain relevant knowledge from the repositories of business intelligence available in organisations, and acquire know-how in response to the demands of their work. It is argued that the availability of environment- and organisation-specific knowledge, as well as a variety of cause-effect relationships, can play an important role in improving decision quality. The value of such knowledge may be seen primarily in its ability to explain past, and anticipate future changes in the behaviour of the variable of interest, thus enabling the decision maker to deal more competently with his or her decision task.

This is a convincing argument for suggesting that the availability of increased amounts of knowledge artefacts in electronic memory systems should increase the decision maker's working knowledge and result in better decision performance. Indeed, the increased amount of task-relevant knowledge may reduce decisional uncertainty; it also may improve the probability that a decision will be made correctly. However, at the same time, increasing the quantity of knowledge artefacts will drive up costs of search and integration into single-decision responses. Most prior research in this area has failed to address the fact that the increasingly sophisticated knowledge management systems increase the complexity of the decision task. Therefore, the main objectives of this study are to empirically examine how people use knowledge assets available in electronic memory systems, and to assess the impact of varying amounts of knowledge assets upon decision performance.

Generally, increasing the amount of task-relevant knowledge artefacts also increases the complexity of decision tasks (Campbell, 1988; Schroder, Driver, & Streufert, 1967; Wood, 1986). The contingency model of human decision behaviour (Beach and Mitchell, 1978) assumes that such behaviour varies according to individual differences and to task demands. The model identifies specific characteristics (e.g., familiarity, ambiguity, complexity) and situational factors (e.g., significance, resources constraints) that affect strategy selection. The model also assumes that strategy selection reflects the individual differences of actors, particularly knowledge, ability, and motivation. Strategy selection is viewed as a "cost/benefit" compromise between the desire to improve task performance and the desire to minimise implementation effort. The model predicts a positive relationship between the demands of the task and the analytical complexity of the strategy used for task performance. The essence of the proposition is that the benefits expected from adopting a complex decision strategy are greater if the task is itself complex rather than simple. However, Christensen-Szalanski (1978) showed that anything that increases task difficulty results in selection of a strategy with lower expected benefit. Therefore, individuals using an electronic memory system must strike a balance between the costs and benefits of available knowledge, and adapt their search behaviour accordingly.

Knowledge Availability and Decision Behaviour

Empirical studies of the impact of knowledge assets availability on acquisition behaviour report mixed results. Some studies find that people respond to increased availability by increasing the amount of artefacts searched, implying increased utilisation (Connolly & Gilani, 1982; Connolly & Thorn, 1987; Levine, Samet, & Brahlek, 1975; Nichols-Hoppe & Beach, 1990). Other studies report reduced and variable search behaviour, suggesting selective utilisation (Biggs, Bedard, Gaber, & Linsmeier, 1985; Cook, 1993; Olshavsky, 1969; Payne, 1976). Connolly and Gilani (1982) indicate that people respond to knowledge availability by increasing the perceived value of available cues. Connolly and Thorn (1987) find a direct (positive) relationship between acquisition effort and number of knowledge items available. In two experiments conducted by Levine et al (1975), results indicate that the number of knowledge requests made prior to a decision increases as the number of total items of knowledge increase. (However, the number of requests represents a smaller proportion of knowledge requested than of total items of knowledge). Similarly, in a preferential choice task context, Nichols-Hoppe and Beach (1990) find more pieces of knowledge are accessed as the number of available alternatives increases.

In contrast to these studies, Payne (1976) finds a significant decrease in knowledge acquisition as the amount of available knowledge increases. His results indicate that knowledge-search activity declines as the number of alternatives and the dimensions per alternative increase. The lower search activity indicates the use of a less analytical strategy. In a similar experiment, Olshavsky (1979) finds that, in addition to experiencing a decrease in the average ratio of references to available knowledge, the average time per unit of available knowledge also decreases as the amount of knowledge increases. Biggs et al. (1985) examine the effect of task size. Results indicate that the percentage of knowledge acquired decreases as task size increases. In a decision task involving the selection of one alternative from a finite set of possible alternatives, Cook (1993) finds a reduced proportion of search activity and increased variability in the proportion of knowledge search across attributes and dimensions. Results also indicate a pattern of search that is more dimensionwise than alternativewise, and suggest that decision makers make greater use of simplifying search strategies as the amount of knowledge available increases.

Knowledge Availability and Decision Performance

With respect to performance, Schroder et al. (1967) establishes an inverted U curve relationship between the level of knowledge processing and the degree of decision accuracy. The shape implies an initial increase in decision performance as a result of increased knowledge processing, but a decline in performance after a certain level of complexity is reached (as a consequence of the limitations in human knowledge processing). Wood (1986) also postulates a curvilinear relationship between complexity and performance, characterised by initial improvement, but a later decline in performance (again as the level of complexity increases). Payne (1982), on the other hand, proposes a gradual decline in decision performance with increased task complexity due to increased amounts of knowledge.

Empirical evidence regarding the impact of knowledge availability upon decision performance is mixed. Some studies report that more knowledge generally increases confidence, even though its effect on accuracy varies. Studies report greater accuracy (Casey, 1980; Peterson & Pitz, 1988), no systematic effect (Levine et al., 1975; Oskamp, 1965; Paese & Sniezek, 1991; Snowball, 1980), and diminished performance (Chervany & Dickson, 1974; Davis, Lohse, & Kottemann, 1994) as a result of increased knowledge availability.

Peterson and Pitz (1988) examine the impact of numbers of relevant units of knowledge provided. They find that increased knowledge leads to greater confidence and greater accuracy. Furthermore, Casey (1980) finds that subjects provided with a moderate amount of knowledge make significantly more accurate predictions than subjects with less knowledge, even though the knowledge rich group did not.

Several other studies report a lack of significant improvement in performance despite a broader knowledge base. Oskamp (1965) and Paese and Sniezek (1991) find that increasing knowledge brings about a significant increase in confidence without an increase in accuracy. However, Snowball (1980) finds that lower amounts of available knowledge are associated with wider confidence intervals around users' predictions.

A few studies associate actual declines in performance with increased amounts of knowledge. Davis et al. (1994) finds that redundant knowledge makes subjects substantially more confident in their forecasts, and that nonredundant knowledge makes them even more confident. Forecast accuracy, however, is substantially diminished with both redundant and nonredundant knowledge. Thus, additional knowledge has the effect of degrading performance while increasing confidence. This indicates that decision makers may be poor judges of the usefulness of newly available knowledge sources. They may be influenced by knowledge that does not improve their performance, under the false impression that knowledge is helpful. The possibly dysfunctional role of increased knowledge also is seen in a study by Chervany and Dickson (1974), who find that those with a larger amount of raw data make poorer quality decisions, but have more confidence in the quality of their decisions. Finally, Connolly and Thorn (1987) report poorer efficiency of knowledge use with increased knowledge.

The lack of substantial improvement in performance reported in some of the studies may be due to decision makers' use of simplification strategies. Such strategies may be invoked to cope with the higher demand on cognitive resources posed by increased amounts of task knowledge. In a series of simulation studies, Payne and his colleagues (Payne, Bettman, & Johnson, 1988; Payne, Johnson, Bettman, & Coupey, 1990) test performance of a number of simplifying heuristics in a choice task context. They find that the level of performance of various heuristics is highly contingent upon task environment characteristics.

Empirical Study

Study Objectives

In view of inconsistent prior findings and concerns expressed, it is of particular interest to this study to examine the situation in which decision makers are provided with a varying amount of highly predictive contextual knowledge (to ensure validity) in regard to the decision response. The question is (1) whether, and how, increased availability of relevant knowledge artefacts will affect decision makers' knowledge acquisition behaviour; (2) whether and what impact the application of the acquired knowledge may have on their subsequent decision performance.

Experimental Task

The experimental task in the current study was a simple production-planning activity in which subjects made decisions regarding daily production of fresh ice cream. The participants assumed the role of Production Manager for a fictitious dairy firm that sold ice cream from its outlet at Bondi Beach in Sydney, Australia. The fictitious company incurred equally costly losses if production was set too low (due to loss of market to the competition) or too high (by spoilage of unsold product). The participants' goal was to minimise the total costs incurred by incorrect production decisions. During the experiment, participants were asked at the end of each day to set production quotas for ice cream to be sold the following day. Subjects were required to repeat this same decision task over a period of 30 consecutive days. Before commencing the task, participants had an opportunity to make five trial decisions (for practice purposes only).

From preexperiment discussions with actual store owners at Bondi Beach, three factors emerged as important in determining local demand for product: the ambient air temperature, the amount of sunshine, and the number of visitors/tourists at the beach. Varying amounts and types of contextual cues were provided to subjects. One third of participants received only one contextual knowledge cue, another third received two cues, and the remaining third received all three cues. All cues were deemed equally reliable in predicting daily product demand. Participants were free to make production decisions based solely on the simulated ice cream demand data that were readily available to them. However, if they wanted to, subjects could obtain other decision-relevant data by explicitly requesting them from an electronic memory system. This could be done by clicking with a mouse on the appropriate knowledge button. On each trial, subjects could access as little or as much knowledge as they wished. Then they were required to set a production quota for the next day's sales.

At the beginning of the experiment, task descriptions were provided to inform subjects about the task scenario and requirements. The given text differed with respect to the amount and type of contextual knowledge provided. In addition, throughout the experiment, instructions and feedback were provided to enable participants to analyse earlier performance and to adjust future strategies.

Experimental Design and Variables

A laboratory experiment with random assignment to treatment groups was used, since it allowed greater experimental control. This made it possible to draw stronger inferences about causal relationships between variables due to high controllability. The only independent variable was *amount of knowledge* (small vs. moderate vs. large). This variable was manipulated by changing the number of the cue time series data (one vs. two vs. three) provided to participants (in addition to a criterion time series data). All cues were decision relevant and equally reliable, with a cue-criterion correlation coefficient set to $r = 0.8$.

Search behaviour variables were the *amount of search*, calculated as the proportion of the available cues searched (PRO-CUE), and *variability of search*, calculated as the standard deviation of the total search requests made per available cue (VAR-

CUE). Amount and variability of search behaviour were used as proxy indicators of knowledge-processing strategies adopted by subjects in making their decisions. Decision performance was evaluated in terms of *decision improvement* and *decision optimality*. Improvement was operationalised as a cumulative relative absolute error (CumRAE) and was calculated as the ratio of the sum of absolute errors of actual decisions to the corresponding sum of errors of the "random walk" (naive) strategy (for details, see Amstrong & Collopy, 1992). Decision optimality was operationalised by an inefficiency index (IND), and calculated as a ratio of the sum of absolute errors in actual production decisions to the corresponding sum of errors of the optimal strategy. Relative measures were used to assess the quality of decisions made by the decision maker, compared to those best achievable with or without the support of an electronic memory system.

Subjects and Procedure

The subjects were 36 graduate students enrolled in either the Master of Commerce or Doctoral courses at the University of New South Wales, Sydney. Twelve subjects were assigned to each of the three treatment groups. Subjects participated in the experiment on a voluntary basis, but received performance contingent monetary incentives in turn for their participation. Generally, graduate students are considered to be appropriate subjects for this type of research (Ashton & Kramer, 1980; Remus, 1996; Whitecotton, 1996). The experiment was conducted in a microcomputer laboratory. On arrival, subjects were randomly assigned to one of the treatment groups by their choice of a microcomputer from a number of units set for the experiment. Before commencing the experimental task, subjects were briefed about the purpose of the experiment and about task requirements. The session lasted about 1 hour.

Results

Data were analysed using one-way ANOVAs (with repeated measures) for each of the dependent variables: knowledge search behaviour (amount of search, variability of search), and performance (decision improvement, decision optimality). Summary results are presented in Table 6.1. Respective means are given in Table 6.2.

Results indicate that the amount of knowledge available via the electronic memory system had a substantial impact on some aspects of the users' knowledge search behaviour and upon their subsequent performance on task. Table 6.1 shows a highly significant effect of knowledge availability upon variability of search ($F(2,33)=14.72$, p=0.000), but not upon amount of search (H1). Multiple comparisons among knowledge availability groups using the Duncan decision rule revealed significant

Table 6.1. Results of one-way ANOVAs for dependent variables: Knowledge search behaviour, and decision performance

Variable	MS between-groups (df=2)	MS within-groups (df=33)	F	p
Amount of Search (PRO-CUE)	0.0417	0.0344	1.2108	0.3109
Variability of Search (VAR-CUE)	0.0091	0.0006	14.7180	0.0000**
Decision Improvement (CumRAE)	0.0495	0.0315	1.5709	0.2230
Decision Optimality (IND)	0.8944	0.2667	3.3541	0.0472*

*Note: * p<0.05, ** p<0.01*

Table 6.2. Means of dependent variables (knowledge search behaviour and decision performance) by experimental group

Amount of Knowledge Available	N	Group			
		PRO-CUE	VAR-CUE	CumRAE	IND
Small	12	0.8778	0.0000	0.6598	1.6426
Moderate	12	0.9611	0.0379	0.5494	1.7970
Large	12	0.9917	0.0535	0.5476	2.1734
Combined	36	0.9435	0.0305	0.5856	1.8710

differences in the variability of search activities between moderate and small (0.04 vs. 0.00) and large and small (0.05 vs. 0.00) knowledge groups. No significant difference was found between large and moderate (0.04 vs. 0.05) groups. Results suggest that subjects in moderate and large knowledge tasks tended to inspect some cues more frequently than others. Such behaviour is consistent with the use of simplifying selective search strategies on more complex decision tasks. In contrast, Table 6.1 shows no significant effect of knowledge availability on the amount of search activity. The subjects tended to inspect similar proportions of cues irrespective of the amount of knowledge available (0.88 vs. 0.96 vs. 0.99). Mean values close to 1 indicate that the subjects made nearly complete examination of available cues. In summary, results suggest knowledge search behaviour characterised by initial broad screening of most available knowledge, followed by more focused, deeper inspection of fewer selected items. Such behaviour indicates the use of a differential weighting knowledge processing strategy.

With respect to decision performance, results indicate that increased knowledge availability had a significant impact on some aspects of decision performance. Table 6.1 shows a significant effect by the amount of knowledge available upon decision optimality, but not on decision improvement (H2). Mean values of CumRAE less than one (0.61 vs. 0.63 vs. 0.73) indicate that there was a real improvement in the accuracy of informed decisions over naive forecasts, across the various knowledge availability conditions. In contrast, results indicate that the increased amount of knowledge available affected decision optimality. Table 6.1 shows a significant effect upon decision optimality ($F(2,33)=3.35$, $p=0.047$). Post-hoc analysis applying the Duncan test revealed that the mean knowledge inefficiency index of large-amount knowledge task subjects was significantly higher than that of their small-amount counterparts (2.17 vs. 1.64). Subjects with a moderate-to-large knowledge base used significantly less of their knowledge potential to enhance performance than did those with a small-to-moderate knowledge base, and therefore performed less efficiently.

Discussion

Main Findings

The findings of this study provide support for the proposition that the utilisation of digitised knowledge is highly contingent upon system design related factors such as the amount of knowledge provided. The current study has demonstrated that increased knowledge availability leads to selective knowledge use, but not to significant improvement in subsequent decision performance. Subjects equipped with moderate and large amounts of knowledge either completely ignored some of their available cues or placed much less importance on them when making decisions. This was demonstrated by significantly greater variability in the number of search requests per cue among the moderate and large knowledge groups, compared to small knowledge amount subjects. These effects were not seen, however, in proportion of cues searched. Subjects initially searched a high proportion of available knowledge, irrespective of knowledge availability. However, they later accessed more frequently some available cues (but not others). Such behaviour is indicative of selective knowledge use, an interpretation further supported by regression models of individuals' processing strategies. In general, findings of the current study are consistent with prior research that suggested a general tendency toward adopting simpler strategies for more complex tasks (Payne, 1982).

Consistent with selective knowledge use, the current study revealed that the increased availability of task-relevant knowledge does not enhance decision performance. This was seen in comparable levels of informed performance in terms of decision improvement compared to naive forecasts, as well as in a decline in decision optimality. Selective use of available knowledge by subjects with moderate and large knowledge resulted in a level of performance approximating that of subjects with small amounts of knowledge. Subjects made similar relative errors (CumRAE) irrespective of knowledge availability. They also had significantly higher knowledge ineffeciency (IND) with moderate-to-large compared to small-to-moderate amounts of knowledge. The lack of significant improvement in performance with more knowledge is in accord with selective knowledge use. This finding also is in accord with Payne's (1982) model postulating a gradual decrease in performance with increasing task complexity, given larger amounts of task knowledge (as indicated by IND). Findings also support the proposition that an initial increase in processing of task-relevant knowledge enhances performance. Results for CumRAE indicate that there is a real improvement in decisions that are made with contextual knowledge vs. naive forecasts, in all knowledge availability conditions.

Overall findings indicate that knowledge is effective regardless of knowledge availability, if effectiveness is evaluated in terms of people's ability to enhance their performance compared to naive forecasts. Subjects tended to use task-relevant knowledge to some extent. A consequence: they performed better than if they had used naive strategy. This was demonstrated by mean cumulative relative error (CumRAE) being less than one in all treatment groups. On the other hand, findings reveal that available knowledge is less effective on task than it could be, if effectiveness is defined in terms of people's ability to achieve optimal performance with available knowledge. Subjects were found to use their available knowledge cues selectively, and as a consequence to achieve less than optimal performance, irrespective of treatment group. This was demonstrated by the mean inefficiency index (IND) being greater than one in all treatment groups. Suboptimal behaviour and performance were more evident in large knowledge amount tasks.

It is possible that the suboptimality demonstrated in knowledge-processing behaviour and decision performance may be attributed to limitations in design of the current study. One of these limitations is the nature of task knowledge used in the experiment. The relatively high reliability of individual cues (r=0.80) and, therefore, the high intercorrelations among cues (r=0.64), may have caused subjects to perceive additional cues in moderate and large availability conditions as largely redundant. This, in turn, may have led to selective knowledge use and to less than optimal performance. Therefore, further study is required to examine individuals' knowledge use and performance across different knowledge reliability contexts.

Limitations

While the current study provides a number of interesting findings, some caution is necessary regarding their generalisability, due to a number of limiting aspects. One of the limitations refers to the use of a laboratory experiment that may compromise external validity of research. Another limitation relates to artificial generation of contextual knowledge that may not reflect the true nature of real business. The subjects chosen for the study were students and not real-life decision makers. The fact that they were mature graduates may mitigate the potential differences. No incentives were offered to the subjects for their effort in the study. Consequently, they may have found the study tiring and unimportant and not tried as hard as possible. Most decisions in real business settings have significant consequences. Further research is necessary that would extend the study to other subjects and environmental conditions in order to ensure the generalisability of the present findings.

Practical Implications and Directions for Future Research

Although limited, the findings of the current study may have some important implications for organisational knowledge management strategies. They suggest that decision makers could potentially benefit from additional knowledge management initiatives that would enhance their understanding of the value of explicit knowledge provided in electronic memory systems. One possible solution is to provide these systems with more meaningful analysis, procedural knowledge, and learning histories that might potentially help such workers better understand what works when and why (Kleiner & Roth, 1998). This, in turn, may result in better performance. Alternatively, organisations may employ specialists trained in analytical and statistical reasoning, who would perform a knowledge-filtering process for professional and managerial knowledge workers (Godbout, 1999).

Initiatives aimed at creating working contexts that encourage communication and culture of knowledge sharing may also potentially have a beneficial effect on enhancing decision makers' working knowledge and performance. Organisations have come to realise that a large proportion of the knowledge needed by the business is not captured on hard drives or contained in filing cabinets, but kept in the heads of people. Sources report that between 40% (AAOTE, 1998) and 90% (Hewson, 1999) of the needed knowledge is (in the lingo of the business) tacit. The spiral knowledge model postulates that the processes of sharing will result in the amplification and exponential growth of working knowledge (Nonaka, 1998; Nonaka & Takeuchi, 1995). Yet, little is known of the ways in which tacit knowledge is actually shared, conditions under which this sharing occurs, and the impact it has on performance.

Conclusion

This chapter is concerned with electronic memory systems. The important role of electronic memory systems is to make organisational knowledge more visible and accessible to employees. The assumption is that the availability of an increased knowledge base via these systems will enhance users' working knowledge and job performance. However, our findings indicate that people tend to effectively utilise only a small portion of the knowledge available in electronic memories. The study suggests that individuals can potentially benefit from additional knowledge management initiatives that would help to better organise and interpret useful knowledge from these stores. The following chapter looks at the impact of one such initiative.

References

A. A. (1998). *The knowledge management practices book.* Australia: Arthur Andersen.

Alavi, M., & Leidner, D. E. (2001). Knowledge management and knowledge management systems: Conceptual foundations and research issues. *MIS Quarterly, 25*(1), 107-136.

Amstrong, J. S., & Collopy, F. (1992). Error measures for generalising about forecasting methods: Empirical comparisons. *International Journal of Forecasting, 8*, 69-80.

Ashton, R. H., & Kramer, S. S. (1980). Students as surrogates in behavioural accounting research: Some evidence. *Journal of Accounting Research, 18*(1), 1-15.

Beach, L.R., & Mitchell, T. R. (1978, July). A contingency model for the selection of decision strategies. *Academy of Management Review*, 439-449.

Biggs, S. F., Bedard, J. C., Gaber, B.G., & Linsmeier, T .J. (1985). The effects of task size and similarity on the decision behaviour of bank loan officers. *Management Science, 31*(8), 970-987.

Campbell, D. J. (1988). Task complexity: A review and analysis. *Academy of Management Review, 13*(1), 40-52.

Casey, C. J., Jr. (1980). Variation in accounting information load: The effect on loan officers' predictions of bankruptcy. *The Accounting Review, 52*(1), 36-49.

Chervany, N. L., & Dickson, G. W. (1974). An experimental evaluation of information overload in a production environment. *Management Science, 20*(10), 62-71.

Christensen-Szalanski, J. J. J. (1978). Problem solving strategies: A selection mechanism, some implications, and some data. *Organisational Behaviour and Human Performance, 22*, 307-323.

Connolly, T., & Gilani, N. (1982). Information search in judgement tasks: A regression model and some preliminary findings. *Organisational Behaviour and Human Performance, 30*, 330-350.

Connolly, T., & Thorn, B. K. (1987). Predecisional information acquisition: Effects of task variables on suboptimal search strategies. *Organisational Behaviour and Human Decision Processes, 39*, 397-416.

Cook, G. J. (1993). An empirical investigation of information search strategies with implications for decision support system design. *Decision Sciences, 24*(3), 683-697.

Davis, F. D., Lohse, G. L., & Kottemann, J. E. (1994). Harmful effects of seemingly helpful information on forecasts of stock earnings. *Journal of Economic Psychology, 15*, 253-267.

Evans, W. F., Gray, P., & Rhodes, J. E. (1994). Executive information systems for manufacturing: A case study. In P. Gray (Ed.), *Decision support and executive information systems.* Englewood Cliffs, NJ: Prentice Hall.

Fayyad, U., & Uthurusamy, R. (2002). Evolving into data mining solutions for insight. *Communications of the ACM, 45*(8), 28-31.

Grover, V., & Davenport, T. H. (2001). General perspectives on knowledge management: Fostering a research agenda. *Journal of Management Information System, 18*(1), 5-21.

Handzic, M. (2004). *Knowledge management: Through the technology glass.* Singapore: World Scientific Publishing.

Levine, J. M., Samet, M. G., & Brahlek, R. E. (1975). Information seeking with limitations on available iformation and resources. *Human Factors, 17*(5), 502-513.

Nichols-Hoppe, K. T., & Beach, L. R. (1990). The effects of test anxiety and task variables on predecisional information search. *Journal of Research in Personality, 24*, 163-172.

Olshavsky, R. W. (1979). Task complexity and contingent processing in decision making: A replication and extension. *Organisational Behaviour and Human Performance, 24*, 300-316.

Oskamp, S. (1965). Overconfidence in case-study judgements. *Journal of Consulting Psychology, 29*, 261-265.

Paese, P. W., & Sniezek, J. A. (1991). Influences on the appropriatenesess of confidence in judgement: Practice, effort information and decision making. *Organisational Behaviour and Human Decision Processes, 48*, 100-130.

Payne, J. W. (1976). Task complexity and contingent processing in decision making: An information search and protocol analysis. *Organisational Behaviour and Human Performance, 16*, 366-387.

Payne, J. W. (1982). Contingent decision behaviour. *Psychological Bulletin, 92* (2), 382-402.

Payne, J. W., Bettman, J. R., & Johnson, E. J. (1988). Adaptive strategy selection in decision making. *Journal of Experimental Psychology*, *14*(3), 534-552.

Payne, J. W., Johnson, E. J., Bettman, J. R., & Coupey, E. (1990). Understanding contingent choice: A computer simulation approach. *IEEE Transactions on Systems, Man and Cybernetics*, *20*(2), 296-309.

Peterson, D. K., & Pitz, G. F. (1988). Confidence, uncertainty and the use of information. *Journal of Experimental Psychology: Learning, Memory and Cognition*, *14*, 85-92.

Probst, G., Raub, S., & Romhardt. K. (2000). *Managing knowledge*. New York: John Wiley & Sons.

Remus, W. (1996). Will behavioural research on managerial decision making generalise to managers? *Managerial and Decision Economics*, *17*, 93-101.

Schroder, H. M., Driver, M. J., & Streufert, S. (1967). *Human information processing*. USA: Holt, Rinehart and Winston Inc.

Standards Australia. (2003). *Interim Australian standard: Knowledge management (AS5037 int)*. Sydney: Standards Australia International Ltd.

Stein, E. W., & Zwass, V. (1995). Actualising organisational memory with information systems. *Information Systems Research,* *6*(2), 85-117.

Watson, H. J, Rainer, R. K., & Koh, C. E. (1991). Executive information systems: A framework for development and a survey of current practices. *MIS Quarterly*, *31*, 13-30.

Whitecotton, S. M. (1996). The effects of experience and a decision aid on the slope, scatter, and bias of earnings forecasts. *Organisational Behaviour and Human Decision Processes*, *66*(1), 111-121.

Wood, R. E. (1986). Task complexity: Definition of the construct. *Organisational Behaviour and Human Decision Processes*, *37*(1), 60-82.

Chapter VII

Visualisation System:
Facilitating Knowledge Interpretation

Abstract

This chapter addresses the role of visualisation in knowledge management. More particularly, the chapter reports the results of an empirical study of the impact of a visualisation system on user's knowledge interpretation and resulting performance in the context of a time-series forecasting. The visualisation system used was based on a decomposition method and line graphs. Results show real reduction in forecast errors due to the visualisation system support, but failure to reach optimal performance. This suggests that there is room for further improvement.

Introduction

The advances of digital technologies for collecting and storing large amounts of knowledge artefacts have resulted in the availability of huge collections in most areas of human endeavour. As more artefacts are added to organisational stores, the need for some sort of a mechanism to help organise and search useful knowledge from these stores becomes clearer. Finding technologies that make stored knowledge effective is one of the most challenging research questions in the field of knowledge management.

Responding to this challenge, KM researchers have suggested a number of different tools and techniques for structuring knowledge content and providing guidance to useful knowledge as a means to improve its effectiveness. For example, O'Leary (2003) proposes that knowledge availability provides a basis to facilitate knowledge assimilation. Massaging knowledge into an appropriate format by a KM system could further help the user to better understand and use knowledge. Furthermore, knowledge can be filtered so that the right knowledge gets to the right people at the right time. Alternatively, KM system can provide guidance to relevant knowledge by making it more visible and accessible. Developing knowledge taxonomies or ontologies and linking knowledge to other knowledge or people and navigation tools are other commonly suggested approaches to improve knowledge assimilation (Handzic, 2004).

Knowledge mapping is another feasible KM method to coordinate, simplify, highlight, and navigate through complex webs of knowledge possessed by institutions (Wexler, 2001). The main purpose of knowledge maps is to locate important knowledge in an organisation (Kim, Suh, & Hwang, 2003) and guide users where to find it (Davenport & Prusak, 1998). They can also be used to identify domain experts (Eppler, 2003) and map knowledge flows (Grey, 1999).

Recent empirical findings indicate that all of these approaches were beneficial. With respect to storage and filtering, our earlier study reported that people managed to improve the quality of their decisions due to available knowledge (Handzic & Bewsell, 2005). However, the amount of improvement was highly contingent upon the quantity of the content, as shown in Chapter VI of this book. Another study found out that filtered knowledge, provided in a knowledge mart instead of a knowledge warehouse, resulted in further improved knowledge use and performance (Handzic & Parkin, 2000). Competency maps were also found to be helpful in locating and acquiring expert's advice (Handzic, 2004). Finally, Chapter X of this book indicates that knowledge rating scores had a positive effect on identifying and using high-quality knowledge.

In this study we take a closer look at the role of visualization as another potentially useful knowledge-massaging technique in KM. The main study objective is to empirically examine the impact of a specific visualization system on users' knowledge interpretation, and its subsequent effect on their performance in a judgmental forecasting task. It is hoped that the current research will provide a deeper insight into the potential and limitations of a knowledge visualisation approach to improving the effectiveness of knowledge repositories in supporting decision making. The assumption is that large, and largely incomprehensible, amounts of content available in knowledge repositories can be presented in a form that can be understood and interpreted by a human through the use of visualisation techniques.

Visualisation System

Vessey (1994) argued that the mode of presentation may influence people's perception of the value of knowledge displayed and, consequently, their readiness to apply that knowledge for problem solving. Unfortunately, past empirical research in this area continues to provide inconclusive and mixed results (Van Toorn, 2004). This suggests the need for further investigation. The current chapter describes a specific visualisation system based on decomposition approach and graphical visualisation, and examines its effectiveness in the time-series-forecasting task. The screenshot of the system studied is presented in Figure 7.1. The system was developed by Handzic and Shek (2004) specifically for the purpose of this investigation.

Decomposition

Decomposition is the term used to denote the separation of time series pattern into several subpatterns, namely trend, seasonality, noise, and cycle (Makridakis & Wheelwright, 1989). A basic premise behind decomposition is the notion that it adds structure to the task. Decomposition may also be seen to be decreasing the complexity of the pattern recognition task by reducing it into smaller and cognitively more manageable parts (MacGregor, 2001).

According to Makridakis and Wheelwright (1989), the trend component is assumed to represent the overall long-term direction of the time series. The trend can be either going upward, steady, or going downward. In practice, the trend is usually associated with the long-term growth or contractions of the economy.

The cycle component in the decomposition model generally reflects any long-term, but irregular, business cycles. It is generally related to demand and supply, sales, GDP, and implementation of monetary and fiscal policies by the government. The main reasons for these cycles are associated with boom and recession periods in the economy.

Figure 7.1 Screenshot of the proposed visualisation system

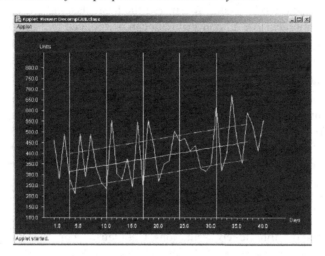

Another important component of the decomposition model is known as seasonality. Typically, seasonality is associated with periods of fixed length that can have an effect on the time-series pattern. In practice, these periods range from yearly to monthly to weekly. Yearly periods, such as the timing of holidays, commemorations, and celebrations or climate changes, may affect the time-series pattern. Weekly periods that can influence the time-series pattern include weekends and paydays. The seasonality component will usually show up as periodic and regular ups and downs.

The final component that the decomposition model assumes is noise. In theory, this component is defined as the component that cannot be explained by either the trend, cycle, or seasonality factors. In practice, it is considered as the error component. The error component can have a detrimental effect on the accuracy of the decomposition model, and every effort is made to minimise this component.

While different decomposition models have been suggested in the literature, this study focuses on the additive model, due to its simplicity. In this model, each time series value is considered as a simple sum of the trend, seasonality, cycle, and error components. These components can be added back together to form the original time-series values. For details of the decomposition model and its use in forecasting, interested readers are referred to Makridakis and Wheelwright (1989).

Visualisation

The review of visualisation literature presented here is based on Handzic (2004). Visualisation is defined as the process by which numerical data, such as surveys, measurements, or simulations, are converted into meaningful images (Marakas, 1999). The usefulness of visualisation lies in the basic assumption that large and normally incomprehensible amounts of data can be reduced to a form that can be understood and interpreted by a human through the use of visualisation techniques (Simoff, 2001).

umans are known to be visual creatures, with most of what they learn coming through sight (Whinston, 1995). It has also been recognised that visual pattern recognition skills exceed human ability to comprehend collections of texts and numbers (Ho & Azvine, 2000). This suggests that technologies and tools using visualisation techniques may be useful in analysing and understanding collections of data in various contexts. A large body of empirical evidence from research on presentation modes indicates that a graphical presentation is particularly useful for the identification of trends and relationships among variables (Handzic, 1996).

Visualisation models can be represented in different ways. They can be classified into geometric and symbolic representations. Geometric techniques include scatter plots, lines, surfaces, and volumes. Symbolic representations are showing the data by graphs (Fayyad, Grinstein, & Wierse, 2002). The simplest form of visualising data is using graphs, charts and tables, and indexing by colouring or symbol codes (Cabena, Hadjinian, Stadler, & Zanasi, 1997). There are other forms that include digital images, geographic systems, graphical user interfaces, multidimensions, virtual reality, 3-D presentations, and animation.

So far, visualisation has been successfully used in many industries including credit scoring and risk analysis in banking, fraud analysis and drug enforcement in government, and customer behaviour analysis in marketing. Empirical findings from our own laboratory studies indicate that 2-D visualisation tools were helpful in improving performance in forecasting trends (Handzic, Aurum, Oliver, & Logenthiran, 2002a), as well as in understanding relationships among multiple contextual cues (Handzic & Li, 2003). Our findings also show that scatter plots were more beneficial than bar charts in visualising two-way relationships among variables (Handzic, Lam, Aurum, & Oliver, 2002b).

Two-dimensional (2-D) and three-dimensional (3-D) visualisations have always been some of the most popular design options when it comes to the layout of a semantic structure. It has been long debated whether a three-dimensional visualisation would indeed offer the user richer semantics and more informative and intuitive controls of the underlying information. Several projects have investigated the relative performance and preference of users for 2-D and 3-D noninteractive graphs. Some studies found no difference in performance between them (Carswell, Frankenberger, & Bernhard, 1991), others found a general preference for 3-D graphs, particularly when they were used for making a memorable impression and when communicating information to others (Levy, Zacks, Tversky, & Schiano, 1996). 3-D visualisations were also useful for examining interactions that could not be expressed by decomposing them into two-way relationships (Poulet, 2000). However, a disadvantage of some 3-D visualisations was the difficulty of precisely locating an element in space. Stephens and Handzic (2004) proposed an interactive 3-D visualisation tool using virtual reality. They found out that it was a useful means to support social network analysis, particularly the discovery of relationships and network structures in an academic work environment.

This review and analysis of previous research clearly demonstrates the usefulness of visualisation technology in a variety of contexts. It also suggests that the effectiveness of a particular tool may be contingent upon the task context. The objective of this study was to test the effectiveness of a 2-D visualisation system, shown in Figure 7.1 in the context of time-series forecasting.

Empirical Study

Study Objectives

The main objective of the current study was to examine the impact of the proposed visualisation system based on time-series decomposition model and line graphs on users' understanding and performance in a judgmental extrapolation task. According to Van Toorn (2004), a decomposed graphical representation of time series may reduce the complexity of the extrapolation task by adding structure to it. This in turn may decrease the overall cognitive load on task doers and maximise their task performance. The current research seeks to empirically test this proposition.

Experimental Task

The experimental task was a modified version of the sales forecasting task used in an earlier chapter (Chapter IV) of this book. As before, the task involved estimating the daily demand of fresh ice cream at Bondi, a famous Sydney surf beach. Participants assumed a role of Sales Manager for a fictitious firm that sold the product from its outlet located at the beach. They were required to make predictions of daily product demand over a period of 30 days. Their goal was to minimise the total cost incurred from untimely and/or incorrect forecasts.

All subjects in the current study were provided with the artificially generated time series representing historic product demand data. However, the task differed with respect to the knowledge management support provided. One half of the subjects were supported by a visualisation system in the form of line graphs for trend and seasonality characteristics. The other half of the subjects received no such support.

On each trial, subjects were required to make estimates of the next day demand. At the beginning of the experiment, instructions were provided to inform the subjects of the task scenario and requirements.

Research Design and Variables

The experiment used a mixed factorial research design with one between-subjects and one within-subjects factor. The first factor was *visualisation system* (with or without), and the second one was *time period* (earlier, later).

The manipulation of the visualisation system factor was achieved by a change in the display format and the inclusion of extra features for those subjects who were in the "with system" treatment condition. These extra features were line graphs that enabled the time-series pattern to be decomposed or structured and thus display individual characteristics of the time series such as trend and seasonality. Experimental time period was divided into two equal blocks of trials termed earlier (trials 1-10) and later (trials 11-20).

The performance was evaluated in terms of *forecast accuracy*. Forecast accuracy was operationally defined by the mean absolute error (MAE). It is obtained by computing the absolute error for each trial, then summing those over time period and dividing by the number of values used (Makridakis, 1993).

Subjects and Procedure

Subjects were final year students from the School of Computer Science and Engineering at the University of New South Wales who participated in the study on a voluntary basis. One group of subjects completed the task without the knowledge visualisation system deemed to be less structured and therefore harder to understand and perform. The other group completed the same task with the support of the visualisation system deemed to be more structured and thus less complex and easier to understand. Data were collected for each treatment condition and time period. Descriptive analysis of collected data was performed and a summary of results presented in Figure 7.2 and 7.3 in the following section.

Results and Discussion

We expected that a visualisation system would have a positive effect on task performance in the judgmental extrapolation of time-series pattern. We believed that the inclusion of the trend and seasonality lines would have assisted subjects with the task and this, in turn, would have led them to produce more accurate results. The findings of the experiment support our contention.

Main Findings

As expected, the overall results indicate that the visualisation system was helpful on the task. The average MAE of subjects who performed the task with the visualisation system support was lower than that of their counterparts without the system (148 vs. 155). The decomposed time-series presentation, using trend and seasonality lines, brought structure to the task, and helped these subjects to better interpret and utilise relevant knowledge to improve the accuracy of their predictions.

On closer examination, the reported difference was greater in earlier than later time period (9% vs. 3%). Subjects undertaking the task with the visualisation system produced significantly better results than those undertaking the task without such support in the earlier time period (148 vs. 157). However, this was not found to hold for forecasts in the later period of time (149 vs. 152). This finding can be attributed to the effect of experiential learning. While subjects with the visualisation system produced similarly accurate forecasts in both earlier and later time periods, their counterparts without the system tended to produce better forecasts as they became more experienced with the task.

The results further indicate that the visualisation system was effective in improving forecast accuracy over naïve. When subjects' results are compared to naïve ones,

Figure 7.2. Subjects' forecast accuracy in four treatment conditions

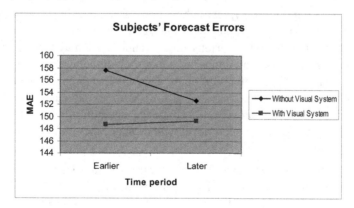

Figure 7.3. Comparative accuracy of actual and nominal naïve and optimal subjects

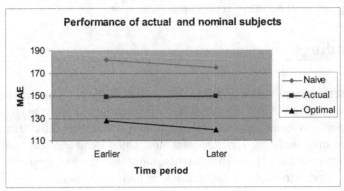

they indicate decrease in forecast errors. The average MAE with the visualisation system was significantly lower than that of their nominal naïve counterparts (148 vs. 178). However, when subjects' results are compared to optimal results, it is clear that there is room for further improvement. The average MAE of the subjects supported by the visualisation system was significantly higher than that of their nominal optimal counterparts (148 vs. 123).

Other Issues

The suboptimal knowledge utilisation, and resulting performance found, suggests that knowledge workers could benefit from additional KM solutions including different "smart" technologies. Typically these systems are enabled by artificial intelligence (AI) and can reason in a narrow domain and in a relatively mechanistic way. Handzic (2004) suggested that various smart technologies may have the potential to augment human abilities by doing tasks that they do better and leaving people to do those tasks they do better. Our study suggests that smart "models" may be more suitable than "heads" for tasks such as time-series extrapolation. Model-based systems can automate the process of knowledge integration and make forecasts instead of people. However, such development may have important ethical and societal implications.

The present study has several aspects that limit the generalisability of its results. In addition to standard limitations inherent in the experimental research design (Huck, Cormier, & Bounds, 1974; Judd, Smith, & Kidder, 1991), undergraduate students were used as subjects and the visualisation system tested was rather simple. Perhaps a more sophisticated visualisation tool for displaying knowledge would further facilitate faster and better understanding of the situation and possibly further help to improve performance.

Conclusion

This chapter explored the effectiveness of a visualisation system in improving knowledge interpretation and utilisation in a time-series-forecasting context. The results indicate that the system was beneficial in reducing the complexity of the forecasting task through decomposed graphical visualisation of the time-series pattern. This, in turn, helped to easier identify trend and seasonality subpatterns and make more accurate predictions. However, these findings are qualified by the number of study limitations. Future research is required to find the best knowledge management systems and tasks alignments.

References

Cabena, P., Hadjinian, P., Stadler, R., & Zanasi, A. (1997). *Discovering data mining from concept to implementation.* Upper Saddle River, NJ: Prentice Hall PTR.

Carswell, C. M., Frankenberger, S., & Bernhard, D. (1991). Graphing in depth: Perspectives on the use of three-dimensional graphs to represent lower-dimensional data. *Behaviour and Information Technology, 10*(6), 459-474.

Davenport, T. H., & Prusak, L. (1998). *Working knowledge,* Boston: Harvard Business School Press.

Eppler, M. (2003). Making knowledge visible through knowledge maps: Concepts, elements, cases. In C. W. Holsapple (Ed.), *Handbook on Knowledge Management, Volume 1* (pp. 189-205). Berlin: Springer-Verlag.

Fayyad, U., Grinstein, G. G., & Wierse, A. (2002). *Information visualisation in data mining and knowledge discovery.* Morgan Kaufmann Publishers.

Grey, D. (1999). *Knowledge mapping: A practical overview.* Retrieved June, 2002, from http://www.smithweaversmith.com/knowledg2.htm

Handzic, M. (1996). The effects of information homogeneity and mode of presentation on utilisation and effectiveness of information systems. In C. D. Keen,

C. Urquhart, & J. Lamp (Eds.), *Proceedings of the 7ᵗʰ Australasian Conference on Information Systems* (pp. 287-298). Hobart: University of Tasmania, Department of Computer Science.

Handzic, M. (2004). *Knowledge management: Through the technology glass.* Singapore: World Scientific Publishing.

Handzic, M., Aurum, A., Oliver, G., & Logenthiran, G. (2002a, September). An empirical investigation of a knowledge discovery tool. In *Proceedings of the European Conference on Knowledge Management (ECKM 2002)*, Dublin.

Handzic, M., & Bewsell, G. (2005). Corporate memories: Tombs or wellsprings of knowledge. In B. Montano (Ed.), *Innovations of knowledge management* (pp. 69-85). Hershey, PA: IRM Press.

Handzic, M., Lam, B., Aurum, A., & Oliver, G. (2002b, September). A comparative analysis of two knowledge discovery tool: Scatterplot versus barchart. In *Proceedings of the International Conference on Data Mining (DM 2002)*, Bologna.

Handzic, M., & Li, W. (2003). Discovering predictive quality of knowledge artefacts in organisational repositories. In *Proceedings of the Australian Conference for Knowledge Management ad Intelligent Decision Support (ACKMIDS 2002)* (pp. 133-144). Melbourne: Australian Scholarly Publishing.

Handzic, M., & Parkin, P. (2000). Knowledge management technology: Examination of information diverse repositories. *South African Computer Journal, 26*, 125-131.

Handzic, M., & and Shek, A. (2004, July). *Forecasting support system: An empirical investigation.* (Working paper), Sydney, Australia: UNSW, School of Information Systems, Technology and Management.

Ho, B., & Azvine, C. (2000, September). Mining travel data with a visualiser. In *Proceedings of ECML'01 Conference*.

Huck, S. W., Cormier, W. H., & Bounds, W. G. Jr. (1974). *Reading statistics and research.* USA: Harper and Row Publishers.

Judd, C. M., Smith, E. R., & Kidder, L. H. (1991). *Research methods in social relations* (6th ed.). Harcourt Brace Jovanovich College Publishers.

Kim, S., Suh, E., & Hwang, H. (2003). Building the knowledge map: An industrial case study. *Journal of Knowledge Management, 7*(2), 34-45.

Levy, E., Zacks, J., Tversky, B., & Schiano, D. (1996). Gratuitous graphics? Putting preferences in perspective. In *Proceedings of CHI '96* (pp. 42-49). Vancouver: ACM Press.

MacGregor, D. (2001). Decomposition for judgemental forecasting and estimation. In J. S. Amstrong (Ed.), *Principles of forecasting.* Norwell, MA: Kluwer Academic Publishers.

Makridakis, S. (1993). Accuracy measures: Theoretical and practical concerns. *International Journal of Forecasting, 9*, 527-529.

Makridakis, S., & Wheelwright, S. C. (1989). *Forecasting methods for management.* New York: John Wiley & Sons.

Marakas, G. M. (1999). *Decision support systems in the 21ˢᵗ century.* New Jersey: Prentice-Hall.

O'Leary, D. E. (2003). Technologies for knowledge storage and assimilation, In C. W. Holsapple (Ed.), *Handbook on knowledge management* (Vol. 2, pp. 29-46). Berlin: Springer.

Poulet, F. (2000, November 19-22). Comprehensibility in data-mining. In *Proceedings of the International Symposium on Data Mining and Statistics*. Germany: University of Augsburg.

Simoff, S. J. (2001, September). Towards the development of environments for designing visualisation support for visual data mining. In *Proceedings of ECML'01.*

Stephens, G., & Handzic, M. (2004, January 5-8). Knowledge discovery through visualising using virtual reality. In *Proceedings of the Thirty-Seventh Annual Hawaii International Conference on System Sciences (HICSS37)* (CD/ROM). Computer Society Press, Ten Pages.

Van Toorn, C. (2004). *Media and technology effects in the forecasting task.* Unpublished Master of Commerce thesis, UNSW, Australia.

Vessey, I. (1994). The effect of information presentation on decision making: A cost-benefit analysis. *Information & Management, 27*(2), 103-119.

Wexler, M. N. (2001). The who, what and why of knowledge mapping. *Journal of Knowledge Management, 5*(3), 249-263.

Whinston, Z. (1995). *Business information visualisation* (Research in Progress). Association for Information Systems.

Chapter VIII

Knowledge Miner:
Assisting in Pattern Discovery and Prediction

Abstract

This chapter addresses the issue of knowledge discovery from data. It reports the results of an empirical investigation of the effectiveness of a specific knowledge-mining tool in discovering and predicting trends from time-series data. The results obtained clearly show that people are capable of enhancing knowledge and subsequent performance using this technology, but they also indicate that there is still room for further improvement. Hence, more research is needed in this area to achieve increased efficiency.

Introduction

The growing amount of data being generated by electronic and traditional transactions between customers, suppliers, and other trading partners represents a potentially valuable source of new knowledge for organisations. Therefore, the discovery of knowledge that is implicit in data is one of the major issues that needs to be addressed in research (Blanning, 2000).

Knowledge discovery has been described as the nontrivial process of identifying valid, novel, potentially useful and ultimately understandable patterns in data (Fayyad, Piatetsky-Shapiro, & Smyth, 1996). The term knowledge mining is often used interchangeably with knowledge discovery (Berry & Linoff, 1997). Patterns in data can be extracted by one or more knowledge discovery tasks. A taxonomy suggested by Shaw et al (Shaw, Subramaniam, Tan, & Welge, 1999) includes five categories: dependency analysis, class identification, concept description, deviation detection, and data visualisation. The focus of this study is on deviation detection in combination with visualisation.

It is argued that discovery systems using statistical techniques, such as linear regression, may help forecasters to detect systematic trends (Makridakis, Wheelwright, & McGee, 1983). The parameters of the linear regression equation minimise the mean error values. Thus, a regression line incorporated into the tool design may be a potentially valuable aid to the knowledge discovery process. To explore the knowledge in data more effectively, data visualisation can be used in association with statistical techniques.

Keim (1996) has provided an elaborate analysis of visualisation techniques and classified them as pixel-oriented, geometric projection, and graph based. Of particular interest in this study are graphs. The basic idea of the graph-based technique is to effectively present a graph using a specific layout algorithm, query languages, and abstraction techniques. It has been shown in past research that graphical presentation enhanced accuracy of novices (Lawrence, Edmundson, & O'Connor, 1985). So, one can assume, for example, that a line graph representing a series of historic sales data points may allow a forecaster to view the underlying pattern in product sales over time and help extrapolate that pattern in an estimate of future sales.

The purpose of this chapter is to address this issue of knowledge discovery by describing and testing a specific knowledge discovery tool in the sales forecasting context. In particular, the study reported here examined: (a) whether and how effective was our knowledge discovery tool in enhancing people's ability to recognise trends in time-series data, and (b) what impact the extracted knowledge had on people's subsequent forecasting performance.

Knowledge Discovery Approaches and Technologies

The overview of various knowledge discovery approaches presented in this section is drawn from Handzic (2004). Typically, knowledge discovery approaches are classified by the function they perform into four major categories: classification, association, sequence, and cluster (Marakas, 1999). Classification seeks the rule that defines whether an item or event belongs to a particular class or set. Association analysis searches for a rule that correlates one set of events or items with another set of events or items. Sequencing is used to relate events in time. Through this analysis, various hidden trends can be discovered that are often predictive of future trends. Clustering groups a set of objects together by virtue of their similarity or proximity to each other.

Technologies associated with these approaches are numerous (Lee & Siau, 2001). They cover statistics, mathematics, database technology, artificial intelligence, economic and decision theory, and visualisation. Statistics can help to detect noise and trends, and traditional modeling techniques, such as regression analysis, are appropriate for building linear predictive models. Multidimensional and relational analytical processing technologies help analysis across multiple dimensions and in drilling down data sets. Neural networks deal with nonlinear relationships and have the ability to learn. Other learning algorithms, such as genetic algorithms and fuzzy logic, can extract patterns and detect trends within highly complex and imprecise sets. Decision trees refer to simple mathematical tools for problem structuring. This technology generates tree-shaped structures that assist in the classification of data. Finally, visualisation enables more clear representation of the found patterns using colors, shapes, sound, and virtual reality.

According to Beccera-Fernandez et al. (Becerra-Fernandez, Gonzales, & Sabherwal, 2004), the many knowledge discovery techniques fall under one of three basic categories: symbolic, connectionist, and statistical. Symbolic techniques use inductive algorithms to build decision trees. Connectionist techniques consist of several processing elements, called neurons, to perform the tasks. The result is a neural network. Statistical methods cover linear regression, k-means, basket analysis, discriminant analysis, and logistic analysis. These knowledge discovery systems have made a significant contribution in scientific fields for years, and have become increasingly popular in business applications over the last decade or so. Typical applications of knowledge discovery include customer, product, and market analysis in retail and banking, fraud detection in government, actuarial modeling in insurance, patient and therapy analysis in health care, and risk and portfolio analysis in asset management (Marakas, 1999).

The suggested benefits range from being better informed about a customer's needs, to higher efficiency, productivity, accuracy in prediction, and better decision making. Our own empirical studies reveal that neural networks, indeed, were helpful in supporting loan officers' application decisions (Handzic et al., 2003). Statistics assisted in discovering predictive quality of knowledge artifacts in organisational repositories (Handzic & Li, 2003) and forecasting sales trends (Handzic, Lam, Aurum, & Oliver, 2002a). Finally, visualisation using virtual reality was useful in social network analysis (Stephens & Handzic, 2004). In the next section, we report one empirical study conducted as part of the ongoing research program in knowledge management at UNSW.

Data-Mining-Tool Description

Based on the literature review and assessment, Handzic et al. (Handzic, Aurum, Oliver, & Logenthiran, 2002b) developed a knowledge-mining tool based on a combination of statistical (linear regression) and visualisation (line graph) techniques, as suggested by data mining (Westphal & Blaxton, 1998) and forecasting literature (Makridakis et al., 1983). The system was designed to accommodate all the needed operations and visual capabilities to provide maximum support to users in a time-series-forecasting task. The software for the tool was written in Microsoft Visual Basic because of its ability to handle several variables; ability to collect, store, and manipulate data; number of visual options present in the package; object-oriented capabilities; the "easy to run" characteristic of "exe" (executable) files; and it is user–friendly and easier than many other languages to program with.

The data files were created separately from the artificially generated set of random numbers. These were drawn from a normal distribution with a mean of 0 and a standard deviation 500 and added to a constant 2000. A sequence of increasing numbers was added to create a 5% upward trend. Finally, trend and standard deviation lines were incorporated in the research instrument, as shown in Figure 8.1.

The trend line shown can be described by two parameters, a and b, in the form: $x = a + b * t$.

The values of a and b that minimize the MSE (mean squared error) can be found by using the formulas: $a = (Sx - b* St) / n$, $b = (n*Stx - St*Sx) / (n*Stt - St*St)$, where the observations, their squares, and products are summed to obtain the following quantities:$St = t1 + t2 + ...+ tn$, $Sx = x1 + x2 + ... + xn$, $Stx = t1*x1 + t2 * x2 + ... + tn * xn$, and $Stt = t1 * t1 + t2 * t2 + ...+ tn * tn$. The standard deviation lines of the trend line have the same gradient (b), but different a value. Hence the formula can be given as: $x = (a \pm c) + b * t$. The value of c is calculated using the formula: $c = sqrt [(n * Sxx - Sx * Sx) / n * (n - 1)]$, where $Sxx = x1 * x1 + x2 * x2 + ... + xn * xn$, and sqrt stands for square root operation.

Figure 8.1. Screenshot of the research instrument

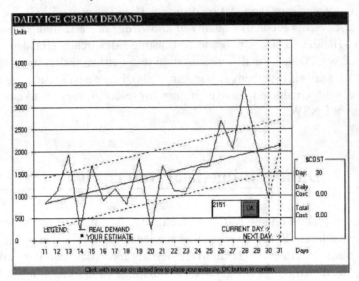

Empirical Study

The tool's effectiveness was tested in the context of a judgmental extrapolation task with an upward trended time series, shown in Figure 8.1. Trends are patterns that persist over a period of time. They could be short-term trends like the sharp increase of sales following a sales campaign. Alternatively, they could be long-term trends like the slow growing of sales of a product over a period of a few months (say after product introduction). A knowledge discovery tool can help detect these sometimes very subtle and hidden trends in the data.

In marketing, trends can be used for evaluating marketing programs or to forecast future sales. Our experimental task involved forecasting daily sales of ice cream in circumstances of slowly increasing product sales over a period of 60 days. The participants assumed the role of the Manager of the fictitious store. Their task was to make their forecasts based on previous sales data. Their goal was to minimise the company's loss due to spoilage or competition by minimising forecast errors.

The manager could consult the company's database and obtain the past sales data graphed as a line against time. An additional trend line, along with the two standard deviation lines, was also given. It was expected that these visual cues would enable individuals to gain a good understanding of the existing upward trend in data and use that knowledge to make better forecasts. In addition, the tool provided continuous feedback on subjects' errors to enable them to analyse their earlier performance and to adjust their future strategies.

The subjects were 47 postgraduate students from a large Australian university. They participated in the study on a voluntary basis and received no monetary incentives. As previously mentioned in Chapter IV, many authors, including Ashton and Kramer (1980), Remus (1996), and Whitecotton (1996), consider graduate students as suitable subjects for research in decision making. The experiment took place in a computer laboratory. Each subject was given a disk containing the data and the tool. The tool incorporated the description of the case study and the task requirements. Subjects were also given an opportunity to make five trial forecasts for practice purpose. The tool automatically recorded all subjects' responses for later analysis. The session lasted approximately 1 hour.

The effectiveness of the tool was measured in terms of the cumulative relative error—CumRAE (Makridakis, 1993). It was calculated as the ratio of the cumulative absolute error of forecasts and the corresponding error of the naive strategy over the total forecasting period. In addition, the corresponding errors of naive and optimal strategies on the task were calculated for the purposes of latest comparison. The naive forecasting method typically produces poor performance by simply determining the future estimate as equal to previous day sales. Optimal (linear regression) error was used as a measure of the maximum knowledge extractable from the historical data using the tool.

Results

The results of the experiment (CumRAE) are presented graphically in Figure 8.2. Mean values of subject errors, as well as naïve and optimal errors, are also depicted for comparison.

The figure reveals that the subjects' mean error falls in between the naïve and optimal. However, it falls closer to optimal than naïve, which indicates that the forecasting efficiency of the experiment was high. This clearly indicates that the knowledge-mining tool did, in fact, improve the forecasting capabilities of the subjects in time series with trend and noise.

The subjects were found to make significantly smaller relative errors compared to their notional naive counterparts ($0.76 < 1$, $p<0.05$). In real terms, subjects' mean prediction error was 662.37 units of sales as compared to naive error of 873.4 units. This suggests that the subjects managed to extract some of the hidden knowledge from data. However, there remained room for possible further improvement. Despite being given an optimal response in the form of a visual cue to guide their perfor-

Figure 8.2. Summary results

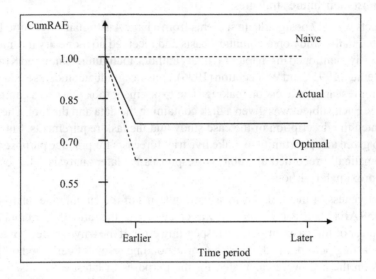

mance, the subjects failed to achieve maximum performance of notional optimal counterparts ($0.76 > 0.65$, $p < 0.05$). In real terms, subjects' average prediction error was 662.37 units of sales, and optimal error was 568.8 units.

From the electronic survey conducted after the experiment, it was found that most people used the features offered by the tool, to a good extent, to identify and utilise patterns. The dominant strategy used was "follow the trend along the trend line between the standard deviation lines" (29.80%), that gives close to maximum performance. The second most-used strategy was "forecast between past maximum and minimum" (27.70%), which would only work well for a flat trend. Several subjects used the worst possible naïve strategy (10.60%). The remaining subjects used a variety of suboptimal heuristics. The use of inadequate strategies had a negative effect on the overall performance.

Discussion

Overall, the results of the analysis performed indicate that the tool was quite effective in enhancing a forecasters' ability to recognise an upward trend pattern existing in sales data.

The subject error was around 76% of the naïve error, indicating a 24% improvement. Considering the fact that, using this specific technique, the optimal error is 65% of the naïve error (35% improvement is possible with optimal performance), the knowledge extracted is substantial. The main reason behind this would be the subjects' ability to see the trend and standard deviation visually. Past research also indicates that graphical presentation enhances accuracy of novices (Lawrence et al., 1985).

From the electronic survey conducted after the experiment, it was found that most people used the features (i.e., trend line and standard deviation lines) offered by the tool, to a good extent, to interpret and utilise discovered patterns. The dominant strategy used by the subjects was the forecasting of future sales based on the trend line of past sales, between the standard deviation lines. It appears that subjects tried to beat the tool and, consequently, performed worse than they could have in theory.

One possible explanation for such a tendency may be the lack of trust in the tool and its outputs. Accordingly, people tried to beat the tool by forecasting around rather than on the line suggested. The presence of the standard deviation lines could have contributed further to distracting subjects' attention off the trend line. This, as a consequence, might have led to suboptimal performance.

In a nondeterministic task problem, such as the one used in this study, no forecasting strategy can ensure a completely error-free forecast. To better understand this issue, people may need additional knowledge management interventions. For example, they may be given the feedback on past performance of the tool to help them analyse its performance compared to other strategies (e.g., their own intuition). This could help in building appreciation and trust on the tool and subsequently, increase reliance. Feedback was generally found to be helpful in cue discovery studies (Klayman, 1988).

It is also possible that additional know-how, in the form of guiding instructions included in the tool design, could be of further assistance. Preliminary findings indicate that by giving people simple written instructions, such as "smooth," it is possible to direct their attention to the systematic trend component, avoid distraction from noise element in the series, and enhance performance (O'Connor, 1998). Full automation of the knowledge discovery process is another potential solution. However, a completely automated system without any human intervention could be detrimental to humans and contribute to deskilling. Our position is that human judgement, interpretation, and implementation are critical to knowledge discovery.

To resolve this issue, organisations may choose to supplement technology-based strategies with other knowledge management strategies. For example, they may conduct specialised professional-development courses for marketing and sales personnel, using modern educational methods. Alternatively, they may buy ready external expertise. In this case, people trained in the area of analytical and statistical reasoning would perform knowledge extraction for other professional and managerial knowledge workers.

It is also possible to encourage a culture of social interaction and collaborative learning. The spiral knowledge model postulates that the process of knowledge sharing will result in the amplification and exponential growth of knowledge (Nonaka, 1998). The preliminary empirical findings conducted in the forecasting context provide support for this proposition (Handzic, 2000). Future research may address some of these and other knowledge discovery issues so that a better understanding of the field can be achieved.

Conclusion

The main concern of this chapter is support for knowledge discovery. The proliferation of information systems and technology has made it inevitable for companies to have the ever-increasing capability to accumulate huge amounts of business data in large databases. However, much of the useful marketing insights into business data are largely untapped and hidden.

The primary objective of the study reported in this chapter was to investigate the human ability to extract and utilise valuable knowledge using time-series analysis. A knowledge discovery tool that displays the historical data graphically, along with the trend and standard deviation lines, was developed to carry out the study.

The findings indicate that the participants were able to discover valuable knowledge hidden in data using the tool. However, their average performance indicated that they could not extract all possible knowledge embedded in data. Hence even though they achieved substantial performance improvement, they still failed to achieve the maximum possible success.

Therefore, it could be concluded that further research and analytical studies should be carried out to achieve a better understanding and more accurate forecasting capabilities to further enhance performance. Further research may also explore the practice of knowledge discovery in other tasks and contexts, and using different subjects in order to generalise and expand these findings.

References

Ashton, R. H., & Kramer, S. S. (1980). Students as surrogates in behavioural accounting research: Some evidence. *Journal of Accounting Research, 18*(1), 1-15.

Becerra-Fernandez, I., Gonzales, A., & Sabherwal, R. (2004). *Knowledge management: Challenges, solutions, and technologies.* Upper Saddle River, NJ: Pearson Education, Inc.

Berry, M. J. A., & Linoff, G. (1997). *Data mining techniques for marketing, sales, and customer support.* New York: John Wiley & Sons.

Blanning, R. W. (2000). Knowledge management and electronic commerce. In *Position Papers on Future Directions in Decision Support, IFIP WK8.3 Working Conference on DSS*, Stochholm.

Fayyad, U., Piatetsky-Shapiro, G., & Smyth, P. (1996). Knowledge discovery and data mining: Towards a unifying framework. In *Proceedings of the Second International Conference on Knowledge Discovery and Data mining (KDD-96)*, OR.

Handzic, M. (2000, October 30-31). Managing knowledge through experimentation and socialisation, In U. Reimer (Ed.), *Proceedings of the Third International Conference on Practical Aspects of Knowledge Management (PAKM 2000)*, Basel, Switzerland.

Handzic, M. (2004). *Knowledge management: Through the technology glass.* Singapore: World Scientific Publishing.

Handzic, M., Aurum, A., Oliver, G., & Logenthiran, G. (2002b, September). An empirical investigation of a knowledge discovery tool. In *Proceedings of the European Conference on Knowledge Management (ECKM 2002)*, Dublin.

Handzic, M., Lam, B., Aurum, A., & Oliver G. (2002a, September). A comparative analysis of two knowledge discovery tool: Scatterplot versus barchart, In *Proceedings of the International Conference on Data Mining (DM 2002)*, Bologna.

Handzic, M., & Li, W. (2003). Discovering predictive quality of knowledge artefacts in organisational repositories. In *Proceedings of the Australian Conference for Knowledge Management and Intelligent Decision Support (ACKMIDS 2002)* (pp. 133-144). Melbourne: Australian Scholarly Publishing.

Klayman, J. (1988). Learning from experience. In B. Brehmer, & C. R. B. Joyce (Eds.), *Human judgement. The SJT view.* Amsterdam: North-Holland.

Lawrence, M., Edmundson, B., & O'Connor, M. (1985). An examination of accuracy of judgemental extrapolation of time series. *International Journal of Forecasting, 1*, 25-35.

Lee, S. J., & Siau, K. (2001). A review of data mining techniques. *Industrial Management & Data Systems, 101*(1), 41-46.

Makridakis, S. (1993). Accuracy measures: Theoretical and practical concerns. *International Journal of Forecasting, 9*, 527-529.

Makridakis, S., Wheelwright, S. C., & McGee, V. E. (1983). *Forecasting: Methods and applications.* Canada: John Wiley & Sons.

Marakas, G. M. (1999). *Decision support systems in the 21st century.* Englewood Cliffs, NJ: Prentice-Hall.

Nonaka, I. (1998). The knowledge-creating company. In *Harvard Business Review on knowledge management.* Boston: Harvard Business School Press.

O'Connor, M. (1999). Improving judgemental forecasting. In *Proceedings of the International Symposium on Forecasting (ISF-99).* Barbados.

Remus, W. (1996). Will behavioural research on managerial decision making generalise to managers? *Managerial and Decision Economics, 17,* 93-101.

Shaw, M. J., Subramaniam, C., Tan, G. W., & Welge, M. E. (1999). Knowledge management and data mining for marketing. In *Proceedings of International Society for Decision Support Systems (ISDSS'99)* (pp. 1-8).

Westphal, C., & Blaxton, T. (1998). *Data mining solutions: Methods and tools for solving real-world problems.* New York: John Wiley & Sons.

Whitecotton, S. M. (1996). The effects of experience and a decision aid on the slope, scatter, and bias of earnings forecasts. *Organisational Behaviour and Human Decision Processes, 66*(1), 111-121.

Chapter IX

E-Learning Portal:
Enhancing User Experience

Abstract

*This chapter looks at the e-learning portal from the perspective of the user. Percep-
tions and attitudes of employees from a large Asian organisation towards their corporate e-learning portal were compared to those towards the traditional classroom
environment. The results indicate overall preference for electronic over traditional
learning environment. However, deeper analysis revealed that e-learning was clearly
preferred only for acquiring explicit knowledge, but not tacit knowledge.*

Introduction

Technological advances, globalization, changing demographics, and privatisation are the main driving forces behind the current transformation of education and training. Market research firms estimate that electronic learning or e-learning is the fastest growing sector of the global education market with an annual growth rate of 10-15% (Hezel Associates, 2005).

The proponents of e-learning argue that such technology-mediated learning (also known as virtual, online, or distance learning) may improve students' achievement, their attitudes toward learning, and their evaluation of the learning experience. They also suggest that e-learning may help to increase student interaction and to make learning more student-centered. In addition, many researchers suggest that e-learning can potentially eliminate geographic barriers while providing increased convenience, flexibility, currency of material, retention of students, individualized learning, and feedback over traditional classrooms (Piccoli, Ahmad, & Ives, 2001). In contrast, some researchers warn that e-learning may lead to the student feelings of isolation, frustration, anxiety, and confusion. Furthermore, inappropriate e-learning practice may result in reduced interest in the subject matter and questionable learner achievement (Schank, 2001).

The literature indicates that current research interests in e-learning fall into three areas: (1) measuring e-learning outcomes, (2) measuring preferences for learning methods, and (3) proposing and evaluating hybrid models. With respect to outcomes, the research has produced mixed evidence regarding the benefits of e-learning (Cho, 2002; Rosenberg, 2001; Urdan & Weggen, 2000; Yoo, 2002). With respect to methods, researchers are seeking to better understand learner preferences for one delivery system over another (Rivera, McAlister, & Rice, 2002). Finally, there is a growing interest in hybrid courses that meet in the traditional classroom for part of the course and meet online for another part (Reasons, 2004; Young, 2002).

The main purpose of this chapter is to address the issue of user preferences for their learning environment in the context of a large Asian organization, and from the knowledge management (KM) perspective. In particular, the paper examines employee-trainees' perceptions and attitudes towards their corporate e-learning portal compared to the traditional classroom environment. The current study is a part of the ongoing research project on corporate e-learning by Handzic and Hoor (2005). The investigation was carried out in Korean Air, a global-sized airline that is ranked 12th for passenger transportation and 1st for cargo transportation in 2003. Korean Air flies to 87 cities in 31 countries and has offices worldwide. The company introduced its first e-learning course in 2001 and is gradually increasing the number of e-learning courses, in order to replace most of its on-site trainings with e-learning eventually. The focus of the current investigation was on the KALCC's (Korean Air Lines cybercampus) Microsoft Word e-learning portal.

E-Learning Portal

According to Handzic (2004), the main objective of any educational portal or Web site is to provide learners with a one-stop point of interaction for all their study needs, a place that students can go to obtain lecture notes, assignments, reference materials, discussions, surveys, search facilities, links, and many other useful features. Different KM features on the Web site can accommodate different types of knowledge (Handzic & Jamieson, 2001). It is assumed that learners respond differently to different types of KM features and if all are available, the productivity and enjoyment of the learning experience is likely to be increased.

With respect to the KALCC's Microsoft Word course portal, Handzic and Hur (2005) note that it contains lecture notes, course outline, resources, announcements, discussion forum, table of contents, search facility, online tests, questions and answers, and progress report. Essentially, the portal captures different quadrants of the knowledge space/matrix, presented in Chapter III of this book, through the use of the suitable KM support. Figure 9.1 shows specific KM features in KALCC's portal categorised into four groups based on the type of knowledge they support.

Explicit know-what features from the KALCC's Microsoft Word course portal include the following knowledge repositories: (1) Course Outline, which gives students an insight into the course content, structure, and assessments weighting; (2) Lecture Notes, which aid in learning specific topics and increasing overall knowledge of the subject; and (3) Resources, which come in the form of recommended texts, case studies, and research papers. Wider knowledge about the subject matter may be gained from these readings. These electronic documents are compared to paper notes, books, and reference materials in the traditional learning environment.

Explicit know-how features found on the KALCC's portal include the following:(1) Table of Contents, which is an efficient means of mapping knowledge concepts,

Figure 9.1. KM features by knowledge types

Types of knowledge	Explicit	Tacit
Know-what	• Course Outline • Lecture Notes • Resources	• Announcement • Discussion Forum
Know-how	• Table of Contents • Search Facility	• Tests • Questions & Answers • Progress Report

competencies, and processes; helps in understanding; and provides guidance; and (2) Search Facility, which is a direct means of access to what students are looking for; it allows students to find knowledge on relevant topics quickly, whether they are looking for course content or trying to find the details of a staff member. These KM features are compared to manuals, guidebooks, FAQ's, and library catalogues used in the traditional learning environment.

Tacit know-what features found on the KALCC's portal include the following: (1) Discussion Forum, which allows students to interact with each other in an asynchronous way. This allows students to post questions regarding assignments, exams, or make general queries in relation to the subject; thus allowing them to transfer and acquire knowledge from each other; and (2) Online Announcements that allow students to keep up to date with everything that is going on in the course on a 24-hour basis, eliminating any delays. These virtual spaces are compared with face-to-face announcements, class discussions and debates in the traditional learning environment.

Tacit know-how features are provided on the on the KALCC's portal in the form of: (1) Online Tests, which allow students to progress through the subject and acquire knowledge at their own pace by allowing them to participate in quizzes in the comfort of their own home and in their own time; (2) Questions & Answers, which is an efficient means of gaining knowledge about most important classes of issues, as well as additional clarifications of assignment queries; and (3) Progress Report, which is a means of gaining up-to-date information such as personal performance results. It also gives students an idea of their relative student ranking. It measures their continuous progress and knowledge of the subject. These KM tools are compared with written examinations, classroom exercises, instructor's feedback, and reports in the traditional learning environment.

Empirical Study

A survey study was conducted to explore employee-trainees' perceptions of effectiveness of their e-learning portal compared to the traditional learning environment in a real-world organisation. The survey was chosen as a preferred research method due to the timeliness, low cost, and convenience factors. Subjects for this study were employees working at Korean Air. A total of 101 employees from worldwide offices were enrolled in KALCC (Korean Air Lines Cyber Campus) Microsoft Word course. Out of these, 80 employees participated in the study. The survey was designed to explore a specific e-learning course in a corporate environment. The main objective was to find out learners' views on the effectiveness of their e-learning portal compared to the traditional learning environment in supporting different types of knowledge. Another objective was to obtain user views on possible improvements in the portal effectiveness.

A two-part questionnaire administered consisted of a mixture of closed and open-ended questions. In Part I, closed questions asked learners to indicate their perceived effectiveness of e-learning portal compared to traditional class in supporting explicit and tacit what and how types of knowledge. Open-ended questions were used to elicit reasons for preferring e-learning. In Part II, the learners were asked to make suggestions for inclusion of additional advanced features that could make the e-learning portal more effective. The survey was designed to allow anonymity so that the subjects could freely express their thoughts and feelings with respect to the KALCC course evaluated. From the responses obtained, the learners' views of e-learning were carefully analysed. The results are presented in Figure 9.2.

Results and Discussion

User Preferences for Learning Environment

The overall results indicate that 55% participants favoured e-learning. They perceived their e-learning portal as more effective than the traditional learning environment in supporting their learning needs. The next 27% participants were neutral. They perceived both e-learning and traditional learning environment as equally effective. Only 18% participants had a preference for traditional learning environment.

The main reasons mentioned for preferring e-learning portal over traditional class are the following:

- Ability to revise/revisit certain areas that the learners wish to study
- Easiness of finding other related supplementary resources
- Learners can study at their own paces
- Ability to concentrate better
- Heighten interests through usage of multimedia (audio/video effects, interactions)
- Approachability
- Less psychological problems (fears or timidity caused by peers/co-learners)

Further analyses of results by different knowledge types indicate that the e-learning portal was perceived as significantly more effective than the traditional class in providing support for acquisition of explicit, but not tacit knowledge.

These results support some earlier findings that course Web sites are an effective means of delivering course content (Handzic & Chumkovski, 2004). Therefore, it comes as no surprise that more than two thirds of the participants clearly preferred e-learning portal over traditional class with respect to acquiring explicit know-what (68% vs. 6%) and explicit know-how (69% vs. 1%).

In contrast, less than half of the participants reported their preference of e-learning portal over traditional class as an effective means to stimulate interactions and learning of tacit know-what (40% vs. 38%) and tacit know-how (45% vs. 25%) by doing. Such results indicate room for further improvement.

Perceptions of E-Learning

Quantitative Analysis

Table 9.1 shows summary results from the descriptive analyses of the responses obtained for users' views on KM features implemented on their e-learning portal. The "mean" score values for various KM features are assigned to categories—"Perceived Importance" and "Felt Satisfaction." Only those facilities that were implemented were considered.

Figure 9.2. Preferences in learning each type of knowledge

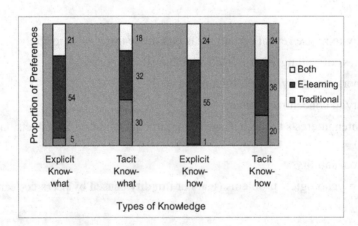

From a quick glance at the importance column, it can be seen that the employees felt that all KM features on their portal were important for their learning experience. All mean scores were greater than 3 (out of 5). However, "Lecture Notes" and "Progress Report" were the most important ones with ratings of 4. "Announcements" came a close third at 3.97, and "Questions and Answers" fourth at 3.91. These were followed by "Table of Contents" at 3.89 and "Course Outline" at 3.85. "Discussion Forum" was eighth with a score of 3.77. "Resources" and "Search facility" were considered as least important KM features with rating scores 3.60 and 3.51 respectively.

Looking at the satisfaction column, one can see that the employees were quite satisfied with the quality of their portal implementation. All satisfaction scores were above 3 (out of 5). However, all satisfaction rates were lower than their corresponding importance scores. Among these, "Progress Report" together with "Questions and Answers" had the highest satisfaction rate amongst the employees of 3.90. These were followed by "Online Tests" at 3.87, "Lecture Notes" at 3.79, "Course Outline" at 3.76, and "Table of Contents" at 3.65. "Announcements" and "Discussion Forum" received equal satisfaction rates of 3.54. Finally, employees were least satisfied with the implementation of "Resources" and "Search Facility." Their mean rating scores were 3.51 and 3.49 respectively.

Overall mean results of 3.83 for importance and 3.67 for satisfaction indicate that this e-learning portal was quite valuable in supporting its learning purpose. How-

Table 9.1. Summary results for implemented KM features

	Knowledge Management Feature	Perceived Importance	Felt Satisfaction
1.	Course Outline	3.85	3.76
2.	Lecture Notes	4.00	3.79
3.	Resources	3.60	3.51
4.	Announcements	3.97	3.54
5.	Discussion Forum	3.77	3.54
6.	Table of Contents	3.89	3.65
7.	Search Facility	3.51	3.49
8.	Online tests	3.90	3.87
9.	Questions & Answers	3.91	3.90
10.	Progress Report	4.00	3.90
	Overall	3.83	3.67

ever, employees agreed that extra functionality provided by advanced KM features could make e-learning even more effective. The four advanced KM features that did not appear on the portal included the "Simulator," "Systematic Search Function," "One-to-One Online Tutor," and "Online Help." Their respective "Perceived Importance" rates of 4.37, 4.21, 3.94, and 4.14 clearly show that all of these were considered as very important by employees.

Qualitative Analysis

Further analyses of employee responses to open-ended questions of the survey provide deeper understanding of the reasons behind positive attitudes towards e-learning found in the study, as well as help in identifying major problems affecting employees' satisfaction.

Mentioned major advantages of e-learning mentioned included: "Can concentrate better"; "Not forced-learning"; "Ability to re-visit my weaknesses at my own pace"; "Interesting contents"; "Ability to replay lectures/tutorials again and again"; "Effective to set up a good foundation to a study"; "No shyness in asking questions/No embarrassments of speaking in front of others"; "Ease of searching relevant information"; "Ability to see one's progress"; "Experiencing multimedia tools (more interesting/exciting)"; "Possibility to study a small part of a large content"; "Accessibility (anytime/anywhere wherever internet is available)"; "Can study at my own pace"; "Usage of various multimedia tools help learners understand better"; and "More efficient time management."

Major disadvantages included: "You cannot always carry your PC around (unlike books/papers)"; "As in the traditional learning environments, course designers must average out the level of students' ability/level of intelligence (Designers cannot design a hundred courses for the same topic to customize all different students). Hence, various other attempts still cannot solve this problem"; and "Even super-advanced communication tools cannot replace same-time same-place one-to-one communications/instructions".

Specific problems with respect to explicit know-what support included: "Insufficient quality and quantity of contents in course notes"; "E-learning is theory-based, so not very practical"; "Lack of real-time communication tools lead to loss of attention/lack of instant feed-backs"; "Not very familiar"; "Very hard to find the key points to the contents (In classroom environments teachers or instructors point out/emphasize key points"; "Similar level of difficulty—need varied levels for different individuals"; "Unlike hard-copies, it is sometimes hard to set-up equipments (Books or journals are easier to carry)."

With respect to the implementation of e-learning support for tacit know-what, typical problems identified were: "Same-time same-place communication is possible in traditional learning environment"; "Face-to-face learning is more effective"; "Learning atmosphere"; "Hard to share knowledge in e-learning (Don't know who possesses what kind of knowledge online)", "Traditional learning has more opportunities for debating, discussing and sharing opinions"; "Difficult to express emotions and feeling online"; and "Lacks direct communication."

"Lack of functions such as 'Add short-cut' where the learners can re-visit their weaknesses anytime they wish" was one of the major implementation weaknesses mentioned with respect to explicit know-how support. Other noted problems included: "Not everyone would work with the same logic/brain structure of individuals may vary. Thus, it is impossible to set up a well-structured search engine"; and "Difficult to find the very information one requires (In traditional environment, rather than going through search engines, you can ask your instructors/teachers for that very information or they can tell you where to find that information)."

Finally, with respect to tacit know-how support, it was suggested that "For tests, a function that can prevent 'cheating' should be implemented for fair and accurate results." Among other problems identified were: "E-learning lacks one-to-one tutorials/mentoring"; "Lack of functions that learners can learn by actually doing something (lack of practical devices)"; "Lack of real-life application opportunities"; "Feedback from the instructors in the traditional environment is perceived to be more detailed and personalized"; "Lack of real-time communication leads to lack of understanding/In order to fully understand the contents, it requires more time and efforts in e-learning."

Group Level Analysis

The clear winner in terms of importance at the group level is KM support for tacit know-how. This is not so much of a surprise as it comprises the progress report, tests, and questions and answers features that received some of the highest importance ratings. With such numbers, it is clear that employees thought that learning by doing is the best way of increasing their overall knowledge of the subject. There is not a lot that separates second and third place. KM features supporting the availability of knowledge and sharing of knowledge were both deemed to be similarly relevant when it came to fostering good learning practices. Finally, KM features supporting knowledge search and discovery were considered the least important category. The potential reason could be a busy work schedule of employees that does not leave them enough spare time for exploration.

With respect to satisfaction, KM support for tacit know-how continued its dominance as the most valuable category in increasing learners' knowledge. This fondness for learning by doing may be due to the fact that it contains three of the most person-alised features on the course Web site (individual tests, progress report, and answers to questions). The progress report has been overlooked in many course Web sites because it is time consuming and hard to maintain, being essentially a database of confidential student records that displays student progress and performance. With respect to the other three categories of KM features supporting knowledge availability, sharing, and discovery, employees felt that they were implemented on the course Web site quite well (all above the neutral 3). However, the fact that the satisfaction ratings never matched their corresponding importance ratings show that there was a general feeling that the design of the course Web site could be improved.

With respect to the perceived importance of individual KM features, participants thought that "Progress Report" and "Lecture Notes" were the most important ones. Similar findings were reported by a recent study from the academic environment (Handzic & Chumkovski, 2004). This is because lecture notes provide students with knowledge in a summarised form that keeps them up to date with the course, while progress reports give students a good idea of their performance, development, and relative standing. Examining the other end of the spectrum, we see that "Resources" and "Search Facility" were seen as being the least important KM features. The explanation for such results can be found in that employee students are extremely busy, engaged in many different tasks at the same time. Hence, they may not have spare time for further exploration. This may also be a reason for the high importance rating given to online announcements. These announcements act as a personal diary or secretary for these students. Employee students are fond of them as they inform them of important dates or changes to the subject that may have slipped their minds.

With respect to the participants' satisfaction scores, "Progress Report" and "Questions & Answers" had the highest rating, highlighting the employees' highly positive feelings towards these KM features. In contrast, participants were least satisfied with "Resources" and "Search Facility." Possibly the most significant discovery was that some of the most advanced KM features, including "Simulator," "Systematic Search Function," "Online Tutor," and "Online Help," did not appear on the course Web site at all. Explanation for these features not being implemented on the course Web site may be in their novelty. Also, the fact that the extra preparation time in implementing features such as these may be seen as too time consuming and possibly not value for money by instructors. Participants in this study, however, find these KM features as quite important in improving the value of e-learning.

Other Issues

When asked for suggestions on how to improve the effectiveness of their e-learning portal, participants identified a number of advanced KM features including a simulator, systematic search functions, one-to-one tutoring, and online help functions.

Based on the results of this study, one can conclude that e-learning portals have a future in corporate education. More importantly, they point out to Web course designers, which KM features are considered strong and useful by corporate learners and which ones are weaker and less useful to them. Designers of Web courses can put these results to good use and provide better and more satisfying e-learning experiences for learners.

While the current study provides some interesting findings, caution is necessary when generalising these results due to a number of limitations. Firstly, the study applied a simple survey questionnaire. While its brief and noncomplex format enabled employee subjects to answer quickly and precisely, it did not allow deeper qualitative analysis of their responses. Therefore, new instrumentation should be developed that asks more in-depth questions about reasons why subjects felt the way they did about e-learning.

Another limitation concerns the nature of the course evaluated. The course Web site in this study did not feature many advanced KM features that subjects considered important in e-learning. Future research is necessary in courses with expanded content and resources.

Finally, the survey took place in a single company. The fact that all learners were employees with similar background means that they share a common mode of thought that would perhaps differ from learners from other organisations or academia. Hence, to overcome this limitation, it would be necessary for future research to be conducted in various other contexts and see how the learners feel about different Web courses.

In summary, future research is needed in this area. We hope that the findings of this study may help to inspire others to undertake both larger-scale and more in-depth research to overcome current limitations and find ways for providing better and more satisfying e-learning experience for the students of Web-based courses.

Conclusion

The main objective of this chapter was to examine perceptions and attitudes of employees from a large Asian organization towards their corporate e-learning portal compared to the traditional classroom environment. The Web-based e-learning portal studied here included various KM features that provided support for explicit and tacit what and how types of knowledge. The study identified overall preference of employees for electronic over traditional learning. At the knowledge category level, e-learning was clearly preferred for acquiring explicit knowledge, but not tacit knowledge.

Due to the exploratory nature of this study and its limitations, further research is suggested to address the issues in different contexts and among different users, as well as to extend current research to other questions, in order to find ways for providing better and more satisfying learning experience for the students of Web-based courses.

References

Cho, E. (2002). *Application of e-learning*. Seoul, Korea.

Handzic, M. (2004). *Knowledge management: Through the technology glass*. Singapore: World Scientific Publishing.

Handzic, M., & Chumkovski, A. (2004). *An empirical evaluation of a knowledge portal in the context of e-learning* (Working paper, April). Sydney, Australia: UNSW, School of Information Systems, Technology and Management.

Handzic, M., & Hoor, H. J. (2005). Corporate e-learning: An empirical evaluation. *Journal of Information & Knowledge Management, 4*(4), 229-235

Handzic, M., & Jamieson, R. (2001). *A knowledge management framework for research in electronic commerce* (SISTM Research Information Paper Series No: RIPS2001-02). Sydney, Australia: UNSW, School of Information Systems Technology and Management.

Hezel Associates. (2005). *Global e-learning opportunities for US higher education*. Retrieved from http://www.hezel.com/globalreport/index.htm

Piccoli, G., Ahmad, R., & Ives, B. (2001). Web-based virtual learning environments: A research framework and a preliminary assessment of effectiveness in basic IT skills training. *MIS Quarterly, 25*(4), 401-426.

Reasons, S. G. (2004). Hybrid courses—Hidden dangers? *Distance Education Report, 8*(7), 3-7.

Rivera, J., McAlister, K., & Rice, M. (2002). A comparison of student outcomes & satisfaction between traditional & web based course offerings. *Online Journal of Distance Learning Administration, 5*(3).

Rosenberg, M. (2001). *E-learning: Strategies for delivering knowledge in the digital age*. New York: McGraw-Hill.

Schank, R. (2001). *Designing world class e-learning*. New York: McGraw-Hill.

Urdan, & Weggen. (2000). *Corporate e-learning: Exploring a new frontier*. WRHambrecht and Co.

Yoo, Y. (2002). *E-world e-learning*. Seoul, Korea: Haneon Community.

Young, J. R. (2002). Hybrid teaching seeks to end the divide between traditional and online instruction. *Chronicle of Higher Education, 48*(28).

Chapter X

Quality Monitor:
Assessing Knowledge Credibility

Abstract

This chapter reports results of an empirical examination of the contribution of a quality monitor system (QMS) to evaluating predictive accuracy of knowledge artifacts in a simulated organizational repository. Thirty-four student subjects participated in the study on a voluntary basis. Results indicate that the tool was quite effective in enhancing user understanding of the absolute and relative predictive power of their knowledge artifacts, and led to improved decision performance. These findings have important implications for the development of effective knowledge management systems.

Introduction

Many enterprise systems acquire large volumes of knowledge artifacts from multiple and often remote sources. The complexity of interrelated knowledge artifacts stored in these systems makes it often difficult for people to comprehend and interpret their meaning. There is also a danger that some of the acquired knowledge may be of poor quality. There is strong evidence that the problems related to the quality of knowledge artifacts are becoming increasingly prevalent in practice (Shanks, 2001). It is therefore not surprising that the issue of quality is becoming an increasingly important topic in research.

Considering that knowledge workers must rely on enterprise systems for their task-related activities, it is critical that they better understand the quality of the knowledge artifacts available in these systems. With a better understanding, they can decide to reject using artifacts of poor quality and, consequently, avoid their detrimental effect on task performance (Chengular-Smith, Ballou, & Pazer, 1999). Unfortunately, most of our own empirical evidence casts serious doubts regarding human ability to effectively recognise and utilise this knowledge from artifacts (Handzic & Aurum, 2001; Handzic & Parkin, 2000).

According to Poston and Speirer (2005), shifting through myriad of content available through knowledge management systems can be overwhelming for knowledge workers when trying to find the content most relevant for completing a task. To address the problem, they proposed that systems designers should include content-rating schemes and credibility indicators to improve users' search and evaluation of content. Knowledge ratings would indicate the quality of specific content, and credibility indicators would describe the validity of the content and/or the ratings.

The main objective of the current chapter is to examine a specific quality monitoring system (QMS) designed to assist users in their knowledge evaluation process, and to improve their performance in the context of a decision-making task. Building on previous work by Handzic and Li (2002), the current study will empirically examine the impact of a QMS based on regression and visualisation techniques in assisting user decision making to deal with similar and diverse predictive quality artifacts. To ensure effective usage, the proposed QMS was designed so that knowledge workers can readily find high-quality content without feeling overwhelmed (Alavi & Leidner, 2001) and without being misled (Resnick, Zeekhauser, Friedman, & Kuwabara, 2000).

Concept of Quality

Shanks and Tansley (2002) define quality in terms of "fitness for purpose." This means that the available knowledge must be usable and useful to users, and support their work effectively. Some of the desirable quality dimensions include accuracy, reliability, importance, consistency, precision, timeliness, understandability, conciseness, and usefulness (Ballou & Pazer, 1985; Wand & Wang, 1996). A more complete perspective on quality is provided by a number of proposed frameworks that organise and structure the concept of quality.

For example, the framework by Strong et al. (Strong, Lee, & Wang, 1997), based on a survey of expert opinions of practitioners, suggests four quality dimensions: intrinsic, contextual, representational, and accessibility. The framework of Shanks and Darke (1998) is based on semiotic theory and Bunge's ontology, and consists of quality goals and measures for consumer stakeholders. Quality goals include syntactic, semantic, pragmatic, and social levels. Syntactic quality concerns the form, semantic quality concerns the meaning, pragmatic quality concerns the usage, and social quality the shared understanding. Other frameworks include Wand and Wang (1996), which is also based on Bunge's ontology, and Kahn et al. (Kahn, Stong, & Wang, 1997), which is based on product and service quality theory.

Shanks and Tansley (2002) suggested that a decision makers' understanding of the quality of the content of their organisational repositories could be significantly enhanced by quality tagging. Empirical evidence provides support for the improved performance resulting from accuracy tagging (Shanks, 2001; Shanks & Tansley, 2002). Tags were found to be particularly suitable for syntactic and semiotic quality levels, but unsuitable for pragmatic and social levels, as multiple stakeholders and purposes are involved in these levels. Empirical studies also provide evidence that quality ratings have a strong influence on content search and evaluation processes, which in turn affect decision performance. Certain credibility factors were found to moderate the relationship between rating validity and knowledge search and evaluation (Poston & Speirer, 2005).

We argue that these approaches have several limitations in situations where the environment is unstable or changing. The most important limitations stem from the static and subjective nature of quality tags and rates, and the additional effort required for their maintenance. Therefore, an alternative approach, in terms of a flexible and objective quality monitoring system, (QMS) is suggested in this study as a means that could potentially eliminate some of the earlier approaches limitations. Such a tool would enable the individual to both better understand the quality of various available artifacts, and also help the person to better predict future events.

Empirical Study

Study Objectives

The focus of the present study is on evaluating predictive quality of artifacts in organizational repositories using a QMS based on visualisation, in terms of line graphs, and statistics, in terms of regression analysis. In combination, these techniques may help to discover highly useful and informative relational patterns among sets of data that can be used to develop predictive models of behaviour in a wide variety of knowledge domains. Given that most business forecasting is conducted judgementally (Dalrymple, 1987; Sanders & Manrodt, 1994), forecasters who have better understanding of external causal influences would have a potential advantage in that they can take into account the effect of these influences and make better judgements. Most empirical findings from unaided knowledge discovery studies cast doubt on people's ability to correctly discover causal influences (Andreassen, 1991; Handzic & Aurum, 2001; Harvey, Bolger, & McClelland, 1994).

It is argued here that users can potentially benefit from a QMS that would help them better locate high-quality knowledge and improve performance. Our preliminary empirical investigation revealed positive effects of scatter plots, bar charts, and lines on user performance in moderately predictive sales forecasting situations (Handzic, Aurum, Lam, & Oliver, 2002a; Handzic, Aurum, Oliver, & Logenthiran, 2002b). The objective of the current study is to extend previous work, and examine whether a QMS based on a regression graph will further enhance understanding and application of knowledge about predictive accuracy of interrelated cues in a product sales forecasting;

Experimental Task

A modified version of the earlier used forecasting simulation was created for the purpose of studying the effect of using a QMS tool to aid understanding of knowledge artifact quality and support decision making. It was implemented in Microsoft Visual Basic language. The new QMS tool was developed and incorporated into the simulation in order to give users a clearer and more understandable model visualisation that could lead to higher-quality decisions.

Users assumed the role of the Production Manager for the Dream Cream dairy company in Sydney. One of their responsibilities was to make decisions on daily production of ice creams sold from the company's outlet at Bondi Beach. Users were required to make accurate sales estimates for ice cream to be sold the following day. Users first completed a 5-day practice period, and then went on to do the task for 30 consecutive days.

Managers' assumed financial remuneration was based on users' performance. At the end of the 30-day period, users earned a bonus amount depending on the accuracy of daily estimates. Bonus was accumulated over time and payable at the end of the 30-day period. Therefore, minimisation of sales estimation error, or in other words, maximisation of the bonus amount, was the goal of the task.

Experimental Design and Variables

A laboratory experiment with random assignment to treatment groups was used, as it allowed for greater experimental control, and made possible drawing of stronger inferences about causal relationships between variables. The only independent variable was: *QMS support* (yes or no).

QMS support was manipulated in terms of tool availability. The manipulation was achieved by developing two different versions of the experimental instrument. In one version, users were provided only with a simulated repository of knowledge artifacts, and in the other version, a QMS was added in the form of a regression graph showing predictive quality of simulated artifacts. A set of simulated artifacts was compiled as follows. The set contained three cue series that were unequally distributed, meaning that some figures fluctuated extremely. One cue had a theoretical predictive accuracy of $r=0.95$ (high), and the remaining two $r=0.35$ (low).

We expected users to rely on QMS to determine whether the actual knowledge content is high quality or not, and then utilize high-quality content to make better judgments.

The dependent variable was decision accuracy evaluated in terms of subjects' cumulative relative absolute error (CumRAE). It was calculated as a sum of absolute difference between subjects' forecasts and actual sales over a period of thirty trials (for details, see Makridakis, 1993), divided by the corresponding error of naive strategy. A naive forecast is one that simply determines the next day's sales as equal to the current day's sales. Such strategy makes no use of any contextual knowledge, and typically produces poor performance. This measure was used to assess improvement in the quality of forecasts due to the correct knowledge content evaluation and usage.

Subjects and Procedure

Thirty-four students from four lab sessions of the Business Intelligence Systems course at UNSW were chosen to take part in the experiment. They participated on a voluntary basis, and received no monetary incentives. Some previous studies indicated that students are appropriate subjects for this type of research (Ashton & Kramer, 1980; Remus, 1996; Whitecotton, 1996).

The experimental session was conducted in a microcomputer laboratory. On arrival, subjects were randomly assigned to one of the two treatment groups by choosing a microcomputer from a number of units set for the experiment. Before commencing the task, subjects were briefed about the purpose of the experiment, and read case study descriptions incorporated in the research instrument. They then performed the task. The session lasted about 1 hour.

Research Instrument

Several features have been implemented in the simulation software to aid users in learning the quality of their repository content and making their predictions as accurate as possible. These features were based on two concepts: regression analysis and graphical visualisation. In addition, a simple questionnaire was included in the simulation software, asking primarily about the tool usefulness.

One of the features involved line curves, shown in Figure 10.1. Time series of four events (sales, temperature, visitors, sunshine) for 20 days were initially provided in order to guide the decision-making process. They were presented in the form of line curves in one consolidated graph. These figures were normalised. The reason for normalisation was to reduce the difficulty of integrating items of different units

Figure 10.1. Screenshot of the research instrument

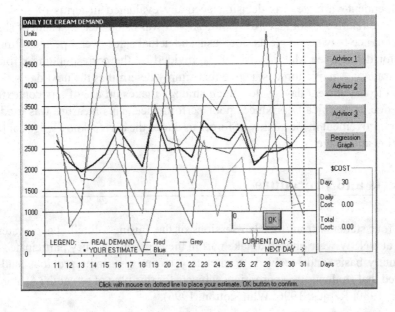

Figure 10.2. Screenshot of the proposed QMS

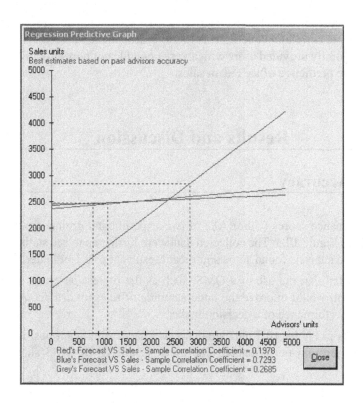

into a single response. In addition, original line curves for temperature, visitors, and sunshine factors were presented in their own windows without being normalised. Finally, three advisors, named Red, Blue, and Grey, provided estimated figures of next day temperature, visitors, and sunshine, respectively. The users were required to evaluate the quality of these estimates and take them into consideration when making sales predictions.

An extra window, shown in Figure 10.2, was provided in one software version to help users find most useful knowledge content. Since all dimensions in our simulation posed some kind of effect on the next day's sales, it was important to know their predictive quality. To do so, the linear regression modeling technique was employed. A new graph was produced containing several components. The first was the three regression lines calculated from historic time-series figures recorded in a repository. Only lines of best fit and no scatter graphs were presented. The second component in the graph was three dotted lines extended from the three regression lines. These dotted lines, extended to both x and y axes. The value cut at the x axis refers to estimated values by three advisers, while the value cut at the y axis refers to the best estimated values based on advisors' past accuracy. The third component included sample correlation coefficients for all independent variables. These three components jointly provided users with a very good idea of how strongly different variables were predictive of ice cream sales.

Results and Discussion

Decision Accuracy

Mean performance scores (CumRAE) of two experimental groups are presented graphically in Figure 10.3. The collected data were further analysed statistically by the T-test. The analysis found some significant results at $p<0.1$ or better.

It was predicted that the use of a QMS, such as the regression graph applied in the experiment, would improve the understanding of relevant artifact quality and increase the performance of a decision maker.

Firstly, results in Figure 10.3 indicate that QMS had a significant positive impact on subjects' decision performance. The mean CumRAE of QMS subjects was

Figure 10.3. Subjects' decision accuracy with and without QMS

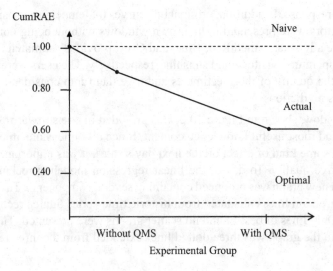

significantly lower than that of their counterparts without QMS support (0.62 vs. 0.84). Subjects using QMS tended to better identify high-quality content and use it to enhance performance than did those without QMS. This effect is quite significant when taking into account that the regression graph was quite simple.

Secondly, mean values of CumRAE less than one indicate that there was a real improvement in the accuracy of actual subjects over naive forecasts (0.84, 0.62 < 1) in both treatment groups. This suggests that subjects tended to use task-relevant content, to some extent, irrespective of QMS. Consequently, they performed better than if they had used naive strategy.

Finally, findings reveal that available QMS was less effective on the task than it could have been. Subjects were found to rely on the available high-quality content far less than they should have and, as a consequence, achieve less than optimal performance, irrespective of the treatment group. This was demonstrated by the subjects' mean CumRAE being greater than optimal in both treatment groups (0.84, 0.62 > 0.24). The potential reason for suboptimal behaviour and performance found in this study may be attributed to human nature to satisfice. Perhaps incentives and rewards may motivate people to invest more cognitive effort in searching, evaluating, and utilizing knowledge resources.

User Responses

Apart from the two hypotheses regarding the effectiveness of QMS on forecasting, it is also important to take into account the feelings of users on the support provided by QMS, as they are the ones who directly utilize this technology. A questionnaire was compiled and incorporated into the simulation program, to be answered by subjects at the end of the task. Here are the nine questions asked in the questionnaire:

1. Indicate your perception of the complexity of the decision task.
2. How useful was the system in making your decisions?
3. How would you describe your level of understanding of the decision task?
4. Indicate your perception of the uncertainty of the daily ice cream sales.
5. How confident did you feel in goodness of your sales estimates?
6. How satisfied did you feel when doing your decision task?
7. How useful was the advisor Red in making your decisions?
8. How useful was the advisor Blue in making your decisions?
9. How useful was the advisor Grey in making your decisions?

The most important finding that can be seen from the answers is that more than 80% of subjects thought that the QMS employed in the simulation was helpful in guiding them to make higher-quality decisions. More than 80% of subjects provided answers with above average rating for question 2. Another important finding is that most of the subjects who took part in the experiment felt quite confident in making decisions when using the QMS. Again, over 70% of subjects provided answers with an above average rating for question 5.

Study Limitations

The present study has several aspects that limit the generalisability of its results. First of all, the investigation took place in a laboratory experiment. The main reason for using a laboratory experiment design was to accomplish a high degree of control over the independent variables. High control maximises the internal validity of the research, and enables drawing of stronger inferences about causal relationships (Huck, Cormier, & Bounds, 1974; Judd, Smith, & Kidder, 1991). However, it may compromise external validity. Data were artificially generated from statistical processes. This was done to allow internal control of different variable characteristics, such as noise level and the form of a relationship among variables of interest, but makes it difficult to generalise to more realistic settings. Linear monotonic dependencies employed in the study may not cover the variety of complex characteristics in the data patterns of real business, or reflect the true relationships between the variables. The increased complexity in the data patterns due to the presence of "broken leg" cues or change over time could seriously reduce the effectiveness of a proposed QMS in practice. Finally, the subjects in the study were students. Their lack of real-life experience on decision-making tasks implies that different strategies may be chosen when comparing with decision makers in industry domains. They also had to learn how the system works. Despite making a serious effort to ensure its ease of use, it is possible that five practice trials were not sufficient to completely familiarise subjects with the system and allow optimal performance.

Future Directions

Due to these limitations, the present study should be considered exploratory, and its conclusions tentative. Replications using experts in their domain as subjects in applied settings are needed to gain deeper insight into people's knowledge discovery process. Additional insight may also be obtained by using real-world data. Several further extensions to the current research are also possible. This study has examined the tool effectiveness in noisy but stable data patterns, characterised by monotonic linear relationships among variables. The proposed QMS was found to be useful in such situations. However, it would be interesting to examine whether, and how, data patterns with instabilities affect tool effectiveness. Some research suggests that more sophisticated methods and tools, including decomposition techniques and machine learning, would be valuable in such circumstances. In addition, the current study has investigated only the extreme situations when all available variables were either very similar or very different. Further studies should incorporate less extreme situations. In particular, one may examine whether moderate contrasts would dilute the effect of a QMS on performance. With respect to tool presentation, the present study used only two-dimensional (regression line) graphs for displaying all variables. Future research may investigate whether multidimensional graphs would facilitate faster and better understanding of the situation and possibly further help to improve performance. Finally, decision performance analysis was employed as a primary method to evaluate the effectiveness of a QMS. Although this method is unobtrusive and robust, other techniques, such as verbal protocols or eye fixation movement, may provide deeper insight into the users' knowledge search and evaluation processes. The results may also be utilised to further validate inferences made in this study.

Conclusion

The results of research presented in this chapter show the influence of a quality-monitoring system (QMS) on users' content evaluation and performance in a forecasting task. From our research findings, one may conclude that using QMS can effectively enhance decision makers' ability to identify and utilize the best content for their task, resulting in improved performance. This work may have important implications for the more effective design and use of knowledge management systems. However, the study is not without the limitations inherent in the experimental approach used. Therefore, further empirical research is recommended, which would eliminate current restrictions and help us to understand how applicable these results may be in different contexts.

References

Alavi, M., & Leidner, D. E. (2001). Knowledge management and knowledge management systems: Conceptual foundations and research issues. *MIS Quarterly*, *25*(1), 107-136.

Andreassen, P. B. (1991). *Causal prediction versus extrapolation: Effects on information source on judgemental forecasting accuracy* (working paper). MIT.

Ashton, R. H., & Kramer, S. S. (1980). Students as surrogates in behavioural accounting research: Some evidence. *Journal of Accounting Research, 18*(1), 1-15.

Ballou, D. P., & Pazer, H. L. (1985). Modelling data and process quality multi-input multi-output information systems. *Management Science, 31*(2), 150-162.

Chengular-Smith, I. N, Ballou, D., & Pazer, H. L. (1999). The impact of data quality information on decision making: An exploratory analysis. *IEEE Transactions on Knowledge and Data Engineering, 11*(6).

Dalrymple, D. J. (1987). Sales forecasting practices: Results from a United States survey. *International Journal of Forecasting, 3*, 379-391.

Handzic, M., & Aurum, A. (2001, September 19-21). Knowledge discovery: Some empirical evidence and directions for future research. In *Proceedings of the 5th International Conference on Wirtschafts Informatics (WI 2001)*, Augsburg, Germany.

Handzic, M., Aurum, A., Lam, B., & Oliver, G. (2002a, September). A comparative study of two knowledge discovery tools: Barchart versus scatterplot. In *Proceedings of the International Conference on Data Mining (DM 2002)*, Bologna, Spain.

Handzic, M., Aurum, A., Oliver, G., & Logenthiran, G. (2002b, September). An empirical study of a knowledge discovery tool, In *Proceedings of the European Conference on Knowledge Management (ECKM 2002)*, Dublin, Ireland.

Handzic, M., & Li, W. (2003). Discovering predictive quality of knowledge artefacts in organisational repositories. In *Proceedings of the Australian Conference for Knowledge Management ad Intelligent Decision Support (ACKMIDS 2002)* (pp. 133-144). Melbourne: Australian Scholarly Publishing.

Handzic, M., & Parkin, P. (2000). Knowledge management technology: Examination of information diverse repositories. *South African Computer Journal, 26*, 125-131.

Harvey, N., Bolger, F., & McClelland, A. (1994). On the nature of expectations. *British Journal of Psychology, 85*, 203-229.

Huck, S. W., Cormier, W. H., & Bounds, W. G. Jr. (1974). *Reading statistics and research.*: Harper and Row Publishers.

Judd, C. M., Smith, E. R., & Kidder, L. H. (1991). *Research methods in social relations* (6th ed). Harcourt Brace Jovanovich College Publishers.

Kahn, B., Stong, D. M, & Wang, R. Y. (1997). A model for delivering quality information as product and service. In *Proceedings of the International Conference on Information Quality* (pp. 80-94). Boston: MIT.

Makridakis, S. (1993). Accuracy measures: Theoretical and practical concerns. *International Journal of Forecasting, 9*, 527-529.

Poston, R. S., & Speirer, C. (2005). Effective use of knowledge management systems: A process model of content ratings and credibility indicators. *MIS Quarterly, 29*(2), 221-244.

Remus, W. (1996). Will behavioural research on managerial decision making generalise to managers? *Managerial and Decision Economics, 17*, 93-101.

Resnick, P., Zeckhauser, R., Friedman, E., & Kuwabara, K. (2000). Reputation systems. *Communications of the ACM, 43*(12), 45-48.

Sanders, N., & Manrodt, K. (1994). Forecasting practices in US corporations: Survey results. *Interfaces, 24*, 92-100.

Shanks, G. (2001, December). The impact of data quality tagging on decision outcomes. In *Proceedings of 12th Australasian Conference on Information Systems*, Coffs Harbour, Australia.

Shanks, G., & Darke, P. (1998, November). Understanding metadata and data quality in a data warehouse. *Australian Computer Journal*.

Shanks, G., & Tansley, E. (2002, July). Data quality tagging and decision outcomes: An experimental study. In *Proceedings of Decision Support in Internet Age Conference (DSIage2002)*, Cork, Ireland.

Strong, D. M., Lee Y. W., & Wang, R. Y. (1997). Data quality in context. *Communications of the ACM, 40*(5), 103-110.

Wand, Y., & Wang, R. (1996). Anchoring data quality dimensions in ontological foundations. *Communications of the ACM, 39*(11), 86-95.

Whitecotton, S. M. (1996). The effects of experience and a decision aid on the slope, scatter, and bias of earnings forecasts. *Organisational Behaviour and Human Decision Processes, 66*(1), 111-121.

Chapter XI

Neural Network:
Automating Knowledge
Application

Abstract

*This chapter deals with neural networks as one of the promising knowledge man-
agement systems for decision support in the loan-granting contexts. The granting of
loans by a financial institution (bank or home loan business) is one of the important
decision problems, which require delicate care. It can be performed using a variety
of different processing algorithms and tools. Neural networks are considered one
of the most promising approaches. In this study, optimal parameters and the comparative efficiency and accuracy of three models: multilayer perceptron, ensemble
averaging, and boosting by filtering, have been investigated in the light of credit
loan application classification. The goal was to find the best of the three neural
network models for this kind of decision context. The experimental results indicate
that committee machine models were superior to a single multilayer perceptron
model, and that boosting by filtering outperformed ensemble averaging.*

Introduction

The granting of loans by a financial institution (bank or home loan business) is one of the important decision problems that require delicate care. Loan applications can be categorized into good applications and bad applications. Good applications are the applications that are worthy of giving the loan. Bad applications are those ones that should be rejected due to the small probability of the applicants ever returning the loan. The institution usually employs loan officers to make credit decisions or recommendations for that institution. These officers are given some hard rules to guide them in evaluating the worthiness of loan applications. After some period of time, the officers also gain their own experiential knowledge or intuition (other than those guidelines given from their institution) in deciding whether an application is loan worthy or not.

Generally, there is widespread recognition that the capability of humans to judge the worthiness of a loan is rather poor (Glorfeld & Hardgrave, 1996). Some of the reasons are: (1) There is a large gray area where the decision is up to the officers, and there are cases that are not immediately obvious for decision making; (2) Humans are prone to bias, for instance, the presence of a physical or emotional condition can affect the decision-making process. Also personal acquaintances with the applicants might distort the judgmental capability; (3) Business data warehouses store historical data from the previous applications. It is likely that there is knowledge hidden in this data that may be useful for assisting the decision making. Unfortunately, the task of discovering useful relationships or patterns from data is difficult for humans (Handzic & Aurum, 2001). The reasons for such difficulties are the large volume of the data to be examined, and the nature of the relationships themselves that are not obvious.

Given the fact that humans are not good at evaluating loan applications, a knowledge-modeling tool, thus, is needed to assist the decision maker to make decisions regarding loan applications. Knowledge management provides a variety of useful tools for discovering the nonobvious relationships in historical data, while ensuring those relationships discovered will generalize to the new/future data (Bigus, 1996; Marakas, 1999). This knowledge, in the end, can be used by the loan officers to assist them in rejecting or accepting applications. Past studies show that even the application of a simplistic linear discriminant technique in place of human judgment yields a significant, although still unsatisfactory, increase in performance (Glorfeld & Hardgrave, 1996).

Treating the nature of the loan application evaluation as a classification (Smith, 1999) and forecasting problem (Thomas, 1998), it was argued by Handzic et al. (Handzic, Tjandrawibawa, & Yeo, 2003) that neural networks may be suitable as knowledge management tools for the task. Therefore, the main objectives of their study presented in this chapter were: (1) To develop a robust knowledge management

134   Handzic

tool, using neural network models, that is both reliable and easy to build, and (2) To compare the performance of the basic neural network model called multilayer perceptron (MLP) with committee machine models (namely ensemble averaging and boosting by filtering) in scoring credit loan applications.

Literature Review

Neural Networks

The initial work on neural networks was motivated by the study on the human brain and the idea of neurons as its building blocks. Artificial intelligence researchers introduced a computing neuron model (depicted in Figure 11.1) to simulate the way neurons work in the human brain. This model provided the basis for many later neural networks developments.

There are literally hundreds of neural network models available to use (FAQ, 2002). The combination of topology, learning paradigm, and learning rules/algorithms define a particular neural network model. The topology can be in the form of feed forward, limited recurrent, and fully recurrent networks. The learning paradigm can be classified as one of these: supervised, unsupervised, and reinforcement. There are different learning algorithms for neural networks, for example, error correction learning, Hebbian learning, competitive learning, and Boltzman learning. Back propagation method and Kohonen feature maps are most popular in knowledge management (Bigus, 1996).

Figure 11.1. Model of computing neuron

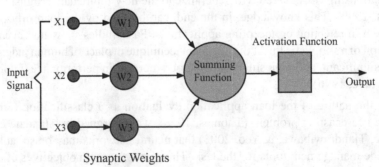

The most important feature of neural networks is their ability to learn. Just like the human brain, neural networks can learn by example and dynamically modify themselves to fit the data presented. Furthermore, neural models are also able to learn from very noisy, distorted, or incomplete sample data, which render other methods useless (Glorfeld & Hardgrave, 1996). Because of this learning ability, neural networks are then seen as appropriate tools for knowledge management. Learning paradigms in neural networks are divided into two categories, supervised and unsupervised. With supervised learning, the model is provided with feedback so that it can learn from its mistakes and try not to repeat the same mistakes in the future. In the unsupervised learning, the neural network model is not given any prior training or feedback. Instead, it is given real data from the beginning and will learn along the way.

Beside its ability to learn patterns, neural networks also have other useful properties and capabilities including: (1) Nonlinearity: A neural network, made up of an interconnection of nonlinear neurons in it is not linear. Nonlinearity is an important property, particularly if the input pattern is inherently nonlinear; (2) Adaptivity: Neural networks have the ability to adapt their synaptic weights to changes in the surrounding environment. This is particularly useful when a neural network model is deployed in a nonstationary environment (an environment that changes with the time, for example, a stock market price); and (3) Generalization: This is perhaps the second most important feature besides learning. Generalization refers to the neural network producing appropriate outputs for inputs that were not encountered during training.

Despite the tremendous benefits offered by knowledge management for businesses, neural networks are not free from criticism. Most neural networks are of the "black box" kind. This means that the tool can only produce conclusions without explanations and justification of the reasons behind such conclusions. This makes accountability and reliability issues difficult to address. That is why one of the main interests in knowledge management research is to find ways to justify and to explain the knowledge management result. Other limitations concern the high computational requirements of neural networks, usually in the form of computer power and training time, and the scarcity of experts in the field, which makes some businesses avoid their use (Marakas, 1999).

Choosing which neural network model to use is not trivial. According to Bigus (1996), there are several criteria that can be followed in order to choose a suitable model. These criteria include data type and quantity, training requirements, and functional requirements. Training requirements are mostly concerned with things such as the tolerable training time and hardware demands for doing such training. Functional requirements are related to the learning function that is expected.

Credit Loan Evaluation

Most of the research on the application of neural networks to credit loan evaluation problem has focused on multilayer perceptron (MLP). The empirical results are mixed. While some studies reviewed here indicate that a neural network approach is better than other techniques (Malhorta & Malhorta, 2001; Nittis, Teachioli, & Zorat, 1998), other studies suggest otherwise (Desai, Convay, Crook, & Overstree, 1997; Galindo & Tamayo, 1997; Yobas, Crook, & Ross, 1997). This makes it hard to draw any general conclusions that would guide practice. The tendency for different experts to argue that they have the best model, whatever model that is, makes this problem even harder (Thomas, 1998).

On a positive side, some studies reinforce Glorfeld's (1996) claim that human performance can be outperformed by simple statistical methods. Nittis et al. (1998) used a neural network as a second-level filter by supplying it with data that already had been approved by loan officers. Their experiments show that the neural network developed was reliable enough to be the first-level filter (replacing loan officers) with only a few cases needing human intervention. Furthermore, Malhorta (2001) discovered a marginal advantage using neural networks over discriminant analysis in classifying consumer loans: the overwhelmingly convincing consistency of neural networks. Also, neural networks outperformed discriminant analysis in recognizing "bad" applications.

In contrast, several studies reported somewhat inferior performance of neural networks compared to other models or found no significant advantage. Galindo and Tamayo (1997), in their empirical study, examined four different techniques: classification and regression trees (CART), neural network models, k-nearest neighbor, and Probi. Neural network models came second after CART in their experimental results. However, the difference in performance between them was small. Desai et al. (1997) concluded that the neural network (feedforward model) involved did not significantly outperform the conventional techniques because the most appropriate variants of the techniques were not used. Yobas et al. (1997) came to a similar conclusion with respect to credit card applications.

Although this review shows that neural networks may not always be the best possible tool for loan application evaluation, it also reveals that it has never been more than marginally outperformed by other methods. The reasons why neural networks do not always come as a winner is these comparison studies are: (1) The most appropriate variants of neural network are not used (Desai et al., 1997). There is still a wide variety of neural network models that have not been tested against the loan application problem; (2) The studies reviewed each used different data. For example, Galindo and Tamayo (1997) used 24 attributes and 4,000 instances, while Malhorta and Malhorta (2001) used data with 6 attributes and 700 instances. The characteristics of the data, for example, number of attributes and the distribution of the data, are all important as they affect the performance of the developing neural network.

Empirical Study

Research Objectives

Based on this review and discussion, this study was set to investigate, on the same collection of real loan data, the comparative performance of two different committee machine models and the basic multilayer perceptron. Ensemble averaging was suggested to be successful in reducing bias and variance of a single expert model (Perrone, 1993; Volker, 2001). Similarly, boosting by filtering was proposed to boost learners' performance by enabling individual experts to learn from others' mistakes (Haykin, 1999; Shapire, 1990). While it was expected that both committee machines would perform reasonably well in loan application evaluation, no prior empirical research was done to establish this.

The current study was carried out in two stages. First, a common MLP model was built and tested for predicting worthiness of loan applications. Then, based on the MLP model built, the study concentrated on developing and testing two static committee machine models, Ensemble averaging and boosting by filtering, to see how much improvement they would provide over MLP. These two models were chosen among other static committee machine models because they were both easy to implement and had the theoretical potential to improve performance over MLP.

Research Method

Tool Design Overview

The knowledge management tool built in this research project consists of five files, each representing a class on its own. The relation of these classes can be seen on the simplified unified modeling language (UML) diagram shown in Figure 11.2. Briefly, MLP implementation was built upon two main modules, BPNN and mlp. BPNN provides backpropagation algorithm, which is then used by mlp. NeuralGUI is an extension of MLP implementation, providing a user with graphical interaction with the program. Committee and boosting modules represent the committee machines implementation. They use MLPs as experts.

Figure 11.2. Neural network tool structure

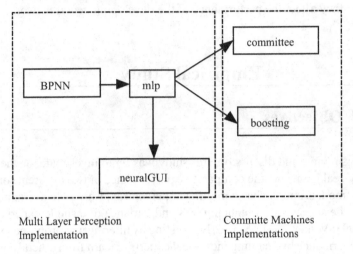

Multi Layer Perception
Implementation

Committe Machines
Implementations

Table 11.1. Result of loan classification

		Results	Application Outcome
Output Neuron Generator		Positive	Good application
			Bad application
		Negative	Good Application
			Bad Application

In designing the tool, the following considerations had to be taken into account. An MLP with one output neuron can produce two different results (binary decision: 0 or 1). Combined with two expected results, bad application and good application, we can have four different combinations of possible prediction result. Thus, result of classification can be divided into four possible outcomes: (1) Negative correctly classified result, the network is rejecting a bad application; (2) Negative incorrectly classified result, the network is accepting a bad application; (3) Positive correctly classified result, the network is accepting a good application; and (4) Positive incorrectly classified result, the network is rejecting a good application.

From these four, we argue that the most important one is the negative misclassified application (highlighted in Table 11.1). Negative data (that is nonloan worthy application) that is misclassified as loan worthy has a more damaging impact than the other types of misclassification. If negative data is misclassified, that means the bank is losing money due to granting loans to wrong applicants. Thus, our experiments were focused on this set of misclassifications and trying to improve the performance of the neural net model in this particular area. However, it is important to recognize that in achieving low error on classifying negative data, there is a cost to pay. There is a trade-off between pursuing best performance on negative misclassified data and pursuing the best performance on all data. That is, in trying to improve the network performance in identifying the negative data, the performance on positive data is going to be worsened.

Multilayer Perceptron Implementation

As mentioned earlier, the first step in this investigative study involved building and testing of the performance of the most widely used neural network model, called multilayer perceptron (MLP), in dealing with credit loan applications. The result of this MLP implementation served as the base for later implementations of combined neural networks.

The design of the MLP module was an adaptation from Tom Mitchell's MLP suite (Mitchell, 1997). BPNN class provided the functionality of backpropagation algorithm, while MLP class provided an interface to integrate these functionalities with the functionalities found in Data module. As the backpropagation learning algorithm requires randomization of initial weights, it was necessary to provide some sort of randomization methods in the program. This was done in such a way to allow the seed to be determined by the user. It is important to notice that the ability to set the seed, and thus control the initial weights for the network, is necessary for reproducing the experiment. Without having the mechanism of reproducing a set of random numbers every time, it would be difficult to compare changes between experiments.

As explained before, the study was conducted with the goal to find a balance in performance trade-off. To achieve the desired performance balance, two threshold variables were included in the program, namely a maximum tolerable error percentage on all data and on negative data. These two thresholds provided an early stopping point for training. Finally, to assist with the experiment, a graphical user interface (GUI) was also provided. Most commercial knowledge management software has GUIs to assist the user of the system. As this project was trying to build a knowledge management tool that was not only robust, but also user-friendly, a simple GUI was thus implemented. The GUI makes it easier for the user to test the constructed neural network model, and the parameters of MLP can be easily set using the GUI.

Ensemble Averaging Implementation

Ensemble averaging was implemented as a combination of several experts, where the individual experts combined were MLPs developed in the earlier stage of the study. Appropriate program modules were built to store and read user specifications, to add an arbitrary number of experts, to train experts, and to combine their assessments. For evaluating a loan application, each expert produces its own assessment on the particular application, and then the combiner takes the average from these assessments to make the final assessment on the loan application.

Boosting by Filtering Implementation

Boosting by filtering was implemented using a simplified version of the boosting algorithm described by Haykin (1999). The simplified algorithm differs from the original in choosing the training data for the second expert. In the original algorithm, the first expert keeps on discarding training instances until it finds the instance suitable for training the second expert, and then the process is repeated until a sufficient number of training instances are reached. In the simplified version, the first expert only needs one pass to gather the necessary instances for training the second expert, and it is done by adding instances from the same set until the set has no more instances.

Experimental Data

In relation to loan application evaluation, the information that is regarded as important (Thomas, 1998) includes: (1) The character of the applicant; credit history of the applicant and his/her family is certainly helpful; (2) The capital' this identifies how much money is being asked by the applicant; (3) The collateral; this refers to what things that the applicant willing to put up from his/her own resources; (4) The capacity; the applicant's repaying ability is one of the most crucial factors, this information can be in the form of how much income does he/she earn, how many jobs does he/she have, or how long has he/she been working in their job; and (5) The condition of current economic market.

The actual data used for this study was taken from the UCI repository; this data is publicly available and can be accessed from the URL ftp://ftp.ics.uci.edu/pub/machine-learning-databases/credit-screening. The data set was compiled by Chiharo Sano, and was generated in accordance to input from a Japanese company that grants credit. All attribute names and values were changed to meaningless symbols to protect confidentiality within the data. However, it was expected that most of the important information (as described earlier) was included in the data set. The last column/attribute was the outcome of the application. If it was "+," that meant the application was a good application. On the other hand, the "-" sign indicated that the application was a bad one. The data set had a total of 690 instances. Of these, 307 instances (44.5%) were good applications, where 383 (55.5%) instances were bad applications. In addition, 37 instances, that is, 5%, had one or more missing attribute values.

Data Preprocessing

Data preprocessing is the first step of the knowledge management process. In this step, data in the data warehouse was preprocessed and then fed to the knowledge management tool. Since neural network models only accept discrete or continuous numerical values, categorical data is needed to translate into numerical values for it to be utilized by the neural network models. This was done using the 1-out-of-N encoding technique (Smith, 1999). The numerical data needs to be normalized in order for it to be used by the neural network. Normalization, in this case, meant dividing an input vector with a norm of the vector. It is a common practice to normalize the input of MLP model to the range of 0 to 1, but there are cases when scaling the inputs to the range of -1 to 1 is a considerably better option (FAQ, 2002). The normalization used in this project is called rescaling, and was done by finding the maximum value of particular numerical attributes and then dividing each of the instances of the attribute by this maximum.

As mentioned earlier, the data set contained 37 instances with one or more missing attribute values. This is sometimes referred to as the noise in the data. Since neural networks have been known for their capacity to handle noisy data, these instances were included as valid cases in the current investigation. The historical data for loan applications after being preprocessed was stored in a file. A data structure was needed to represent the information stored in this file during the running of the program. The data structure was described in the Data module. The Data class encapsulated the application data in the form of lists of values in a Data object. The Data object also stored other information such as the number of negative applications, the number of instances, and so forth.

To prevent the MLP model becoming biased towards the data set used for training, a data partitioning technique was used. The commonly used technique is called cross validation. It is, basically, an approach where the input data is divided into two sets; one set is used for training the MLP model, as can be referred to as the training set. The rest is for validating the performance of the model; this is called the test set. Training set is used for the model to converge to an empirical optimal, and the other set is used to decide when to terminate the convergence process (Perrone, 1993). This study applied 50:50 divisions (346 for training set and 344 for data set). Both training and test sets contained half negative data and half positive data. The training set having at least half of all its data negative allowed the network to learn to classify the negative data properly (Smith, 1999). The special program module provided a function to create two sets that had an equal percentage of negative data.

As is often the case with many boosting algorithms, a method to apply random sampling was required. The samples were generated from the list from which the Data object was created. The sample was taken with replacement; thus, in the resulting set, duplicates were possible. Finally, an appropriate method was provided to produce statistical information on a data column. This information consisted of the sum of all the column values, average values, maximum and minimum values, and was used during the preprocessing of the data.

Experimental Results

Optimal MLP Parameters

Finding the best parameters for MLP model is a crucial issue. The optimal MLP would have a combination of parameters that minimize the classification error. The goal of the MLP experiments, therefore, was to find these combination parameters that were best for evaluating loan applications. In determining optimal MLP parameters, average values from a series of repeated experiments were used. Taking the average results is an approach applied to lessen the instability inherited by the MLP model.

Number of Hidden Neurons

The aim of the first series of experiments was to find the number of hidden neurons needed for the network to be able to evaluate loan applications with the highest accuracy possible, given a fixed number of training epochs. The experiments started by using one hidden neuron, then the number of hidden neurons was increased until the performance improvement was no longer observed. For each experiment, six runs of the network were used; each run had different weight initialization. The result of a particular experiment was the average from the runs. A run was finished when the training epochs reached 500.

An MLP with 15 hidden neurons had the best performance compared to other numbers of hidden neurons. The study found that the network reached its peak performance when 15 hidden neurons were used, and then the network suffered a decrease in performance when more hidden neurons were added. This result confirms the theory that having too many or too few neurons in a hidden layer can have a negative effect on the network performance.

Weight Initialization

The next series of experiments was conducted to test the extent of performance variations due to weight initialization. In theory, the variations of initial weights will result in variations in network performance. Ten experiments were conducted, each using MLP with different weight initializations. These experiments were measuring the number of training periods needed to reach a desired error percentage.

From the 10 experiments conducted, one of the networks was unable to meet the thresholds after 1,500 epochs, while the other 9 were able to do so with an average of 716.4 epochs. From this finding, the significance of weight initialization is apparent. A network with bad weight initialization results in slower converge (more training epochs are needed); in fact, there is no guarantee that this network will converge at all to the performance thresholds. Despite this, the chance of a network in getting the "wrong" weights initialization is quite small (1 out of 10 in this experiment). Our results confirm Smith's (1999) finding that the effect of weight initialization for most applications is not significant.

Momentum

The aim of the momentum experiments was to find momentum that effectively helps the network to avoid local minima and speed up the convergence. For each experiment there were five runs, each run with different weight initialization. With the error threshold set on, a network would terminate training when the error percentage falls below the threshold, or when, after 1,000 epochs, the network was still unable to reach the desired performance.

The results indicate that having a momentum value in the range between 0.6 and 0.7 contributed to speeding up the network's pace of learning. When momentum was set to 0.8, few runs were unable to meet the thresholds after 1,000 epochs. For the rest of experiments, 0.6 was used as an optimal value. Setting the momentum to above 0.7 makes the network too volatile, causing it to fail to descend to better minima.

Learning Rate

Several experiments were carried out to find a learning rate that effectively controls the extent of weight modification during training epochs. For each experiment, there

Table 11.2. Optimal MLP configuration

Parameters	Value
Number of Data in Training Set	346
Number of Data in Test Set	344
Number of Hidden Neurons	15
Seed	0
Learning Rate	0.2
Momentum	0.6
Training epochs	1000

were six runs of the network. Then, the average epochs needed to reach the desired threshold value were calculated. If, after 1,000 epochs, the network is still unable to reach the desired performance, the training would be stopped.

The results show a somewhat nonlinear behavior of the impact of learning rate on performance; hence, it is difficult to find a general trend. In later experiments (after experimenting with a learning rate of 0.5), some of the experiments did not converge within the 1,000 epochs. Interestingly, some earlier research, using a learning rate greater than 0.5 produced networks that required 150 training epochs. This suggests that a learning rate greater than 0.5 causes the network to have volatile performance; hence, for loan application problem, it is desirable to use a learning rate lower than 0.5. For the rest of this study, the learning rate was set at 0.2. This value was chosen as it is close to what commercial neural network packages use (Smith, 1999). Given these justifications for choosing the parameters for MLP model, an optimal configuration is presented in Table 11.2.

Credit Scoring Performance

After determining the optimal parameter combination for the MLP model, the next step was to determine its credit-scoring performance, and compare it with that of the two committee machines. The credit scoring performance of all three models was measured against the test data, and was evaluated in terms of their accuracy and speed.

Two measures of accuracy used were percentage error on negative data and percentage error on all data. These metrics were used to assess the ability of the network to reduce error. Percentage error on negative data measures misclassified negative data against the number of negative data in the set. Percentage error on all data measures misclassified data (both positive and negative) against the number of all data in the set.

The two measures of speed were number of epochs and training time. These metrics were used to assess how fast the network could learn, and also how much training was needed for the network to perform according to the training requirements. The results are as follows:

MLP Results

The combination of parameters presented in Table 11.1 provided us with an MLP model that is customized for predicting bad loans and, at the same time, performance in predicting or classifying other classes of loan applications is not overly sacrificed.. The test results indicate that the average percentage errors achieved by MLP were 1.81% on negative data and 2.38% on all data. This was achieved in less than 1,000 epochs (600) and in a short training time (13 sec). These results are better than Smith (1997), whose experiment produced MLP that was able to classify bad applications correctly 46.7% of the time and good applications 90.9% of the time.

Ensemble Averaging Results

A static committee machine model, called ensemble averaging, was the subject of the following experiment. It is argued that ensemble averaging brings stability in performance. Different weights can lead to better or worse performance, and ensemble averaging compromises the two extremes by lessening the effect of choosing "wrong" weight combinations. It has been proven to be able to enhance MLP performance in other applications, like medical reports. The purpose of the current study was to find out the degree of improvement that ensemble averaging could provide over MLP in the context of loan application evaluation. The committee machine was built upon the 10 experts from MLP experiments. The combiner program used simple voting for combining the results from these experts. As a committee, the model achieved 1.73% error on negative data, and 2.06% on all data. However, it came at the cost of increased training time (245 sec).

Boosting by Filtering Results

To test the performance of the boosting by filtering committee machine in classifying loan applications, three experts were used. Each of the experts was MLP, with optimum configuration based on the result from MLP experiments. Each expert was trained with 500 epochs. The first expert on average produced 278 training instances for the second expert. The first and second expert together, on average, produced 38 training instances for the third expert. This shows that there were roughly 38 cases that were hard to classify, and the third expert concentrated on these cases. The average performance of boosting by filtering indicated small error scores of 1.32% on negative data and 1.65% on all data within a reasonable training time (32 sec).

Comparative Performance Analysis

The overall results of the study are presented in Table 11.3, and clearly suggest that MLP performance in classifying loan applications can be further improved by committee machines models. In particular, ensemble averaging has been shown to be able to reduce the percentage error due to the bias-variance problem inherited by MLP model. However, on average, the improvement ensemble averaging brings on negative data classification is not great. This is evidenced by marginal 0.09% improvement on negative data. The performance on all data was more convincing with 0.32% improvement. While ensemble averaging was able to produce lower percentage errors, it did so at the cost of training time, as evident in the training time for this model compared to other models.

Furthermore, the results indicate that boosting by filtering outperformed other models in this study. It was able to improve the performance of MLP model by 0.49% on negative data and 0.73% on all data. The boosting by filtering committee machine was the best performer in this experiment, in that it was able to produce the least percentage error. This was done at a comparatively low training-time cost.

Table 11.3. Comparative model performance

Neural Network Model	Number of Epochs	Percentage Error on Negative Data	Percentage Error on All Data	Average Training Time
Multilayer Perceptron	600	1.81 %	2.38 %	13 sec
Ensemble Averaging (10 MLPs)	6800	1.73 %	2.06 %	245 sec
Boosting by Filtering (3 MLPs)	1500	1.32 %	1.65 %	32 sec

Overall, the small percentage error produced by neural network models in this experiment (1.32% - 1.81% average percentage error on negative data and 1.65%-2.38% average percentage error on all data) confirms that neural network models are well suited for loan application evaluation. The boosting by filtering committee machine shows that training different experts on hard to classify applications brings a significant performance improvement. Boosting by filtering also shows that these performance improvements can be achieved at a low cost (less training time and computational cost).

Conclusion

This research project reported in this chapter was concerned with the development and experimentation of a knowledge-management tool using neural network models in relation to loan application evaluation. Given the short time available to do the project, a knowledge-management tool has been built, the tool consisting of three neural network models: a multilayer perceptron, an ensemble averaging committee machine and a boosting by filtering committee machine. The tool was tailored for loan applications evaluation. The experimental results confirm that committee machines are able to perform in superior manner compared to MLP, with boosting by filtering outperforming the ensemble averaging model. With their high accuracy in classifying loan applications, all neural network models implemented in this project can certainly be helpful for the decision-making process. However, more trust is necessary before neural networks can gain broader acceptance in business world.

Despite interesting findings, the study faced some limitations. The main difficulty was in determining the best possible set of model parameters. For instance, the model requires foundational knowledge of consumer behavior to be factored in. Neural network models have a very high degree of freedom. What this means is that there is a wide range of different combinations of parameters that can affect the performance of a particular network. This causes difficulties because there are still no really fixed and justified ways to set the values of parameters, so it is expected that the user, the company, or the decision making team will need a period time to find the most suitable or near-perfect parameters of any given neural network model. Future studies could include longitudinal studies of "successful" loan applications so as to analyze the factors of repayment success. Also, it would be interesting to conduct a comparative study of positive data misclassified as bad application vs. negative data misclassified as good application.

A newly developed genetic algorithm has been proposed to be a solution for parameter selection problem. Integrating such elements into the knowledge management tool should enhance the performance of the tool (Marakas, 1999). Furthermore, a genetic algorithm may improve the efficiency of the knowledge-management tool as it should provide an automated procedure to find better parameter selections. In addition, providing a visualization component to obtain a more sophisticated graphical user interface (GUI) would be a useful thing to pursue, as it would provide the decision maker with a greater justification of network performance. The explanatory capability of neural networks is still a weak point. A knowledge-management tool using a neural network that is also self-explanatory would certainly be of major interest to the business world.

References

Bigus, J. P. (1996). *Data mining with neural networks: Solving business problems from application development to decision support.* McGraw Hill.

Desai, V. S., Convay, D. G., Crook, J. N., & Overstree, G. A. (1997). Credit scoring models in the credit union improvement using neural networks and genetic algorithms. *IMA J Mathematics applied in Business and Industry, 8,* 323-346.

FAQ. (2002). Retrieved June, 5, 2002, from http://ftp.sas.com/pub/neural/FAQ.html

Galindo, J., & Tamayo, P. (1997). *Credit risk assessment using statistical and machine learning methods as an ingredient for financial intermediaries risk modeling.* Retrieved June, 5, 2002, from http://www.defaultrisk.com/pp

Glorfeld, L. W., & Hardgrave, B. C. (1996). An improved method for developing neural networks: The case of evaluating commercial loan creditworthiness. *Computer Operation Research, 23*(10), 933-944.

Handzic, M., & Aurum, A. (2001, September 19-21). Knowledge discovery: Some empirical evidence and directions for future research. In *Proceedings of the 5th International Conference on Wirtschafts Informatics (WI 2001),* Augsburg, Germany.

Handzic, M., Tjandrawibawa, F., & Yeo, J. (2003, June 24-27). How neural networks can help loan officers to make better informed application decisions. In *Proceedings of Informing Science and IT Education Conference (InSITE 2003),* Pori. Finland (pp. 97-108).

Haykin, S. (1999). *Neural networks: A comprehensive foundation.* Englewood Cliffs, NJ: Prentice-Hall.

Malhorta, R., & Malhorta, D. K. (2001). *Evaluating consumer loans using neural networks.* Retrieved June, 5, 2002, from http://www.efmaefm.org/Malhorta-Davinder/MalhortaDavinder1.pdf

Marakas, G. M. (1999). *Decision support systems in the twenty-first century.* Englewood Cliffs, NJ: Prentice Hall.

Mitchell, T. (1997). *Machine learning.* McGraw Hill.

Nittis, F. D., Teachioli, G., & Zorat, A. (1998). *Consumer loan classification using artificial neural networks.* Retrieved June, 6, 2002, from www.neuricam. com/neuricam/docs/papers/EIS98.pdf

Perrone, M. P. (1993). *Improving regression estimation: Averaging methods for variance reduction with extensions to general convex measure optimization.* PhD thesis, Brown University, Rhode Island. Retrieved June 5, 2002, from http://citeseer.nj.nec.com/perrone93improving.html

Shapire, R. E. (1990). The strength of weak learnability. *Machine Learning, 5,* 197-227.

Smith, K. A. (1999). *Introduction to neural networks and data mining for business applications.* Australia: Eruditions Publishing.

Thomas, L. C. (1998). *A survey of credit and behavioural scoring: Forecasting financial risk of lending to customers.* Retrieved June, 6, 2002, from www. bus.ed.ac.uk/working_papers/full_text/crc9902.pdf

Volker, T. (2001). Committee machines. In *Handbook for neural network processing.* CRC Press.

Yobas, M. B., Crook, J. N., & Ross, P. (1997). *Credit scoring using neural and evolutionary techniques* (Working Paper 97/2). Credit Research Centre, University of Edinburgh. Retrieved June 5, 2002, from http://www.dai.ed.ac. uk/papers/documents/mt9687.html

Section III

Studies of Socially-Oriented Knowledge Management Initiatives

Chapter XII

Exercising Space:
Facilitating Learning Through Experimentation

Abstract

This chapter reports results of an empirical examination of the facilitating role of experimentation in enhancing individual knowledge and performance in decision making. A laboratory experiment was conducted using 14 graduate students as voluntary subjects. Performance of actual subjects was compared with that of their nominal naive and optimal counterparts. Results indicate that the opportunity for independent experimentation contributed to individual knowledge enhancement and led to improved decision performance. Subjects performed better than notional naive subjects who applied random walk decision strategy. However, the results indicate room for further improvement. Subjects failed to reach performance of notional optimal counterparts who used linear decision strategy. The results also suggest the need for a holistic approach to managing knowledge by combining and integrating various initiatives to create even higher levels of knowledge and performance.

Introduction

In Chapter III of this book, we introduced the concept of knowledge space based on Nonaka and Konno's (1998) original concept of "ba." We presented major types of knowledge spaces and described their characteristics. We also emphasized that different types of knowledge spaces are suited to different types of knowledge processes. In general, these spaces offer platforms for specific steps in the knowledge spiral process that speed up knowledge development. The awareness of the different characteristics of knowledge spaces can facilitate successful support of knowledge processes. Eventually, the knowledge generated within each individual space forms a part of the shared knowledge base of organizations.

Knowledge spaces can be established by systematic organizational effort. In general, knowledge space is where management intervenes in the process of knowledge creation through the special design. For example, some organizations employ "teams" as a platform to support knowledge creation, some create a special "division" as a space for cross-functional knowledge creation, others ground knowledge creation in the company's "culture" and "structure." While organizationally different, all these initiatives are consistent with the theory of knowledge creation in that they emphasise the knowledge space as the enabler of this creation process.

The goal of this chapter is to address one type of knowledge space, namely "exercising space," as a platform for enhancing individual learning in the context of decision making. According to Nonaka and Konno (1998), exercising space supports the internalisation process from the knowledge development cycle. It facilitates the conversion of explicit knowledge to tacit knowledge. It consists primarily of continued exercises that stress certain patterns and working out of such patterns. Learning by continuous self-refinement and active participation is stressed. Knowledge is continuously enhanced by exercise in either real-life situations or simulated applications.

Experiential Learning

The following review presents and discusses relevant past theoretical and empirical literature on learning, and develops specific research questions of interest for the present study. In a recent study, Nissen (2006) defines learning as knowledge in motion. He uses this term to characterize the creation or acquisition of new knowledge. However, he warns that "newness" of knowledge should be understood relative to the acquirer and the context. For example, students may acquire knowledge new to them from their class instructor who already knows the subject matter.

Two closely related concepts to learning are knowing and doing. Knowing refers to knowledge in action, while doing refers to knowledge-based activity. According to Nissen (2006), knowing and learning processes are mutually reinforcing. He suggests that more learning will lead to greater knowledge stocks; greater knowledge stocks will result in better knowing and performance through action; and greater knowledge stocks will lead to faster learning.

Learning theorists further suggest that people should learn from experience gained through task repetition and from feedback to adjust their behaviour and improve performance over time. In decision making, some authors (Payne, Bettman, & Johnson, 1988) claim that adaptivity may be crucial enough to individuals that they would guide themselves to it without the need for an external prod. Other authors (Hogarth, 1981) believe that the availability of immediate feedback, in addition to the opportunity to take corrective action, is critical for effective learning. Adequate feedback is considered especially important for the correct assessment of the previous responses in situations where the subject is unfamiliar with the task or topic (O'Connor, 1989).

Empirical studies indicate mixed findings. Some studies reported modest learning from experience in a series of judgement tasks in which participants were provided with multiple pieces of cues of varying accuracy at a cost (Connolly & Gilani, 1982; Connolly & Serre, 1984; Connolly & Thorn, 1987). Behavioural patterns of real participants were consistent with computer simulation and resulted in improved effectiveness with experience. Although the improvement was real, a serious deviation from optimality remained. In contrast, a study conducted in a similar multivariate judgement task reported no learning at all (Connolly & Wholey, 1988), while the results of a judgemental adjustment study (Lim & O'Connor, 1996) indicated that knowledge seeking strategy even worsened and consequently, performance declined over time. Many studies performed in the multiple-cue probability-learning (MCPL) paradigm have concluded that people can not learn when multiple cues are involved or nonlinear relationships exist (for review see Brehmer, 1980).

It has been suggested that feedback may enhance learning by providing knowledge about the task, task outcome, individual's performance and/or decision process. From this knowledge through task repetition, an individual may learn to adapt, that is, maintain, modify, or abandon strategy to improve task performance. In his review of a number of laboratory and field studies on the impact of feedback on task performance, Kopelman (1986) reported that objective feedback (defined as knowledge about task behaviour or performance that is factual and inconvertible) had a positive effect on performance. But it was stronger and more sizeable in the field than in laboratory. In choice task setting, Creyer, Bettman, and Payne (1990) speculated that for an individual to adapt decision strategy to a particular decision task, he or she had to have at least some vague ideas about the degree of effort and accuracy characterising his or her decision process. They examined how decision-makers learned to adapt when presented with explicit accuracy feedback and/or explicit effort feedback. The results indicate that feedback on accuracy led to more normative-like processing of cues and improved performance. The role of accuracy feedback was greater when the decision problem was more difficult. Explicit effort feedback, on the other hand, had no impact on processing or performance regardless of the difficulty of the problem.

In contrast, findings from MCPL studies with feedback, reported by Klayman (1988), indicate that people have difficulties learning from outcome feedback in these tasks, but they can learn more effectively when they are provided with cognitive feedback, such as summary analysis of how their past predictions differed from optimal. Feedback was found to have induced learning in the so-called cue discovery tasks. People were found to perceive the existence and direction of a cue-criterion relation, but have difficulties in learning its shape. A significant improvement in predictive success over time was attributed to cue discovery rather than accurate weighting.

In a study examining the impact of several types of feedback on the accuracy of forecasts of time series with structural instabilities, Remus, O'Connor, and Griggs (1996) found that task feedback (showing the underlying structure of the task) with or without cognitive feedback (prompting on desirable behaviour) gave significantly better forecasting performance than the baseline simple outcome feedback. Adding cognitive feedback to task feedback did not improve forecasting accuracy. The study also found that performance outcome feedback (prompting with graphical indicator or words expressing levels of forecasting accuracy) was not superior to outcome feedback. The results for task and cognitive feedback largely replicated those by Balzer, Sulsky, Hammer, and Sumner (1992) and Balzer, Hammer, Sumner, Birchenough, Martens, and Raymark (1994).

Some studies have found a detrimental effect of feedback on performance. In a complex probability task, a large error on a particular trial might imply poor strategy, or merely the fact that occasional errors are due to be expected in the probability task. As a consequence, outcome feedback may sometimes have a detrimental effect on strategy selection. Peterson and Pitz (1986) discovered that outcome feedback increased the amount by which the decision maker's estimates deviated from the model. Participants made predictions about a number of games won by a baseball team during the year on the basis of a number of performance indicators. These findings were further reinforced by Arkes, Dawes, and Christensen (1986), who found that the omission of feedback was effective in raising performance. Those without feedback relied more on helpful classification rule that enabled them to judge well in 70% of their decisions, than those with feedback who tried to outperform the rule and consequently performed worse.

In summary, findings concerning the impact of experience and feedback on learning and decision performance in multivariate judgement tasks are mixed and inconclusive. The findings suggest that the quality of performance may be conditional upon the type of feedback, task difficulty, time period, and whether participants are allowed to experiment.

Empirical Study

Failure to learn in judgement and decision making tasks described by "pessimists" and adaptive nature of decision making emphasised by "optimists" are quite informative for knowledge management research. They provide a basis for its interventionist approach to knowledge processes, as they identify points of concern and suggest adaptive directions. The focus of the current study is on one knowledge management initiative, namely "experimentation" aimed at fostering working knowledge of individual decision makers. This initiative has been suggested as central activity of a knowledge-creating company (Garvin, 1998; Nonaka & Takeuchi, 1995). Exercising space encouraging experimentation is assumed to foster individual learning. The objective of this study based on Handzic (2000) is to empirically test this assumption. More specifically, the study will attempt to answer the following research questions: (1) whether and how an opportunity for individual experimentation of decision makers affect their working knowledge, and (2) what impact this initiative has on their subsequent decision performance.

Experimental Task

The experimental task in the current study was an adaptation of a simulated production-planning activity in which participants made decisions regarding daily production of fresh ice cream. The participants assumed the role of Production Manager for a fictitious dairy firm that sold ice cream from its outlet at Bondi Beach in Sydney, Australia. The fictitious company incurred equally costly losses if production were set too low (due to loss of market to the competition) or too high (by spoilage of unsold product). The participants' goal was to minimise the costs incurred by incorrect production decisions. During the experiment, participants were asked at the end of each day to set production quotas for ice cream to be sold the following day. Before commencing the task, participants had an opportunity to make five trial decisions (for practice purposes only).

To aid their decision making, participants were provided with task-relevant variables including actual local demand for product and three contextual factors that emerged as important in determining demand levels: the ambient air temperature, the amount of sunshine, and the number of visitors/tourists at the beach. All contextual factors were deemed relatively similarly important. The task provided challenge because it did not stipulate exactly how information should be translated into specific judgement. The participants were provided with the meaningful task context, sequential historic information of task-relevant variables to provide some cues to causal relationship, and forecast values of contextual variables to suggest future behaviour. However, they were not given any explicit analysis of the quality of their information, or rules they could apply to integrate the available factual information.

Instead, all participants had an opportunity to learn from their own experience through task repetition and from feedback. Each participant was required to make 30 experimental production decisions over a period of 30 consecutive simulated days. At the beginning of the experiment, task descriptions were provided to inform participants about the task scenario and requirements. In addition, throughout the experiment, instructions and immediate performance feedback, as well as the history of past errors, were provided to each participant to analyse earlier performance and to adjust future strategies.

Experimental Design and Variables

A laboratory experiment was used in the current investigation because it allows drawing of stronger causal inferences due to high controllability. All experimental subjects were provided with an opportunity to individually experiment and learn the task by trial and error. Their performance was compared with that of nominal naïve and nominal optimal decision makers. These are completely ignorant and ideally knowledgeable people who produced their decisions using naive (random walk) and optimal (linear) strategies respectively.

The dependant variable was decision performance. It was evaluated in terms of decision accuracy and operationalised by mean *absolute error* (MAE). Mean absolute error was calculated as an absolute difference between the units of sales produced and the units of the product actually demanded (in hundreds of sale units) on each trial, and averaged over a period of 30 trials. MAE is a popular accuracy measure suggested by forecasting literature (Makridakis, 1993; Makridakis and Wheelwright, 1989). In addition, the corresponding errors of nominal naive and nominal optimal decision makers were calculated.

Participants and Procedure

The participants were 14 graduate students enrolled in the Master of Commerce course at The University of New South Wales, Sydney. Students participated in the experiment on a voluntary basis and received no monetary incentives for their performance. All experiments reported in this book, including the current one, make extensive use of graduate students, as they were suggested to be particularly suitable subjects for this type of research by other authors (Ashton & Kramer, 1980; Remus, 1996; Whitecotton, 1996). This experiment was conducted in a microcomputer laboratory. On arrival, participants were briefed about the purpose of the study, read case descriptions, and performed the task. The session lasted about 1 hour.

Results

The collected data were analysed using a series of statistical T-tests to compare decision performance (MAE) among three experimental groups of subjects (notional naives, actual subjects as independent experimenters, and notional optimals). Results are presented graphically in Figure 12.1.

Results of the analyses performed indicate significant improvement in decision performance due to individual experimentation. Independent experimenters tended to make significantly smaller decision errors (MAE) than their notional naive counterparts (3.84 vs. 5.18, $p<0.05$). There was a real drop in error by 26%. However, the results of the analyses indicate that participants failed to achieve optimal performance. Independent experimenters tended to make significantly larger decision errors than their notional optimal counterparts (3.84 vs. 0.87, $p<0.05$). These participants were able to acquire and apply only about 31% of the knowledge possessed by a fully knowledgeable decision maker on the same task.

Discussion

Main Findings

In summary, the main findings of the present study indicate that knowledge management initiatives, such as exercising space aimed at providing opportunities for

Figure 12.1. Decision performances by experimental groups

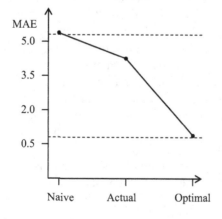

experimentation, were useful in enhancing individual decision makers' working knowledge and performance in a judgemental decision-making task. However, performance gains were less than possible given an expert knowledge of the task.

The study demonstrated that experimentation had a significant positive impact on individual knowledge and performance. Independent experimenters were found to make significantly smaller decision errors than notional naive decision makers. In real terms their error scores dropped by 26%. This finding suggests that subjects allowed time and opportunity to experiment on their own were able to acquire enough relevant knowledge of the decision problem and solving strategies to improve performance. As a result, they significantly reduced decision errors.

This finding provides a more optimistic view of human ability to learn multivariate probabilistic judgement tasks through experience than suggested by earlier research (for review, see Brehmer, 1980) It is possible that graphical presentation of historic data used in this study enabled subjects to more easily identify the existence and direction of relationships among various task variables. Such proposition is consistent with the earlier finding by Lawrence, Edmundson, and O'Connor (1985), that graphical presentation form enhances the accuracy of novice decision makers. It is also possible that the subjects in this study were given sufficient time for experimentation that enabled them to appropriately adjust their strategies through task repetition and from feedback. Klayman (1988) also reported that people could learn, reasonably well, cue discovery over a larger number of trials.

With respect to overall performance, the study revealed serious deviations from optimal performance, irrespective of the knowledge management initiative implemented. Independent experimenters were found to make significantly larger decision errors than they could have. Further analysis revealed that, on average, they acquired and applied only one third of the knowledge assets of an expert decision maker through experimentation.

One potential explanation for the failure to achieve optimal performance may be the difficulty of learning optimal functional forms among given variables. According to Klayman (1988), people can learn, reasonably well, the existence and direction of a cue-criterion relationship, but have difficulties in learning its shape. As a result, they tend to perform suboptimally. Alternatively, the failure could be attributed to the moderately predictive power of contextual factors. Hoch and Schkade (1996) have theoretically proved that pattern-matching strategy cannot produce good results in environments that are not highly predictive. Finally, the participants in the study were not expert decision makers, but novices. Garvin (1998) suggests that to become an expert, each individual must pass through a number of stages of knowledge. In this context, experimentation might have helped push participants from lower to higher stages. However, examples from literature suggest that for maximum effectiveness, other initiatives, including transfer of knowledge through education and training programs, are essential.

Limitations and Implications

While the current study provides a number of interesting findings, some caution is necessary regarding their generalisability due to a number of limiting factors. One of the limitations refers to the use of a laboratory experiment that may compromise external validity. Another limitation relates to artificial generation of information that may not reflect the true nature of real business. The participants chosen for the study were students and not real-life decision makers. The fact that they were mature graduates may mitigate the potential differences. No monetary incentives were offered to the participants for their effort in the study. Consequently, they could find the study tiring and unimportant and would not try as hard as possible. Most decisions in real business settings have significant consequences.

Although limited, the findings of the current study may have some important implications for organisational knowledge-management strategies. Firstly, they provide information about one valuable knowledge management initiative (exercising space for experimentation) that facilitates knowledge creation and improves performance of organisational knowledge workers. Secondly, they point to the need to consider relative importance and limitations of this initiative in planning knowledge-management strategies to prevent unrealistic expectations. Finally, they suggest the need for additional initiatives (e.g., knowledge transfer through education and training) to enable even higher levels of knowledge and performance. According to Davenport and Prusak (1998), only by taking a holistic approach is it possible to realise the full potential of knowledge ecology.

Future research is necessary to empirically investigate the potential of other various individual or combined and integrated knowledge management initiatives to further enhance knowledge and enable optimal performance. One possible direction for future research is to explore the potential contribution of instruction (e.g., coaching and mentoring) to enhancing individual tacit know-how. Future research may also examine the role of explicit analytical and procedural knowledge embedded in organisational repositories. Technology may play an important role in capturing and distributing organisational knowledge, as well as in promoting human interaction and knowledge sharing. Therefore, future research may examine the potential of various information and telecommunication technologies to enable and facilitate knowledge processes. Finally, future research may look at how different knowledge management initiatives interact to create potential synergy effects. These suggested directions are neither prescriptive nor exhaustive, but represent only a small selection of issues that are currently of interest to the author.

Conclusion

The main objective of this chapter was to investigate whether and how the opportunity for individual experimentation may affect decision makers' working knowledge and performance in a specific judgemental decision task. The findings of the experimental study conducted indicate that experimentation was beneficial in enhancing decision makers' working knowledge and subsequent decision performance. The opportunity to experiment led to enhanced decision accuracy compared to naive strategy. However, optimal performance was not achieved. These findings indicate room for improvement. They also suggest that nonexpert professional knowledge workers in judgement and decision-making tasks could benefit from other additional knowledge management initiatives. Therefore, further research is necessary to systematically address various combined and integrated initiatives in different tasks and contexts, and among different knowledge workers, if a better understanding of the field is to be achieved.

References

(AAOTE) Arthur Andersen Office of Training and Education. (1998). *BC knowledge management*. Arthur Andersen.

Arkes, H. R., Dawes, R. M., & Christensen, C. (1986). Factors influencing the use of a decision rule in a probabilistic task. *Organisational Behaviour and Human Decision Processes, 37*, 93-110.

Ashton, R. H., & Kramer, S. S. (1980). Students as surrogates in behavioural accounting research: Some evidence. *Journal of Accounting Research, 18*(1), 1-15.

Balzer, W. K., Hammer, L. B., Sumner, K. E., Birchenough, T. R., Martens, S. P., & Raymark, P. H. (1994). Effects of cognitive feedback components, display format, and elaboration on performance. *Organisational Behaviour and Human Decision Processes, 58*, 369-385.

Balzer, W. K., Sulsky L. M., Hammer, L. B., & Sumner, K. E. (1992). Task information, cognitive information, or functional validity information: Which components of cognitive feedback affect performance? *Organisational Behaviour and Human Decision Processes, 58*, 369-385.

Baxter, J., & Chua, W. F. (1999). Now and the future. *Australian Accounting Review, 9*(3), 3-14.

Brehmer, B. (1980). In one word: Not from experience. *Acta Psychologica, 45*, 223-241.

Connolly, T., & Gilani, N. (1982). Information search in judgement tasks: A regression model and some preliminary findings. *Organisational Behaviour and Human Performance, 30,* 330-350.

Connolly, T., & Serre, P. (1984). Information search in judgement tasks: The effects of unequal cue validity and cost. *Organisational Behaviour and Human Performance, 34,* 387-401.

Connolly, T., & Thorn, B. K. (1987). Predecisional information acquisition: Effects of task variables on suboptimal search strategies. *Organisational Behaviour and Human Decision Processes, 39,* 397-416.

Connolly, T., & Wholey, D. R. (1988). Information mispurchase in judgement tasks: A task driven causal mechanism. *Organisational Behaviour and Human Decision Processes, 42,* 75-87.

Creyer, E. H., Bettman, J. R., & Payne, J. W. (1990). The impact of accuracy and effort feedback and goals on adaptive decision behaviour. *Journal of Behavioural Decision Making, 3*(1), 1-16.

Davenport, T. H., DeLong, D. W., & Breers, M. C. (1998, winter). Successful knowledge management projects. *Sloan Management Review,* 43-57.

Davenport, T. H., & Prusak, L. (1998). *Working knowledge.* Boston: Harvard Business School Press.

Devlin, K. (1999). *Infosense: Turning information into knowledge.* New York: W.H. Freeman and Company.

Drucker, P. F. (1993). *Post-capitalist society.* New York: Harper Business.

Drucker, P. F. (1998). The coming of the new organisation. In *Harvard Business Review on Knowledge Management.* Boston: Harvard Business School Press.

Garvin, D. A. (1998). Building a learning organisation. In *Harvard Business Review on Knowledge Management.* Boston: Harvard Business School Press.

Grayson, C. J., & O'Dell, C. (1998). Mining your hidden resources. *Across the Board, 35*(4), 23-28.

Handzic, M. (2000, October 30-31). Managing knowledge through experimentation and socialisation. In U. Reimer (Ed.), *Proceedings of the Third International Conference on Practical Aspects of Knowledge Management (PAKM 2000),* Basel, Switzerland.

Hastie, R. (1986). Experimental evidence on group accuracy. In B. Grofman, & G. Owen (Eds.), *Decision Research* 2 (pp. 129-157).

Heath, C., & Gonzalez, R. (1995). Interaction with others increases decision confidence but not decision quality: Evidence against information collection views of interactive decision making. *Organisational Behaviour and Human Decision Processes, 61*(3), 305-326.

Hewson, D. (1999, November). Start talking and get to work. *Business Life*, 72-76.

Hoch, S. J., & Schade, D. A. (1996). A psychological approach to decision support systems. *Management Science, 42*(1), 51-65.

Hogarth, R. M. (1981). Beyond discrete biases: Functional and dysfunctional aspects of judgemental heuristics. *Psychological Bulletin, 90*(2), 197-217.

Janis, I (1982). *Groupthink: Psychological studies of policy decisions and fiascoes.* Boston: Houghton-Miffin.

Klayman, J. (1988). Learning from experience. In B. Brehmer, & C. R. B. Joyce (Eds.), *Human judgement. The SJT view.* Amsterdam: North-Holland.

Kleiner, A., & Roth, G. (1998). How to make experience your company's best teacher. In *Harvard Business Review on Knowledge Management.* Boston: Harvard Business School Press.

Kopelman, R. E. (1986). Objective feedback. In E. A. Locke (Ed.) *Generalising from laboratory to field settings.* Lexington Books.

Lawrence, M., Edmundson, B., & O'Connor, M. (1985). An examination of accuracy of judgemental extrapolation of time series. *International Journal of Forecasting, 1*, 25-35.

Lim, J. S., & O'Connor, M. J. (1996). Judgemental forecasting with interactive forecasting support systems. *Decision Support Systems, 16*, 339-357.

Makridakis, S. (1993). Accuracy measures: Theoretical and practical concerns. *International Journal of Forecasting, 9*, 527-529.

Makridakis, S., & Wheelwright, S. C. (1989). *Forecasting methods for managemen,* (5th ed.). New York: John Wiley and Sons.

Marakas, G. M. (1999). *Decision support systems in the 21ˢᵗ century.* Englewood Cliffs, NJ: Prentice Hall Inc.

Nissen, M. (2006). Harnessing knowledge dynamics: Principled organizational knowing and learning (pp.70-90). Hershey, PA: IRM Press.

Nonaka, I. (1998). The knowledge-creating company. In *Harvard Business Review on Knowledge Management.* Boston: Harvard Business School Press.

Nonaka, I., & Konno, N. (1998). The concept of ba: Building a foundation for knowledge creation. *California Management Review, 40*(3), 40-54.

Nonaka, I., & Takeuchi, H. (1995). *The knowledge creating company: How Japanese companies create the dynamics of innovation.* New York: Oxford University Press.

O'Connor, M. J. (1989). Models of human behaviour and confidence in judgement: A review. *International Journal of Forecasting, 5*, 159-169.

Panko, R., & Kinney, S. (1992). Dyadic organisation communication:Is the dyad different? In *Proceedings of the 25ᵗʰ Hawaii International Conference on Systems Sciences*, HI (pp. 244-253).

Payne, J. W., Bettman, J. R., & Johnson, E. J. (1988). Adaptive strategy selection in decision making. *Journal of Experimental Psychology: Learning, Memory and Cognition, 14*(3), 534-552.

Peterson, D. K., & Pitz, G. F. (1988). Confidence, uncertainty and the use of information. *Journal of Experimental Psychology: Learning, Memory and Cognition, 14*, 85-92.

Remus, W. (1996). Will behavioural research on managerial decision making generalise to managers? *Managerial and Decision Economics, 17*, 93-101.

Remus, W., O'Connor, M., & Griggs, K. (1996, January). *Does feedback improve the accuracy of recurrent judgemental forecasts* (Working paper). HI: University of Hawaii.

Sauer, C. (1993). *Why information systems fail: A case study approach*. Henley-on-Thames: Alfred Waller.

Schwartz, D. (1995). The emergence of abstract representation in dyad problem solving. *The Journal of the Learning Sciences, 4*(3), 321-345.

Senge, P. (1990). *The fifth discipline*. New York: Doubleday.

Sniezek, J. A, & Buckley, T. (1995). Cueing and cognitive conflict in judge-advisor decision making. *Organisational Behaviour and Human Decision Processes, 62*(2), 159-174.

Stasser, G., Taylor, L. A., & Hanna, C. (1989). Information sampling in structured and unstructured discussions of three- and six-person groups. *Journal of Personality and Social Psychology, 57*, 67-68.

Stewart, T. A. (1997). *Intellectual capital: The new wealth of organisations*. New York: Doubleday.

Swanson, E. B. (1988). *Information systems implementation*. Homewood: Irwin.

Whitecotton, S. M. (1996). The effects of experience and a decision aid on the slope, scatter, and bias of earnings forecasts. *Organisational Behaviour and Human Decision Processes, 66*(1), 111-121.

Yates, J. F. (1991, November). *JDM conference presentation*. San Francisco.

Chapter XIII

Social Environment:
Promoting Knowledge Sharing
Through Personal Interaction

Abstract

This chapter addresses the role of social environment and knowledge sharing in decision performance. It reports the results of an empirical investigation of the effectiveness of knowledge sharing through socialisation in enhancing the accuracy of judgemental forecasting. The results obtained clearly show that people perform better when sharing knowledge with others, but they also indicate that there is still room for improvement. Hence, more research is needed in this area to investigate the effect of knowledge sharing on decision performance.

Introduction

Throughout this book, the idea has been promoted that the development of knowledge is the result of the dynamic knowledge processes whose effectiveness is impacted by a number of social and technological factors. The focus of this chapter is on one social influence, namely social environment, as an important enabler and facilitator of knowledge sharing.

Nonaka and Konno (1998) consider physical, face-to-face experiences as the key to conversion and transfer of tacit knowledge. They stress the importance of an open organisational design and customer interfaces as providers of strong ecological stimuli through direct encounter between individuals. They see social environment as "ba" (space), where individuals share feelings, emotions, experiences, and mental models. It is the environment where an individual sympathises or further empathises with others, removing the barrier between the self and others. They claim that from this world emerge care, love, trust, and commitment.

Recently, some KM practitioners have implemented the concept of ba in the form of the knowledge café. The term knowledge café is coined by Gurteen (2005) to denote the place where people gather for the purpose of learning in order that they may make a difference. Essentially, knowledge café is about networking, knowledge sharing, and learning from each other. The outcome for the participants is what they take away as individuals that they can act on and do differently. Gurteen knowledge cafes are regular miniworkshops opened worldwide. A full list of regional events is available at the URL http://www.gurteen.com/gurteen/gurteen.nsf/id/kcafes.

Some KM authors suggest that new knowledge always begins with the individual, but that making personal knowledge available to others is the central activity of the knowledge-creating company (Nonaka & Takeuchi, 1995). The spiral knowledge model assumes that the process of sharing will result in the organisational amplification and exponential growth of working knowledge. Others propose that in order to build a learning organisation, the first step should be to foster environment conducive to individual learning, that is, allow experimentation to gain experience, and second, to open up boundaries and stimulate exchange of ideas (Garvin, 1998). Handzic and Zhou (2005) also argue that organisations must nurture a supportive organisational environment in addition to technical infrastructure to facilitate knowledge sharing and transfer.

However, given the current infancy of knowledge management research, there is little empirical evidence regarding the ways in which tacit knowledge is actually shared, and the impact it has on performance. The purpose of this chapter is to address this issue in the context of decision making.

Knowledge Sharing Through Social Interaction

Decisions in social environments can be made individually or in groups. The literature suggests that people make the majority of important personal decisions individually, but after significant social interaction (Heath & Gonzales, 1995). Individuals often seek to consult with others before deciding what jobs to take, what cars to buy, or what changes to make in their personal life. Managerial decision makers also follow similar interactive procedures when making business decisions. They collect information and opinions from their subordinates, peers, and superiors, but make final decisions alone. Because they make their final decisions individually, decision makers can use or ignore the information they collect during social interaction. In contrast, group decision making requires groups to reach a consensual decision.

The information exchange model of social process suggests that people interact primarily for the purpose of information collection. The situation-theoretic approach to interaction (Devlin, 1999) assumes that, for most conversations, the aim of each participant is to take new information about the focal object or situation into his or her context. The contextual situations can be represented graphically by ovals on a conversation diagram. The overlapping portions represent the contexts that the participants share. The interaction can be viewed geometrically as a gradual pushing together of the participants' contexts so that the overlapping portion becomes larger.

The persuasive arguments perspective (Heath & Gonzales, 1995) assumes that an individual's position on any given issue will be a function of the number and persuasiveness of available arguments. It assumes that individuals come up with a few arguments of their own, but during interaction they collect novel arguments and may shift their initial opinions.

The group decision-making approach recognises the collaborative nature of the interaction act and suggests the potential synergy associated with collaborative activity (Marakas, 1999). However, much of earlier research into group interactions questions the relative virtues of collaborative over individual decision making due to the groupthink phenomenon. According to Janis (1982), members of cohesive long-term groups strive for unanimity, and do not realistically appraise alternative courses of action. This results in unfavourable outcomes.

It is argued that situations, where individual decision makers interact in a social environment but make their own decisions, should be free from groupthink-style outcomes. In such situations, interaction is assumed to allow individuals to more accurately assess their information and analysis, and improve individual decision performance. A small number of prior empirical studies investigating the issue indicate inconclusive findings. Heath and Gonzalez (1995) cited some earlier studies where interaction improved accuracy in general knowledge questions (Yates, 1991) and predictions domain (Hastie, 1986).

However, their own research showed that individual performance did not improve much after interaction. Two studies on sport predictions showed that interaction did not increase decision accuracy or metaknowledge (calibration and resolution), while one study found little responsiveness in risky shift dilemmas. Instead, interaction produced robust and consistent increases in people's confidence in their decisions. The authors offered a rationale construction explanation for their findings. It suggests that interaction forces people to explain choices to others, and that explanation generation leads to increased confidence.

In contrast, Sniezek and Buckley (1995) reported mixed effects of interaction on individual performance within the judge-advisor system. In a given choice task concerning business events, judges provided final team choices and confidence assessments independently or after being advised by two advisors. In particular, dependent judges made decisions as advised, cued judges made their own decisions after being advised, and independent judges made initial decisions before and final decisions after being advised. Results showed that the effect of advice was dependent upon advisor conflict. With no-conflict, advice was generally beneficial. When conflict existed, it had either adverse (cued and dependent) or no effect at all (independent) on the judge's final accuracy.

In summary, interaction sometimes had positive, sometimes negative, and sometimes no systematic effect on individual performance. The equivocal effects of interaction may be potentially attributed to differences in size of interacting groups, expertise and status of the participants, or the characteristics of the tasks involved. Some studies indicate that as the number of participants increases, the likelihood of discussing unshared information decreases (Stasser, Taylor, & Hanna, 1989). According to recent studies on collaborative problem solving, teams of two people (dyads) are more successful than larger groups (Panko & Kinney, 1992; Schwartz, 1995). It has also been suggested that nonexperts who are less informed about a decision problem should be more responsive to information collected and pooled through interaction (Heath & Gonzalez, 1995).

Empirical Study

Study Focus

The focus of this study is on the role of social interaction and knowledge sharing in enhancing decision-making performance. As seen from this discussion, decision making involves a significant amount of social interaction. Interaction is assumed to allow individuals to more accurately assess the knowledge sources and analysis, and improve individual decision performance. The objective of this study, based on Handzic and Chen (2006), is to test these assumptions. In particular, the study will examine (1) whether opportunities for interaction among decision makers will lead to changes in their initial decisions, and (2) whether and what impact these changes will have on the quality of final decisions.

Experimental Task

A suitable forecasting-task simulation was created for the current study of the effect of social interaction on knowledge gain and decision-making support. The experimental task and instrument implemented in Microsoft Visual Basic are based on previous studies (e.g., Handzic, 2004;

Handzic, Aurum, Oliver, & Logenthiran, 2002). A slight modification is added towards the software to increase flexibility and convenience, the central core part of the program has not been changed.

Users are assumed to be the Production Manager from the ice cream company in the Sydney area. Their sole responsibility is to make decisions on the units of ice cream to be produced for sale in the company's outlet at Bondi Beach, Sydney. Users were required to make decisions for 10 consecutive simulated days.

All users were provided with a 20 days record of previous product sales to suggest future behaviour. The task was created to discover the effect of knowledge sharing on the accuracy of their production decisions. First, users were asked to independently make 10 predictions. Then, users, in a small group of two people, shared the available information, options, and their initial predictions within the group. Users then could revise or update their initial predictions.

Maximisation of accuracy was the goal of the task. Over and under estimation errors were equally costly. The user's prediction before the interaction and after was compared and analysed to determine the direction and size of the knowledge sharing performance effects.

Experimental Design and Variables

A laboratory experiment was used as the preferred research method, as it allowed for greater experimental control and made possible drawing of stronger inferences about casual relationships between variables. The experiment had one within-subject factor design. The only factor was social environment (noninteractive vs. interactive). A noninteractive social environment was manipulated by completely constraining, and interactive by maximally encouraging (through dialogue) sharing of ideas and information while making decisions.

Decision performance was evaluated in terms of (1) cost operationalised by absolute error (AE) expressed in dollar terms; and (2) accuracy operationalised by symmetric absolute percentage error (SAPE). AE was calculated for each trial as an absolute difference between subjects' forecasts and actual sale values. SAPE was calculated by dividing AE by an average of actual and forecast values, and multiplying the result by 100% (for details and justification see Makridakis, 1993). Subjects' decision behaviour was evaluated in terms of before and after the peer interaction.

Time Series Generation and Optimal Strategy

The product sales time series were artificially generated with the following conditions: The data files were created from an artificially generated set of random numbers. These were drawn from a normal distribution with a mean of 0 and a standard deviation 500 and added to a constant 2,000. Finally, a sequence of increasing numbers was added to create a 5% upward trend. There were no regular seasonal patterns of demand occurring. This process was replicated from Handzic et al. (2002).

The optimal response required subjects to detect and decompose the time series provided into trend and noise elements and take these into account in future predictions. This meant that they needed to follow the general direction of the demand line (trend), and avoid being influenced by the random ups and downs (noise).

Subjects and Procedure

Twelve PhD students in Information Systems at UNSW participated in this experiment. They attended on a voluntary basis and received no monetary reward for making predictions. As in our previous experimental studies (e.g., see Chapter VI, VIII and XII), the use of graduate students as subjects is justified by recommendations about their appropriateness for this type of research given by other authors (Ashton & Kramer, 1980; Remus, 1996; Whitecotton, 1996). Although the software was generated to be used by subjects, to make the experiment easier and shorter to conduct, hard copies of the experimental task were printed out and handed to the students upon the commencement of the experiment.

Prior to that, students were randomly assigned into six pairs. Then, each person was given an experiment sheet and performed the task as stated in the sheet independently. After the completion of the independent task, the group members discussed with the other colleague in the group their decisions and strategies applied when performing the tasks. Then they had a chance to revise and update their previous decisions independently, but were not required to reach the consensus decision. All the experiment sheets were collected and data entered into the spreadsheet file for further analysis by the researcher. The session lasted for about 30 minutes.

Research Instrument

The research instrument used for the current investigation was based on the software adapted from the author's earlier experimental work. As before, the software was written in Microsoft Visual Basic. It included a task simulator, a decision support component, and a data collection component. A slight modification was added to the program later on by a research student. A printed version of the research instrument shown in Figure 13.1 was used in this particular study, due to the laboratory time and space constraints.

The instrument simulated a time-series forecasting task in a repetitive decision environment. Entry of the decision could be drawn as a dot in the special dotted line corresponding to the appropriated date. A written-down numerical value above or below the dot indicated the prediction number.

Several features have been implemented in the instrument to aid the user in learning the sales pattern and making accurate decisions. These features were based on two concepts: time series analysis and graphical visualisation. Time series of sales events for 20 days were initially provided as line curves in the graph. With the line graph of past sales, the users had a reasonable amount of knowledge to make ac-

Figure 13.1. Screen shot of the research instrument

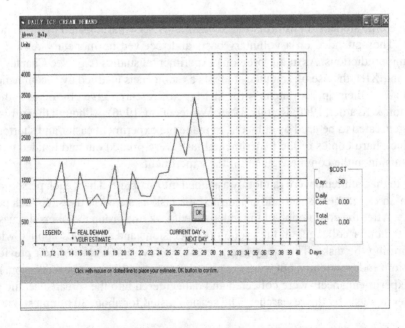

curate future decisions. Graphical visualisation was used as Daily Ice Cream Unit of Sales vs. Days Plot. This was assumed to allow users to quickly understand the issue and determine prediction strategies.

Using the regression equation, it was possible to find the optimal prediction scores for the 10 consecutive days forecasting period. These optimal results were compared with the decision makers' actual prediction scores of before interaction and the scores of after interaction. These were used to evaluate individual performance against the theoretically best possible on the task.

Results

Comparative Analysis and Results

From Figure 13.2, it can be seen that the number of Revised/Changed Scores in the total number of Prediction Scores is only 26/120=21.67%, and the remaining 94/120 (78.33%) scores remained unchanged.

These results indicate that many people were reluctant to change ideas once they had put them down in a written form. While an interaction between group members could have contributed to sharing the knowledge developed from performing the same knowledge task, it did not greatly affect the behaviour, as the users were not likely to change once they made their decisions.

Figure 13.3 shows No. of Negative, No. of Positive, and total No. of Changes of Score. The No. of Positive Changes means the revised scores performed better than initial scores after interaction within group, the No. of Negative Changes means the opposite. From the results shown, it is clear that the No. of Positive changes was much greater than negative ones. The ratio was 19/26 = 73.08%. The high rate of positive changes indicates that interaction can help to improve the decision performance.

Descriptive results (means) for cost and accuracy variables by experimental groups are presented in Figure 13.4 and 13.5. For comparison purposes, the linear regression prediction (optimal score) is presented as well.

The results indicate a significant positive effect of knowledge sharing on both cost and accuracy. The mean AE of the subjects after interaction was significantly smaller compared to those before interaction (661.31 vs. 758.67). Similarly, the mean SAPE of the subjects after interaction was significantly smaller than before interaction (33.90% vs. 37.55%). However, optimal (linear regression) strategy tended to perform the best. The mean AE of the optimal strategy was smaller compared to that

Figure 13.2. Amount of changes after interaction

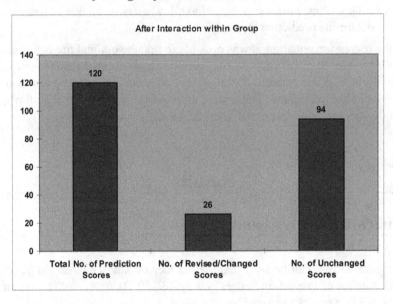

Figure 13.3. Nature of changes after interaction

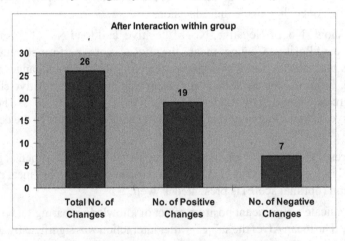

of subjects after interaction (558.21 vs. 661.31). The same was true for the SAPE (25.07% vs. 33.90%).

Discussion

The main findings of this study make two important contributions to the development of KM theory: (i) identify knowledge sharing as a strategy, which improves the performance for solving uncertain decision problems. (ii) suggests that the use of automated (intelligent/statistical) models may overcome the deficiencies of human judgment.

Knowledge-Sharing Effects

The current study found a positive impact of knowledge sharing on performance. Revised score after interaction tended to be much better than the Initial score before interaction. Figures 13.4 and 13.5 show the graphical visualisation of the decision performance under three circumstances. Performance after interaction was far better than before interaction. However, the best performance was obtained from the

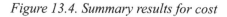

Figure 13.4. Summary results for cost

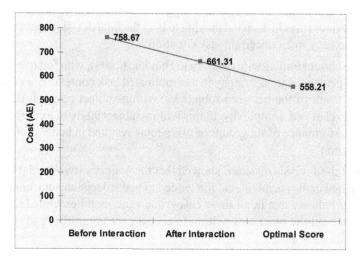

Figure 13.5. Summary results for accuracy

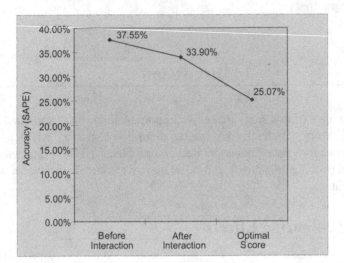

statistical model. Despite this, surveys in real-world business environment reveal that judgment is preferred over models (Dalrymple, 1987).

The beneficial effect of knowledge sharing found in this study agrees with Nonaka's (1998) knowledge creation theory, which emphasises the critical importance of the process of socialisation for tacit knowledge transfer. The results also agree with Handzic and Low (2002), who found positive effect of socialisation on performance in complex task contexts. Such findings suggest that more participants should be involved in various roles in decision making to help the final decision maker achieve maximum accuracy in an uncertain task situation.

However, the current findings are contrary to Handzic (2004), who found no significant effect of personalisation strategy in a complicated task context. The difference could be the result of the between-subject vs. within-subject research design, or altering the level of task complexity. In this within-subject study of a complex task, the average performance of six groups of two people resulted in better performance due to interaction.

The results of the analysis by teams showed that the majority (two thirds) of teams who participated in the social interaction tended to make decision adjustments. The results further indicate that in all these cases, one team member tended to rely on own decisions, and the other was willing to accept peer arguments and revise the scores. Such results provide strong support for the persuasive arguments perspective on socialisation (Heath & Gonzales, 1995). In the remaining teams (one third), both participants tended to ancor on their own decisions and reject peer arguments to revise the scores.

However, the fact that revised scores represent a relatively small part of total prediction scores (21.67%) suggests room for further improvement. A chat between peers is assumed to foster the development of trust, and to provide a foundation for creative working. An individual position and decision may shift as a result of interaction with others due to the collection of persuasive arguments. However, various interests, knowledge, back group, personal experiences may have an adverse effect on performance. Another possible explanation for the conservative behaviour exhibited may lie in the predictable propensity of humans towards irrationality and bias (Arnott, 2002).

Other Issues

The current study showed relatively poor overall performance for all the strategies. This could be for two reasons: First, the competitive and uncertain nature of many business processes is hard to predict, and the use a simple heuristics and methods in a short time cannot generate a very good result. Decision makers faced with complex decision tasks may greatly benefit from various strategies, but this does not guarantee that decision makers can make the most accurate prediction possible. Second, the current experiment is only volunteer based without monetary incentives. The participants may not have tried their best in this situation to investigate and make decisions. Other similar studies (Handzic, 1997; Sniezek & Buckley, 1995) provided their students with substantial monetary reward for their performance. By not giving monetary incentives, this study attempted to prevent knowledge "hoarding," and promoted cooperation rather than competition among the participants. It was assumed the PhD students would treat the experiment seriously and contribute/try their best by the intrinsic interest in the subject matter. Most decisions in real business have significant consequences.

Some caution is also necessary regarding the generalisability of the study findings due to artificial generation of time series that may not reflect the true nature of real business. There is also a limitation, in terms of the small number of participants involved in the experiment, that may affect confidence in the experimental results. Overall, when considering the results and analysis of this study, it is important to be aware of these limitations.

Conclusion

The results of the study presented in this chapter were able to show the usefulness of social interaction and knowledge sharing in improving the understanding and enhancing decision makers' performance of a forecasting task. The research showed that social environment encouraging interaction had a positive effect on their performance in terms of improving decision accuracy and reducing the cost of error in the context of an uncertain decision task. However, people failed to reach the optimal performance of the statistical model. The findings suggest that creating the opportunities for socialisation need to be taken with careful consideration and analysis, in conjunction with other possible approaches to reach the maximum possible outcome.

References

Arnott, D. (2002). *Decision biases and decision support systems development* (Working

Paper. No. 2002/04). Melbourne, Australia: Monash University, Decision Support Systems Laboratory.

Ashton, R. H., & Kramer, S. S. (1980). Students as surrogates in behavioural accounting research: Some evidence. *Journal of Accounting Research, 18*(1), 1-15.

Dalrymple, D. J. (1987). Sales forecasting practices: Results from a United States survey. *International Journal of Forecasting, 3,* 379-391.

Devlin, K. (1999). *Infosense: Turning information into knowledge.* New York: W.H. Freeman and Company.

Garvin, D. A. (1998). Building a learning organisation. In *Harvard Business Review on Knowledge Management* (pp. 47-80). Boston: Harvard Business School Press.

Gurteen, D. (2005). Spur organisational learning with a knowledge café. *KM Review Magazine,* October.

Handzic, M. (1997). Decision performance as a function of information availability: An examination of executive information systems. In H. Rehesaar (Ed.), *Proceedings of the 2nd New South Wales Symposium on Information Technology and Information Systems.* Sydney: UNSW.

Handzic, M. (2004, July 1-3). Decision support through knowledge management: An empirical examination of two strategies. In *Proceedings of the IFIP WG8.3 Working Conference on Decision Support Systems*, Prato, Italy.

Handzic, M., Aurum, A., Oliver, G., & Logenthiran, G. (2002, September). An empirical investigation of a knowledge discovery tool. *European Conference on Knowledge Management (ECKM 2002)*, Dublin.

Handzic, M., & Chen, F. (2006, July). The impact of knowledge sharing on decision performance. In *Proceedings of Knowledge Management Aston Conference (KMAC 2006)*, Birmingham, UK.

Handzic, M., & Low, G. (2002). The impact of social interaction on performance of decision tasks of varying complexity. *OR Insight, 15*(1), 15-22.

Handzic, M., & Zhou, A. Z. (2005). *Knowledge management: An integrative approach.* Oxford, UK: Chandos Publishing.

Hastie, R. (1986). Experimental evidence on group accuracy. In B. Grofman, & G. Owen (Eds.), *Decision Research* 2 (pp. 129-157).

Heath, C., & Gonzalez, R. (1995). Interaction with others increases decision confidence but not decision quality: Evidence against information collection views of interactive decision making. *Organisational Behaviour and Human Decision Processes, 61*(3), 305-326.

Janis, I. (1982). *Groupthink: Psychological studies of policy decisions and fiascoes.* Boston: Houghton-Miffin.

Makridakis, S. (1993). Accuracy measures: Theoretical and practical concerns. *International Journal of Forecasting, 9*, 527-529.

Marakas, G. M. (1999). *Decision support systems in the 21ˢᵗ century.* Englewood Cliffs, NJ: Prentice Hall Inc.

Nonaka, I. (1998). The knowledge-creating company. In *Harvard Business Review on Knowledge Management* (pp. 21-45). Boston: Harvard Business School Press.

Nonaka, I., & Konno, N. (1998). The concept of ba: Building a foundation for knowledge creation. *California Management Review, 40*(3), 40-54.

Nonaka, I., & Takeuchi, H. (1995). *The knowledge creating company: How Japanese companies create the dynamics of innovation.* New York: Oxford University Press.

Panko, R., & Kinney, S. (1992). Dyadic organisation communication: Is the dyad different? In *Proceedings of the 25ᵗʰ Hawaii International Conference on Systems Sciences*, HI (pp. 244-253).

Remus, W. (1996). Will behavioural research on managerial decision making generalise to managers? *Managerial and Decision Economics, 17,* 93-101.

Schwartz, D. (1995). The emergence of abstract representation in dyad problem solving. *The Journal of the Learning Sciences, 4*(3), 321-345.

Sniezek, J. A., & Buckley, T. (1995). Cueing and cognitive conflict in judge-advisor decision making. *Organisational Behaviour and Human Decision Processes, 62*(2), 159-174.

Stasser, G., Taylor, L. A., & Hanna, C.(1989). Information sampling in structured and unstructured discussions of three- and six-person groups. *Journal of Personality and Social Psychology, 57,* 67-68.

Whitecotton, S. M. (1996). The effects of experience and a decision aid on the slope, scatter, and bias of earnings forecasts. *Organisational Behaviour and Human Decision Processes, 66*(1), 111-121.

Yates, J. F. (1991, November). *JDM Conference presentation.* San Francisco.

Chapter XIV

Task Contingencies:
Examining if Two Heads are Always Better Than One

Abstract

This chapter investigates the value of social interaction in promoting people's working knowledge and performance in decision making in relation to task complexity. The results of an empirical study undertaken indicate that social interaction was highly beneficial for enhancing people's knowledge and performance of complex decision tasks. However, the results indicate that social interaction made no difference to people's performance of simple decision tasks. These findings make two important contributions to the development of theory: they support the contingent nature of social interaction effects on decision-making knowledge and performance, and identify component task complexity as an important contingent factor.

Introduction

In Chapter XIII of this book, we discussed the enabler, the process, and the impact of socialisation and knowledge sharing in the context of decision making. From the significant positive effects found, one could conclude that knowledge sharing through socialisation is universally good knowledge-management practice that should always be encouraged.

According to Becerra-Fernandez, Gonzales, and Sabherwal (2004), much of the current literature on knowledge management promotes such universalistic view of knowledge management. In general, this view of knowledge management implies that there is one best way to manage knowledge in all organisations and under all circumstances. In contrast, a contingency view of knowledge management suggests that no one approach is best under all circumstances. Instead, individuals and organisations need to choose, among multiple possible paths, that one which fits best their set of circumstances. The assumption is that only the choice of the appropriate path will lead them to the ultimate success.

Drawing on previous theoretical and empirical research, Handzic (2004) suggested several contingency factors that influence knowledge management effort in the context of decision making. These include various decision tasks, decision environment, and decision maker characteristics. The author then used the gaming approach to knowledge management to explore how these contingency factors affected the effectiveness of various computer-based knowledge-management systems. Some of the major advantages of the gaming approach over other more conventional exploratory methods is that gaming allows for complex and realistic cases to be made, sequences of actions and events to be represented, and different players to be involved in the game, thus providing the variety of possible situations (De Hoog et al., 1999). Simulation games are considered particularly useful for conveying complex relationships to a knowledge worker, and for exploring what-if scenarios in an interactive format. The user can view and manipulate the parameters involved and observe the effect (Bergeron, 2003).

This chapter attempts to extend the author's earlier work on contingent nature of technology-based knowledge management initiatives to socially-orientated ones. Given that various sources report between 40% and 90% of the needed knowledge in organisations as being tacit (e.g., AAOTE, 1998; Hewson, 1999), socially orientated mechanisms are particulary focused on promoting socialisation among people. It is argued that people's behaviour and values contribute most to the circulation of tacit knowledge in organisations. The spiral knowledge model (Nonaka & Takeuchi, 1995) assumes that the processes of socialisation and knowledge sharing will result in the organisational amplification and exponential growth of working knowledge.

Given the early stage of knowledge management research, little is known about the actual success of socialisation and knowledge sharing initiatives, returns resulting from them, or the potential moderating factors. The focus of this chapter is on one task-related moderator, namely task complexity.

Task Complexity

The literature provides several conceptualisations of complexity. Some investigators define complexity in terms of objective task qualities. Schroder et al. (Schroder, Driver, & Streufert, 1967) identify load, diversity, and rate of change as three primary properties of a complex task. Payne (1976) defines complexity as a function of both the number of alternatives and the number of attributes on which the alternatives are compared. Similarly, Beach and Mitchell (1978) define task complexity in terms of the number of different components of the decision problem, such as the number of alternatives and the amount of relevant knowledge artefacts to be considered, the number of criteria on which the problem would be judged, and the degree to which the problem would influence future decisions. A more comprehensive definition of task complexity was developed by Wood (1986). He proposed a multidimensional construct comprising component, coordinative, and dynamic complexity. The component complexity is viewed as a direct function of the number of knowledge artefacts or cues and the number of distinct acts required for the task performance. Coordinative complexity refers to the form and strength of the relationship between cues, acts, and products of acts, such as sequencing of inputs and timing, frequency, intensity, and location of acts. Dynamic complexity involves change in the component and coordinative of the task over time.

Other approaches mentioned by Campbell (1988) treat complexity as a primarily psychological experience or an interaction between task and person characteristics. The former emphasise the subjective reaction of the individual to the task rather than the objective task characteristics, while the latter acknowledge the importance of both the person and the task. In the integrative framework proposed by Campbell (1988), task complexity is related to both the objective task characteristics that increase load, diversity, and change, and cognitive demands that those factors place on the person. The task characteristics that contribute to complexity include multiple paths, uncertain outcomes, conflicting interdependencies among paths, uncertain or probabilistic linkages, and associated characteristics such as ill-structured, ambiguous, and difficult tasks. The framework also recognises that experienced complexity, although merely a reaction to task characteristics, may be evoked for reasons other than the task, such as context, anxiety, or fear. Design characteristics of the supporting knowledge management system, such as presentation format, may also affect the perceived complexity of the task (Te'eni, 1989).

The Beach and Mitchell (1978) model proposes a positive relationship between the level of task complexity and the level of analytic complexity of the decision strategy selected for the task performance. The essence of the model proposition lies in the fact that the difference in the expected benefit associated with a complex vs. simple decision strategy is larger in its application to a more complex than to a less complex task. While the model recognises the benefit of using a complex decision strategy for a more complex decision problem, it does not recognise the effect of cost, which may be much larger in the application of the strategy in a more complex problem than in a less complex one. Thus, from the cost perspective, a person may be more likely to select less complex strategies for more complex problems, and more complex strategies for less complex problems. Christensen-Szalanski (1978), who formalised the cognitive cost/benefit model of problem solving strategy selection, showed analytically that anything that increases difficulty of the task results in a rise of the cost curve associated with the performance of the task and consequently, selection of a strategy with lower level of expected benefit.

Empirical findings from a study conducted by Smith et al. (Smith, Mitchell, & Beach, 1982) on the effect of task complexity on choice of an analysis method for the investment task involving different number of investment alternatives are consistent with the selection mechanism proposed by Christensen-Szalanski (1978). The evidence from the preferential choice research also indicates that decision makers tend to use less complex decision strategies for more complex problems (Payne, 1976, 1982). Typically, when faced with a task involving many alternatives described by many attributes, subjects tended to use noncompensatory decision strategies. In a task involving a small number of alternatives, the tendency to use compensatory decision strategies was evident. Compensatory strategies involve trade-off between high value on some dimensions relevant to a decision alternative, and low value on other dimensions. They are expensive strategies to use as they demand multiple comparisons and extensive memory to retain the outcomes. In contrast, noncompensatory strategies ignore trade-offs and by doing so, simplify search and reduce the expense of cognitive processing (Nichols-Hoppe & Beach, 1990).

Empirical Study

Study Focus

The focus of this study is on relationships between task complexity, socialisation, and performance. In view of the small number of equivocal prior findings, it is of particular interest for the current study to examine the impact of pairwise interaction on decision performance of nonexpert individuals with no social ties with each other, across decision tasks of varying complexity. Specifically, the current study will examine: (1) whether the opportunity for social interaction will affect the individual decision maker's processing efficiency with respect to the task artefacts, and his or her subsequent decision accuracy; and (2) whether the impact of social interaction will be influenced by the complexity of the decision task due to the increasing volume of task-related knowledge artefacts.

Experimental Task

The experimental task in the current study was a simple production planning activity in which subjects made decisions regarding daily production of fresh ice cream. The participants assumed the role of Production Manager for a fictitious dairy firm that sold ice cream from its outlet at Bondi Beach in Sydney, Australia. The fictitious company incurred equally costly losses if production was set too low (due to loss of market to the competition) or too high (by spoilage of unsold product). The participants' goal was to minimise the costs incurred by incorrect production decisions. During the experiment, participants were asked, at the end of each day, to set production quotas for ice cream to be sold the following day. Subjects were required to make 30 production decisions over a period of 30 consecutive days. Before commencing the task, participants had an opportunity to make five trial decisions (for practice purposes only).

The task differed with respect to social interaction and task complexity. One half of the subjects were encouraged to share (in pairs) their information and opinions with others while making decisions, but were not required to reach a consensual decision. The other half made decisions independently, without any interaction with others. One half of the participants performed a simple decision problem based on a single contextual information cue, and another half performed a complex decision problem based on multiple contextual cues.

The task provided a challenge because it did not stipulate exactly how information should be translated into specific decision response. The participants were provided with a meaningful task context, sequential historic information of task relevant variables to provide some cues to causal relationship, and forecast values of contextual variables to suggest future behaviour. However, they were not given any explicit analysis of the quality of their information, or rules they could apply to integrate the available factual information.

For the purpose of the study, the product demand time series was artificially generated as a series of random numbers ($DEMAND_i \sim N(25,5)$, $i=1,2,...,n$) to provide a realistic demand dimension. The contextual cues were created from demand data by adding random error terms ($CUE_i = DEMAND_i + e_i$, $e_i \sim N(0,3.75)$, $i=1,2,...,n$) to provide theoretical cue-criterion correlation coefficients of $r=0.80$. Derivation of optimal strategies was based on linear regression model, with contextual cues as independent and demand as dependent variables in the equation. The results of stepwise regressions showed R-square values of 0.66 ($F(1,28)=55.62$, p=.000) with one cue, and 0.87 ($F(3,26)=56.82$, p=.000) with three cues in the equation.

At the beginning of the experiment, task descriptions were provided to inform subjects about the task scenario and requirements. The given text differed with respect to the quantity of contextual information provided and the form of communication allowed. In addition, throughout the experiment, instructions and feedback were provided to each participant to analyse earlier performance and to adjust future strategies.

Experimental Design and Variables

A laboratory experiment with random assignment to treatment groups was used, since it allowed greater experimental control. This made it possible to draw stronger inferences about causal relationships between variables due to high controllability. The experiment had a 2×2 factorial design with two independent factors: (1) *social interaction* (constrained vs. encouraged), and (2) *decision task* (simple vs. complex).

Social interaction was manipulated by completely constraining or maximally encouraging (through dialogue) sharing of ideas and information while making decisions. Decision task was manipulated by changing the volume of task relevant contextual information (one vs. three) provided to participants in a computerised database. All information cues were decision relevant and relatively equally reliable.

Individual performance was evaluated in terms of *processing efficiency* of the task information and *decision accuracy* achieved as a result. Processing efficiency was operationalised by a relative to optimal error (ROE), and was calculated as a ratio of an absolute error of a person's decision to the corresponding error of the "optimal strategy." Decision accuracy was operationalised by a relative to naive error (RNE), and was calculated as a ratio of an absolute error of a person's decision to the corresponding error of the "random walk" (naive) strategy (for details, see Amstrong & Collopy, 1992). Relative measures were used to compare individual performance with the theoretically best possible on the task, with and without the given information.

Subjects and Procedure

The subjects were 56 graduate students enrolled in the Master of Commerce course at The University of New South Wales, Sydney. Subjects participated in the experiment on a voluntary basis and received no monetary incentives for their performance. Graduate students are used as appropriate subjects in experimental research throughout this book, as well as in similar decision-making studies by other authors (Ashton & Kramer, 1980; Remus, 1996; Whitecotton, 1996). The current experiment was conducted in a microcomputer laboratory. On arrival, subjects were assigned randomly to one of the treatment groups by picking up a diskette with an appropriate version of the research instrument to be used. The instrument was specifically developed by the book author in Visual Basic. Subjects were briefed about the purpose of the study, read case descriptions, and performed the task. The session lasted about 1 hour.

Results

The results of a preliminary two-way analysis of variance indicated significant interaction effects between social interaction and decision task on both processing efficiency and decision accuracy. In view of the significant interaction effects, further analysis was performed using T-test method to examine simple main effects of social interaction on two dependent variables of interest.

The analysis reveals a highly significant positive effect of interaction on processing efficiency (ROE) with the complex, but not simple task. The mean ROE of the subjects in the encouraged interaction group was significantly smaller than that of the subjects in the constrained interaction group (3.51 vs. 4.00, t=2.09, p<.05). No significant difference between the two groups was found among subjects with the simple decision task (2.80 vs. 2.70, ns). Mean values greater than 1 indicated that subjects processed task information less efficiently than they could have irrespective of social interaction.

The analysis also shows a highly significant effect of interaction on decision accuracy among subjects with the complex task. The subjects in the encouraged interaction group had a significantly smaller mean RNE than their counterparts in the constrained interaction group (.81 vs. 1.15, t=3.49, p<.05). The difference between the two groups was not statistically significant among the subjects with the simple task (1.12 vs. .94, ns). Mean values less than 1 indicated slight improvements in decision accuracy over naive strategy due to information processing.

Discussion

The findings of this study make two important contributions to the development of theory: support the contention that the value of social interaction in improving decision making is highly contingent upon the characteristics of the decision task, and identify component task complexity as an important contingent factor. More specifically, the study has demonstrated that encouraging social interaction improved processing efficiency and decision accuracy in a more complex decision task involving multiple interrelated cues. However, it made no difference in performance of a simple decision task involving only one cue.

Main Effects

Subjects performing a more complex decision task were found to process their task information more efficiently and consequently, make more accurate decisions when they were allowed to interact and share ideas with others while handling the large amounts of information, than when they performed the same task without such interaction. On the other hand, the findings indicate that interaction did not improve either of the two aspects of the individual performance (efficiency or accuracy) of subjects performing a simple decision task with small amounts of task information. This suggests the highly contingent nature of the performance impact of social interaction upon the complexity of the task due to information load.

The beneficial effect of social interaction found in a more complex task is consistent with the theoretical expectations suggested by the knowledge management literature (Marakas, 1999; Nonaka & Takeuchi, 1995). It also agrees with anecdotal evidence from "real world" organisations (Hewson, 1999). However, the results obtained in this study contradict findings of an earlier study that investigated the issue in a similarly complex predictive task domain (see study 2 in Heath & Gonzales, 1995). The difference between the two findings can be potentially attributed to the characteristics of the task context in which the investigation was carried out. The current study provided an iterative task context with performance feedback. Earlier empirical research indicated the beneficial effect of feedback on learning (for review, see Kopelman, 1986). Participants might have brought their personal analysis and know-how to the task, acquired information about their partner's arguments, jointly generated new ideas, and considered all in making final decisions. Immediate performance feedback might have enabled participants to evaluate alternative views and adjust future strategies accordingly. Generating and sharing personal tacit knowledge through interaction, coupled with the opportunity to test its contribution to performance over time, might have enhanced learning and resulted in greater accuracy.

Additional analysis of the collected data across two equal blocks of trials (later vs. earlier) was done to test this proposition. The results confirm a significant learning effect on decision accuracy in the interactive environment. As suggested, subjects who interacted with others tended to exhibit significant learning, which led to improved quality of their decisions over time. This was demonstrated by significantly smaller relative decision errors found among these subjects in the later than in the earlier period of the task (.67 vs. .96, t=2.70, p<.05). No significant learning effect was found in the noninteractive environment (1.11 vs. 1.19, ns).

The current study also tried to avoid a potential adverse effect of advisor conflict by limiting the individual's social interaction to one other person. It has been reported that in a two-advisor system with conflict, advice did not improve judge's accuracy, and resulted in deteriorated performance in some circumstances (Sniezek & Buckley, 1995). In addition, the participants in the current study had dual judge-advisor roles. Because of their equal status in the interactive act, it is possible that the participants jointly generated some new ideas previously nonexistent in their individual contexts. Previous research indicated that teams of two people were successful in performing collaborative activities (Panko & Kinney, 1992; Schwartz, 1995).

With respect to a simpler decision task, with smaller amounts of task information, the current study found no significant social interaction impact. The lack of any significant impact is contrary to expectations. The results also contradict some earlier empirical findings. In a similarly simple task involving choice between two alternatives (Sniezek & Buckley, 1995), there was a positive effect of advice on judge's accuracy when given in a no-advisor-conflict situation. The difference in findings between the two studies could potentially be attributed to the level of expertise about the problem brought by the participants to the interactive act. Participants bringing similarly high levels of expertise to the interaction act are likely to enhance only confidence, but not accuracy of their decisions (Heath & Gonzales, 1995). Subjects in the current study could get a reasonably good understanding of the task and develop an appropriate strategy for solving the problem from the available computerised information. They were provided with sequential historic information to show causal relationships between the two task variables, as well as the forecast value of one variable to suggest future changes in the other. An earlier study (Handzic, 1997) reported that participants in a similar task were able to use most of the potential of their computerised information to improve decision quality. However, our analysis showed that participants in this study performed far worse than they could have, leaving room for further improvement.

With respect to overall performance, the study revealed relatively inefficient processing of the available information across all treatments, which consequently resulted in little or no real improvement in decision accuracy over naive strategy. The relatively poor overall performance could be potentially attributed to the lack of monetary incentives. Other studies (Handzic, 1997; Sniezek & Buckley, 1995) provided their students with substantial monetary rewards for their performance. It is possible that without monetary incentives, the subjects did not try as hard as possible to use the full potential of their information to improve decisions. By not giving extrinsic incentives, this study attempted to prevent information "hoarding," and promote cooperation rather than competition among the participants. It was also assumed that graduates chosen from the pool of students attending an advanced Master's level course should be motivated to do their best on the task by the intrinsic interest for the subject matter.

Alternatively, poor overall performance could be attributed to the characteristics of the task information and the task performers. Computerised information repositories available to participants in the current study contained only factual information with little analysis, and had no procedural information. Internalising factual information into "explicit" knowledge was not sufficient to perform well on the task. The participants also needed analytical information, such as an evaluation of the predictive validity of each contextual factor, as well as the relevant know-how to integrate factual information into a decision response. This crucial information was assumed to be a part of individual "tacit" knowledge. However, nonexpert participants were not likely to have high levels of the required "tacit" knowledge to perform well on the task without prior training or experience. An encouraging finding is that individual performance did improve over time through task repetition with feedback for more complex tasks.

Study Limitations

While the current study provides a number of interesting findings, some caution is necessary regarding their generalisability, due to a number of limiting factors. One of the limitations refers to the use of a laboratory experiment that may compromise external validity of research. Another limitation relates to artificial generation of information that may not reflect the true nature of real business. The subjects chosen for the study were students and not real-life decision makers. The fact that they were mature graduates may mitigate the potential differences. No incentives were offered to the subjects for their effort in the study. Consequently, they could find the study tiring and unimportant and would not try as hard as possible. Most decisions in real business settings have significant consequences.

Although limited, the findings of the current study may have some important implications for organisational knowledge management strategies. They indicate that the decision makers, overwhelmed by the complexity of their decision problem and no opportunity to communicate with others, may resolve to extremely simple decision strategies, completely avoid the use of their information, and make intuitive decisions. Creating working contexts that encourage communication and a culture of information sharing may potentially have a beneficial effect on performance by partially alleviating the negative effects of task complexity due to information overload.

Conclusion

The main objective of this chapter was to investigate the effect of social interaction on people's working knowledge and use of that knowledge to improve performance in a specific decision-making context. In summary, the findings of the study presented here indicate a beneficial effect of social interaction on performance of a more complex decision task with larger amounts of task information. The encouraged interaction was useful in such a task, and resulted in improved processing efficiency of the task information, and enhanced decision accuracy. Interaction made no significant contribution to the performance of a simpler decision task with smaller amounts of task information. These findings have important implications for organisations, as they emphasise the importance of communication among people for effective knowledge management in circumstances of increasing complexity of knowledge work and information supply enabled by new technology. Further research is required that would extend the study to other subjects and environmental conditions in order to ensure the generalisability of the present findings.

References

(AAOTE) Arthur Andersen Office of Training and Education. (1998). *BC knowledge management.* Arthur Andersen.

Amstrong, J. S., & Collopy, F. (1992). Error measures for generalising about forecasting methods: Empirical comparisons. *International Journal of Forecasting, 8*, 69-80.

Ashton, R. H., & Kramer, S. S. (1980). Students as surrogates in behavioural accounting research: Some evidence. *Journal of Accounting Research, 18*(1), 1-15.

Baxter, J., & Chua, W. F. (1999). Now and the future. *Australian Accounting Review, 9*(3), 3-14.

Beach, L. R., & Mitchell, T. R. (1978, July). A contingency model for the selection of decision strategies. *Academy of Management Review*, 439-449.

Becerra-Fernandez, I., Gonzales, A., & Sabherwal, R. (2004). *Knowledge management: Challenges, solutions, and technologies.* Upper Saddle River, NJ: Pearson Education, Inc.

Bergeron, B. (2003). *Essentials of knowledge management*, Hoboken, NJ: John Wiley & Sons.

Campbell, D. J. (1988). Task complexity: A review and analysis. *Academy of Management Review, 13*(1), 40-52.

Christensen-Szalanski, J. J. J. (1978). Problem solving strategies: A selection mechanism, some implications, and some data. *Organisational Behaviour and Human Performance, 22*, 307-323.

Davenport, T. H., DeLong, D. W., & Breers, M. C. (1998, winter). Successful knowledge management projects. *Sloan Management Review*, 43-57.

Davenport, T. H., & Prusak, L. (1998). *Working knowledge*. Boston: Harvard Business School Press.

De Hoog, R., van Heijst, G, van der Spek, R., Edwards, J. S., Mallis, R., van der Meij, B., et al. (1999). Investigating a theoretical framework for knowledge management: A gaming approach. In J. Liebowitz (Ed.), *Knowledge management handbook*. Boca Raton: CRC Press.

Devlin, K. (1999). *Infosense: Turning information into knowledge*. New York: W.H. Freeman and Company.

Drucker, P. F. (1993). *Post-capitalist society*. New York: Harper Business.

Goffee, R., & Jones, G. (1999). What holds the modern company together? In *Harvard Business Review on Managing People*. Boston: Harvard Business School Press.

Grayson, C. J., & O'Dell, C. (1998). Mining your hidden resources. *Across the Board, 35*(4), 23-28.

Handzic, M. (1997). Decision performance as a function of information availability: An examination of executive information systems. In H. Rehesaar (Ed.), *Proceedings of the 2nd New South Wales Symposium on Information Technology and Information Systems*. Sydney: UNSW.

Hastie, R. (1986). Experimental evidence on group accuracy. In B. Grofman, & G. Owen (Eds.), *Decision research 2* (pp. 129-157).

Heath, C., & Gonzalez, R. (1995). Interaction with others increases decision confidence but not decision quality: Evidence against information collection views of interactive decision making. *Organisational Behaviour and Human Decision Processes, 61*(3), 305-326.

Hewson, D. (1999, November). Start talking and get to work. *Business Life*, 72-76.

Janis, I. (1982). *Groupthink: Psychological studies of policy decisions and fiascoes*. Boston: Houghton-Miffin.

Kopelman, R. E. (1986). Objective feedback. In E. A. Locke (Ed.), *Generalising from laboratory to field settings*. Lexington Books.

Marakas, G. M. (1999). *Decision support systems in the 21ˢᵗ century.* Englewood Cliffs, NJ: Prentice Hall Inc.

Nichols-Hoppe, K. T., & Beach, L. R. (1990). The effects of test anxiety and task variables on predecisional information search. *Journal of Research in Personality, 24,* 163-172.

Nonaka, I., & Takeuchi, H. (1995). *The knowledge creating company: How Japanese companies create the dynamics of innovation.* New York: Oxford University Press.

Panko, R., & Kinney, S. (1992). Dyadic organisation communication:Is the dyad different? In *Proceedings of the 25ᵗʰ Hawaii International Conference on Systems Sciences,* HI (pp. 244-253).

Payne, J. W. (1976). Task complexity and contingent processing in decision making: An information processing and protocol analysis. *Organisational Behaviour and Human Performance, 16,* 366-387.

Payne, J. W. (1982). Contingent decision behaviour. *Psychological Bulletin, 92* (2), 382-402.

Remus, W. (1996). Will behavioural research on managerial decision making generalise to managers? *Managerial and Decision Economics, 17,* 93-101.

Schroder, H. M., Driver, M. J., & Streufert, S. (1967). *Human information processing.* Holt, Rinehart and Winston Inc.

Schwartz, D. (1995). The emergence of abstract representation in dyad problem solving. *The Journal of the Learning Sciences, 4*(3), 321-345.

Smith, J. F., Mitchell, T. R., & Beach, L. R. (1982). A cost-benefit mechanism for selecting problem-solving strategies: Some extensions and empirical tests. *Organisational Behaviour and Human Performance, 29,* 370-396.

Sniezek, J. A., & Buckley T. (1995). Cueing and cognitive conflict in judge-advisor decision making. *Organisational Behaviour and Human Decision Processes, 62*(2), 159-174.

Stasser, G., Taylor, L. A., & Hanna, C. (1989). Information sampling in structured and unstructured discussions of three- and six-person groups. *Journal of Personality and Social Psychology, 57,* 67-68.

Stewart, T. A. (1997). *Intellectual capital: The new wealth of organisations.* New York: Doubleday.

Te'eni, D. (1989). Determinants and consequences of perceived complexity in human-computer interaction. *Decision Sciences, 20*(1), 166-181.

Whitecotton, S. M. (1996). The effects of experience and a decision aid on the slope, scatter, and bias of earnings forecasts. *Organisational Behaviour and Human Decision Processes, 66*(1), 111-121.

Wood, R. E. (1986). Task complexity: Definition of the construct. *Organisational Behaviour and Human Decision Processes, 37*(1), 60-82.

Yates, J. F. (1991, November). *JDM Conference presentation*, San Francisco.

Chapter XV

Communities of Practice:
Enhancing Collective Effectiveness

Abstract

The objective of this chapter is to explore the social dynamics and the effectiveness benefits that a community of practice creates for its members in a knowledge-intensive IT industry. Social dynamics is examined in terms of informal and organised forms of socialisation processes. Effectiveness benefits were evaluated in terms of commitment, friendship, community satisfaction, process satisfaction, and trust. The results of the study indicate that organised socialisation had a significant positive impact on all aspects of community effectiveness, but no particularly outstanding effect. The results further indicate that informal socialisation had a stronger positive impact on community effectiveness than organised socialisation, except for process satisfaction. These findings confirm the value of socialisation for effective knowledge organisations, and suggest the need for strategies that would provide encouragement without overformalisation.

Introduction

Knowledge intensive organisations, as well as extraorganisational groups of professionals, are often structured as communities of practice (CoP). These are groups of people that engage in activities that encompass a common interest or goal, and ongoing learning through practice (Hasan & Crawford, 2003). Typically, they employ common practices, use the same tools, communicate in common language, and hold similar beliefs and values.

Most studies concentrate on investigating communities inside an organisation. There is an increasing awareness that knowledge creation and innovation in organisations can be achieved through knowledge sharing among members of such communities of practice (Wenger, 1998). In addition to being creative work units and learning, communities also represent important social structures in organisations. As such, they enable and constrain the actions of individual members through reinforcing preferred-shared beliefs and behaviours and discouraging less preferred ones. In short, they shape the organisational social capital including its norms and relationships. It is assumed that social capital is beneficial as it reduces the cost of doing business and creates opportunity by facilitating coordination and cooperation (Standards Australia, 2001).

The wide range of benefits of communities of learning and practice are so significant that government and corporations are seeking ways to encourage their establishment and continued existence (Mentzas, Apostolou, Young, & Abecker, 2001). Knowledge management (KM) can be used to encourage development of social capital. Socialisation is assumed to enable tacit knowledge, values, and beliefs to be transferred between individuals through shared experience, space, and time (Nonaka, 1998). Through socialising, community members develop relationships. Interactive sessions, including spending time, working together, or attending informal social meetings, provide a chance for participants to relax, have fun, and develop trust. Socialisation is a way to establish an individual status in terms of abilities, skills, and knowledge relative to other members. Interaction also drives the creation and growth of the personal tacit knowledge base of individuals. By seeing other people's perspective and ideas, a new interpretation of what one knows is created.

Many knowledge workers have both organizational and professional affiliations. They are both employees of the organization in which they work and members of professional associations that extend beyond organizational borders. Typically, these extraorganizational communities of practice are groups of individuals who are linked by what they do rather than where and for whom they work (Viehland, 2005). Of particular interest to this study is "IT community of practice," made up of professionals who either work directly in the IT industry or are heavily involved in IT activities at their respective workplaces. So far, there has been very little research conducted on knowledge sharing within such extraorganisational broad, professional-oriented communities of practice. Therefore, the purpose of this chapter is to address the issue by examining empirically the social dynamics and benefits of IT community of practice to its members.

Social Aspects of Communities of Practice

The Concept of Community of Practice

The introductory section of this chapter defines communities of practice (CoPs) as groups in which two or more people regularly engage in sharing and learning, based on common interests (Lesser & Storck, 2001). These communities are usually established in order to provide value to organisations. They are believed to improve business performance by fostering an environment with shared mental models, common understanding, high levels of trust, and mutual obligation (Lesser & Storck, 2001). Such an environment is important for effective person-to-person interactions to take place. It leads to effective knowledge sharing among community members.

According to Handzic and Zhou (2005), trust, group norms, and a sense of common identity are all important factors in building a community of practice. This approach to organisational structuring advocates the formation of centres of expertise for each knowledge domain, discipline, or subject matter speciality. As such, communities of practice can be organised around geographic areas, client industries, types of service, practice specialisations, and so on. They can also be structured around projects and related activities. Within a community, organisations often use a variety of online and off-line discussion means to transfer tacit knowledge among members. The suggested benefits include shared perspective, common language, and context that help individuals to better resolve problems (Sharratt & Usoro, 2003).

Although virtual communication is becoming a popular mode of interaction, many agree that face-to-face conversation remains the most effective method of knowledge transfer. Hence, in addition to utilising information technologies for virtual interaction, some organisations pay attention to the design of physical office space to create a supportive work environment for knowledge sharing and creation. The total work area can be configured into a culturally encouraging working environment. Tea rooms, hot spots, or coffee stations provide social spaces that allow ideas to arise from informal contact and conversations among different groups of people within the organisation. Seating staff, identified as knowledge experts, at key interaction points can also stimulate communication and collaboration.

Social Dynamics

In Chapter XIII we referred to socialisation as the process of communication and interaction between people. We also discussed the function of socialisation from the knowledge exchange perspective (Devlin, 1999), persuasive argumentation theory (Heath & Gonzales, 1995), and group decision-making approach (Marakas, 1999).

More recently, through the work of Weick (1995), the idea of sense making as collective meaning creation has slowly protruded into the world of organisational cognitive science and decision making. Popular interpretations of the term annotate it as mental activities whereby individuals make sense of themselves, others, institutions, and events. It is where individuals reflect and create meaning, based on interpretations of both external and internal interactions. Individuals place themselves within the context of their current situation. It necessitates interaction with others (i.e., social behaviour), which provides both the situational context and opportunities for self-reflection. Sense making is often constructed on cultural pilings held unconsciously in long-term memory.

One of the key differentiating aspects of sense making is that it is necessarily a social phenomenon: its conduct is contingent on the conduct of others, whether those others are imagined or physically present (Woodside, 2001). Sense making is described as a social-constructionist concept (Craig-Lees, 2001). Meaning is created in relation to a social circumstance. Socialisation enables people to create and share their realities and context, not just to transfer discrete information or data. Social participants reinterpret the world and the environment they live in. In addition, the study of sense making is in the throws of a paradigm shift from positivist to constructivist approaches, and it is thus increasing its complexity. It is driven by plausibility rather than accuracy: it does not aim to reduce and deconstruct, but to holistically appreciate and understand. The feasibility of adopting a constructivist concept within a positivist philosophy of organisational cognitive science has been called into question (Craig-Lees, 2001), and empirical evidence has been mixed (Solomon, 1997).

In knowledge management, the SECI model of knowledge creation (Nonaka, 1998) suggests that knowledge creation starts with socialisation, which is the process of converting new tacit knowledge through shared experiences in day-to-day social interaction. Socialisation within the originating "ba" (Nonaka & Konno, 1998) provides a rich and meaningful platform for face-to-face natural interaction. Sometimes labelled as colocated communication, this enables a medium in which multiple senses and means (e.g., tone, eyes, body) can be used to convey knowledge. A chat between employees may well foster the development of trust and provide a foundation for vital creative working.

Collective Effectiveness

There is a large body of group work research dating back through the decades. One widely adopted model is McGrath's (1991) time, interaction and performance (TIP) theory. This theory argues that communities embedded in organisations perform three functions, namely production, well-being, and member support. The production function consists of tasks, such as idea generation and decision making, that contribute to the whole organisation. Community well-being consists of activities that contribute to the development of the community's shared values and behavioural norms. Member support consists of activities that contribute to community members' individual growth and relationships with others.

Another enduring model, which has been well cited and adopted over the years, is authored by Richard Hackman (Thomas, 1999; Vinokur-Kaplan, 1995). Hackman suggests that three criteria drive community effectiveness. First, the results from the community's effort must be of a high enough quality to exceed the standards set for them. For a community to be considered effective, it must produce outcomes that are useful and fulfil the objectives and criteria of the task. Secondly, the social process, which allows the community to function, must maintain or enhance the capability of community members to work together. The community needs to develop personal bonds to build trust and cohesion. A successful community that burns out and refuses to work together again is not effective. This idea that cohesion is important for community effectiveness is quite common (Warkentin, Sayyed, & Hightower, 1997; Watson & Michaelson, 1988). Lastly, the community experience must satisfy the personal motivations of community members. The community must contribute to the growth and development of the individuals, allowing members to learn new things and to satisfy their private needs. Hackman's idea is well supported by Rushmer (1997), who states that an effective community "enhances their own personal growth, quality of life and job satisfaction." Other commentators, like Daft (1992), similarly commented that the important factors of effective communities were "trust, open confrontation of problems, employee empowerment and participation, the design of meaningful work, cooperation between communities, and the full use of human potential."

Furthermore, satisfaction with different facets of the community dynamics is important for effectiveness (Hackman & Oldham, 1975). This includes happiness with members' relationship with other people, or with the community in general. Perceptions of decision-making processes are also relevant (Chidambaram & Kautz, 1993). If a community member is happy with the way the community operates, this will generally result in lower conflict and increased trust, leading to better effectiveness overall. The idea of general cohesion is further explored through examining the level of cooperation and the level of "organisational citizenship." Organisational citizenship is doing things that have not been prescribed as part of any specific person's formal role. It is where people show performance beyond what is required. This includes helping others and other altruistic behaviours such as courtesy and conscientiousness (Organ, 1988). The amount of commitment and trust that the individuals feel towards the community are also important. If the individual is willing to trust the abilities of their community members, a much more inclusive "give take" environment will emerge and people will communicate better. The facilitation of communication could then lead to personal bonds developing and an improvement in community effectiveness.

IT Community Description

The emphasis in this study is on an extraorganisational community of Australian IT professionals whose members either work directly in the IT industry or are heavily involved in IT activities at their respective workplaces. According to Marcus (2001), they are knowledge workers who share the following characteristics: (1) do similar work in different settings and produce knowledge for each other's use; (2) seek new knowledge to understand how to handle a new and/or particularly challenging or unusual situation; (3) require quality assurance for successful knowledge acquisition and incentives for successful knowledge contributions; (4) use networks of contacts to locate experts/expertise; and (5) have little difficulty applying the expertise, once it has been acquired.

To find out how such a community of practice operates and produces value for its members, we surveyed 93 professionals from a variety of companies who all had first-hand everyday experience of work in the IT industry or related activities. The focus was on grassroots people who have to deal with the everyday problems and challenges of work as opposed to management. This was preferred since their roles are more suited for the study of community behaviour than a possibly noninvolved leadership role, which could be the case with management. While this IT focus may potentially limit the general applicability of our findings, it is our assumption that the findings would typically apply to many group work situations. Consequently, results of this study may have applicability to areas beyond the boundaries of just the IT industry.

The membership profile is examined in terms of gender, age, work experience, and field of work. Of the total of 93 surveyed IT professionals, 63% were male and 37% were female. The ratio of female respondents was surprisingly high for a study of the IT industry. Most were within the 21-29 age group (76%), and more than 91% of all respondents were under the age of 30. Given the relatively young age of the sample, the level of work experience is accordingly low. Eighty-five percent of the respondents have had 3 or less than 3 years of work experience. This bias may have an effect on the generalisability of the findings. All the respondents' fields of work were associated with IT in some form. Most were from IT administration/programming (55%) and consulting (17%). The remaining ones were spread among various other areas including customer service, education/training, and engineering (28%). In summary, the average IT community member can be described as being a young male with 3 or less years of experience in the IT industry, and having administration/programming positions.

Empirical Study

Objectives of this Study

When describing the socialisation phase of the knowledge spiral, Nonaka et al. (Nonaka, Toyama, & Konno, 2000) also mentioned the building of personal bonds. Socialisation and originating ba are said to be the source of trust and empathy. Socialisation helps to build relationships, goodwill, and understanding. Through empathy, bonds develop, trust builds, and barriers are broken down. Where there may have been personal conflicts before, there are now constructive dialogues. Through socialisation, an individual transcends the self (Nonaka & Konno, 1998). In simple terms, socialisation builds relationships by "putting yourself in another's shoes" and trying to understand others from their perspective. Interestingly, the "care, love, trust and commitment" that result from socialisation (Nonaka & Konno, 1998) also form a key part of "social processes" in Hackman's model for group effectiveness (Hackman, 1987, 1990) and McGrath's (1991) group well-being and member support functions. In essence, Nonaka implied that socialisation will lead to the appropriate social conditions for effective work groups. Our proposition is that both informal and organised forms of socialisation, emerging from the originating ba, affect group effectiveness. Through building of personal bonds and relationships, trust, commitment, and understanding emerge. The main objective of the current study is to test this proposition empirically.

Research Design and Variables

The general design of this research is that of an exploratory industry survey distributed electronically. We have taken this approach since we feel that while there seems a wealth of anecdotal evidence for KM theories dealing with socialisation, there have been relatively few attempts at industry level empirical validations. The exploratory-survey-based approach is most appropriate, given the nature of the independent variable being examined. Socialisation is, by its nature, a voluntary activity that does not flourish under controlled and restrictive environments, such as those present in laboratory studies.

Drawing from prior literature, we devised new instruments for measuring socialisation and group effectiveness constructs, which are outlined in the following paragraphs. Participants indicated the extent of their agreement with scale items on a five-point Likert scale anchored by values of five (strongly agree) and one (strongly disagree). The scale is essentially self-reporting. A series of rigorous tests were applied to ensure that a reasonable level of reliability and validity is achieved before data analyses were performed.

Socialisation was operationalised by two variables, informal socialisation and organised socialisation, that were the basis of earlier instruments by Bennet (2001) and Anakwe and Greenhaus (1999). The first variable, "informal socialisation," tests the level of socialising and casual interaction. Informal socialisation represents the most innate form of socialisation that occurs naturally. Organised socialisation refers to the amount of socialisation that occurs as part of an organised event by the workplace. This variable attempts to capture the amount of socialisation that occurs as part of company organised events. For further details, see Handzic and Chaimungkalanont (2003).

Community effectiveness was operationalised by six variables: commitment; friendship, community satisfaction, organisational citizenship, process satisfaction, and trust. These were adapted by Chaimungkalanont in a pilot study from the original instrument used by Thomas (1999). The adapted instrument included two variables, "commitment" and "friendship," extracted by a factor analysis from the original cohesion factor and supplements from the pilot study. The instrument used in this study was further modified, compared to previous instruments, by omitting negative aspects of community effectiveness (e.g., conflict) and focusing on positive ones only. A complete list of survey items for group effectiveness is provided in the Appendix to this chapter.

The reliability of the responses to all instrument items was assessed by means of Cronbach alpha coefficients. The informal socialisation instrument obtained a coefficient of 0.77, and organised socialisation 0.72. Commitment showed a reliability score of 0.83, friendship 0.73, community satisfaction 0.75, process satisfaction 0.66, organisational citizenship 0.57, and trust 0.79. Scores above 0.6 are considered to be adequate (Nunnelly, 1978). Only the organisational citizenship construct showed poor reliability, and was consequently excluded from further analysis.

Results

The Pearson r-correlations were computed for all variables of interest in order to determine the extent of the relationships between them. The Pearson r-value represents the effect size or the strength and magnitude of the relationship between two variables (Judd, Smith, & Kidder, 1991). Values of r can range between 0 and 1. Larger values indicate stronger relationships. According to Cohen (1988), r-values greater than 0.5 are considered "large," between 0.5 and 0.3 "moderate," and less than 0.3 "low." A conventional level of $p<0.05$ was adopted to establish statistically significant correlations.

The results of the analysis performed indicate that informal socialisation was significantly correlated with all dependant variables. This is not a surprising result, considering that effective interpersonal bonds play a significant role in all of these factors. Some relationships were not merely significant, but also of an appreciable magnitude. The r-value for overall community effectiveness (0.51) indicates a large relationship with informal socialisation. The r-values for commitment (0.44), community satisfaction (0.48), and trust (0.48) also show a significant amount of covariance between these factors and informal socialisation. The r-values for friendship (0.34) and process satisfaction (0.25) show somewhat weaker relationships of informal socialisation with these variables.

The analysis further found that organised socialisation was significantly correlated with all community effectiveness variables, but had no particularly outstanding relationship. The r-value for overall community effectiveness (0.41) indicates a moderate relationship with organised socialisation. The r-values for commitment (0.35), friendship (0.29), community satisfaction (0.36), process satisfaction (0.31), and trust (0.26) show similarly weak relationships. It appears that organised socialisation is a poorer indicator of community effectiveness than informal socialisation, as organised socialisation had lower correlations on all but one of the variables measured-process satisfaction.

In summary, the results of this study have shown that (1) there is a positive and significant relationship between community effectiveness and socialisation; and that (2) community effectiveness is more strongly associated with informal socialisation than with organised socialisation.

Discussion

In this chapter, we have addressed the issue of social dynamics and group effectiveness in the context of IT community of practice. We have adopted Nonaka's (1998)

SECI model as a theoretical framework for our empirical investigation, and focused on the idea of utilising socialisation to improve an organisation's social capital. The results of the study indeed reinforce the idea that socialisation is important for community effectiveness in knowledge intensive organisations.

As expected, a higher level of socialisation meant a higher level of community effectiveness. Socialisation tends to further develop personal bonds between team members as individual people, not just as coworkers. Through empathy and personal bonds, factors that are important to the inner workings of the team, like trust and commitment, grow and strengthen. Implications for managers include increasing the use of socialisation-inducing techniques in order to improve a team struggling with low morale and lacking cohesion.

The key finding of this study is a large and significant relationship between informal socialisation and community effectiveness. Socialisation was found to be a particularly important factor to commitment, community satisfaction, and trust. There is also significant support for organised socialisation. A moderate, but significant relationship was found between organised socialisation and community effectiveness. An interesting finding is that organised socialisation was more strongly associated with process satisfaction than informal socialisation. Overall, these are particularly significant and important findings in a KM landscape that is rich in theory and rhetoric, but scarce in empirical evidence.

The strong and significant finding relating informal socialisation and community effectiveness is indicative of why management would be so interested in maximising the level of socialisation. The idea itself is not revolutionary. The ancient Greek philosophers tended to gather around town squares to socialise and contemplate. However, informal "water-cooler" socialisation in the workplace has long been ignored as an important value-creating process for a company (Yavuz & Heidelman, 1999).

The explanation for organised socialisation's relatively poorer showing may be found in that communities of practice and learning blossom in an open climate, and that formalisation can often serve to constrict this blooming rather than promote it. Yet, knowledge management dictates that we attempt to harness the power of socialisation by finding methods to encourage an increase in socialisation. This form of socialisation was termed organised socialisation in that it artificially manufactured situations where employees have an opportunity to socialise. In a way, it is formally creating an environment fit for informal relationships to develop. The results of this study indicate that organised socialisation does contribute significantly to community effectiveness, as shown by the correlation coefficients. Thus, organised socialisation does indeed, to a point, influence the levels of collective effectiveness in the workplace, as predicted by our theoretical model. This provides support for the notion that organised socialisation works, albeit at a much lower level of effectiveness than informal.

While this research has established a clear relationship between socialisation and community effectiveness, an unanswered question remains relating to the relationship between community effectiveness and business performance. Some authors suggest that a communal organisational culture increases the firm's capacity to learn, grow, and improve (Handzic & Agahari, 2003). Other authors dispute the ability of work communities to create new knowledge, and suggest that such groups can learn only knowledge that is already embedded in the community, bounded by their task, culture, and history (Von Krogh, Ichijo, & Nonaka, 2000). A recent case study demonstrates that communities of practice and learning may have a wide range of benefits (Hasan & Crawford, 2003). However, more work is needed in order to determine if such communities are economically and socially viable in specific situations.

Finally, some caution must be exercised when interpreting current research findings, due to a number of limiting factors. One of the limitations of a quantitative study like this is that while it is able to establish a relatively clear picture of relationships between phenomena, it is less adept at explaining the reasons behind it. Future qualitative research needs to be conducted to explore the exact reasons why sociali-sation tends to lead to a higher level of community effectiveness. Other limitations include the use of a relatively undeveloped measuring instrument, the inability to establish causality, the limited demographic and relatively small sample size in the study. Future research is necessary to address these limitations and extend current study to other KM contexts and issues.

Conclusion

This study, reported in this chapter, has demonstrated the importance of informal socialisation for the effectiveness of communities of practice, especially for com-mitment, community satisfaction, citizenship, and trust. These findings make several important contributions to knowledge management research and practice.

For research, they contribute important and previously lacking empirical evidence confirming the value of informal socialisation in effective knowledge organisations. Management often finds theoretical, qualitative research insightful, but is wary about basing decisions on it, fearing the fallibility of the logic and the, often, lack of strongly quantified data (Nancarrow, Moskvin, & Shankar, 1996). These presented results represent a small step towards filling the huge void of empirical data in KM. They clearly show that the informal unstructured nature of socialisation is critical for promoting community effectiveness.

For practice, they suggest that a set of interrelated strategies, enabling and encourag-ing continued informal socialisation, need to be formulated. The key is to provide encouragement without delving into overly formal or even coercive practices.

Organisations must strike a balance between giving too little encouragement to socialisation and enforcing socialisation. Spontaneous and informal socialisation can only occur if the environment is right. Organisations should strive to provide the best environment for encouraging and fostering socialisation and, by extension, community effectiveness. Only then will free-flowing socialisation emerge, and the full value of knowledge management be realised.

References

Anakwe, U. P., & Greehaus, J. H. (1999). Socialisation of employees: Content perspective. *Journal of Managerial Issues*, *11*(3).

Bennet, R. (2001). Ba as the determinant of sales force effectiveness: An empirical assessment of the applicability of the Nonaka-Takeuchi model to the management of the selling function. *Marketing Intelligence and Planning*, *19*(3).

Chidambaram, L., & Kautz, J. A. (1993). Defining common ground: Managing diversity through electronic meeting systems. In *Proceedings of the 14th Annual Conference on Information Systems*.

Cohen, J. (1988). *Statistical power analysis for the behavioural science* (2nd ed.). NJ: Lawrence Erlbaum.

Craig-Lees, M. (2001). Sense making: Trojan horse? Pandora's box? *Psychology and Marketing*, *18*(5).

Daft, R. (1992). *Organisation theory and design* (4th ed.). St Paul, MN: West.

Devlin, K. (1999). *Infosense: Turning information into knowledge.* New York: W.H. Freeman and Company.

Hackman, J. R. (1990). *Groups that work (and those that don't): Creating conditions for effective teamwork.* San Francisco: Jossey-Bass.

Hackman, J. R. (1987). The design of work teams, In Lorsch (Ed.) *Handbook of Organisational behaviour.* Englewood Cliffs, NJ: Prentice-Hall.

Hackman, J. R., & Olham, G. R. (1975). Development of the job diagnostic survey. *Journal of Applied Psychology*, *60*, 159-170.

Handzic, M., & Agahari, D. (2003, July 14-15). A knowledge sharing culture. In *Proceedings of the Knowledge Management Aston Conference (KMAC 2003)*, Birmingham, UK (pp. 31-41).

Handzic, M., & Chaimungkalanont, M. (2003, September). The impact of socialisation on organisational creativity. In *Proceedings of the European Conference on Knowledge Management (ECKM 2003)*, Oxford, UK.

Handzic, M., & Zhou, A. Z. (2005). *Knowledge management: An integrative approach.* Oxford, UK: Chandos Publishing.

Hasan, H., & Crawford, K. (2003). Distributed communities of learning and practice. In H. Hasan, & M. Handzic (Eds.), *Australian studies in knowledge management.* Wollongong: UOW Press.

Heath, C., & Gonzalez, R. (1995). Interaction with others increases decision confidence but not decision quality: Evidence against information collection views of interactive decision making. *Organisational Behaviour and Human Decision Processes, 61*(3), 305-326.

Judd, C. M, Smith, E. R., & Kidder, L. H. (1991). *Research methods in social relations.* FL: Harcourt Brace.

Lesser, E. L., & Storck, J. (2001). Communities of practice and organisational performance. *IBM Systems Journal, 40*(4), 831-41.

Marakas, G. M. (1999). *Decision support systems in the 21st century.* Englewood Cliffs, NJ: Prentice Hall Inc.

Markus, M. L. (2001). Toward a theory of knowledge reuse: Types of knowledge reuse situations and factors in reuse success. *Journal of Management Information Systems, 18*(1), 57-93.

McGrath, J. E. (1991). Time, interaction and performance (TIP): A theory of groups. *Small Group Research, 22*(2), 147-174.

Mentzas, G., Apostolou, D., Young, R., & Abecker, A. (2001). Knowledge network: A holistic solution for leveraging corporate knowledge. *Journal of Knowledge Management, 5*(1), 94-106.

Nancarrow, C., Moskvin, A., & Shankar, A. (1996). Bridging the great divide the transfer of technique. *Marketing Intelligence and Planning, 14*(6).

Nonaka, I., & Konno, N. (1998). The concept of ba: Building a foundation for knowledge creation. *California Management Review, 40*(3), 40-54.

Nonaka, I. (1998). The knowledge-creating company, In *Harvard Business Review on knowledge management.* Boston: Harvard Business School Press.

Nonaka, I., Toyama, R., & Konno, N. (2000). SECI, ba and leadership: A unified model of dynamic knowledge creation. *Long Range Planning, 33.*

Nunnelly, J. C. (1978). *Psychometric Theory* (2nd ed.). New York: McGraw Hill.

Organ, D. W. (1988). *Organisational citizenship behaviour: The good soldier syndrome.* Lexington Books.

Rushmer, R. (1997). How do we measure the effectiveness of team building? Is it good enough? Team management systems—A case study. *Team Performance Management, 3*(4).

Sharratt, M., & Usoro, A. (2003). Understanding knowledge-sharing in online communities of practice. *Electronic Journal of Knowledge Management, 1*(2), 187-96.

Solomon, P. (1997). Discovering information behaviour in sense making. *Journal of The American Society for Information Science, 48*(12).

Standards Australia. (2001). *Knowledge management: A framework for succeeding in the knowledge era.* Sydney: Standards Australia International Limited.

Thomas, D. (1999). Cultural diversity and work group effectiveness: An experimental study. *Journal of Cross-Cultural Psychology, 30*(2).

Viehland, D. (2005). ISExpertNet: Facilitating knowledge sharing in the information systems academic community. *Issues in Informing Science and Information Technology,* 441-450.

Vinokur-Kaplan, D. (1995). Treatment teams that work (and those that don't): An application of Hackman's model to interdisciplinary teams in psychiatric hospitals group effectiveness. *Journal of Applied Behavioural Science, 31*(1).

Von Krogh, G., Ichijo, K., & Nonaka, I. (2000). *Enabling knowledge creation.* New York: Oxford University Press.

Warkentin, M. E., Sayyed, L., & Hightower, R. (1997). Virtual teams versus face-to-face teams: An exploratory study of Web-based conference system. *Decision Sciences, 28*(4).

Watson, W.E., & Michaelson, L. K (1988). Group interaction behaviour that affect group performance on an intellectual task. *Group and Organisation Studies, 13,* 495-516.

Weick, K. (1995). *Sensemaking in organisations.* Thousand Oaks, CA: Sage.

Wenger, E. (1998). *Communities of practice.* Cambridge: Cambridge University Press.

Woodside, A. G. (2001). Editorial: Sense making in marketing organisations and consumer psychology; Theory and practice. *Psychology and Marketing, 18*(5).

Yavuz, E. M., & Heidelman, D. (1999). Knowledge management: The office water cooler of the 21st century. *Medical Marketing and Media, 34*(4).

Appendix: List of Survey Items
for Group Effectiveness

1. I would like to do things with members of my team outside work

2. Sometimes I think I will not be able to express my ideas in front of my team members

3. I feel like I am friends with other members of the group

4. I feel that everyone gets along well

5. On the whole, I would be willing to work with my team members on another company project

6. I am satisfied with the amount of support and guidance I receive from the team

7. On the whole, I would be willing to have my team members represent me

8. I am satisfied with the chance that being on this team gives me to know people better

9. There is good communication between the team members

10. An atmosphere of trust exists in my team

11. I feel that my team is more interesting to work with than   most

12. I am satisfied with the overall quality of my relationship with the team

13. Members of my team take time to listen to each other's problems and worries

14. I feel involved and part of the team

15. I am satisfied with the way my team makes decisions

16. Members of my team cooperate to get the work done

17. I always say what is on my mind at team meetings

18. Members of my team help others who have heavy workloads

19. Members of my team are very willing to share information with other team members about work

20. The group was able to work effectively together to get the task done

21. If I was given the opportunity I would switch to another team

22. I am satisfied with who is on my team

23. I am satisfied with the degree of respect and fair treatment I receive from other team members

24. I am satisfied with the way conflicts are resolved in my team

25. The individual personalities of the members of my team seem compatible

26. I would like to work with the members in my group again

27. The group enabled me to pick up/learn things easier

28. We are comfortable with the roles we play in our team

29. Members of my team help others who have been absent

30. I am satisfied with the way work is divided in my team

31. On the whole, I would rely on my team members in an emergency situation

32. In team meetings, I often don't speak up even though I have a good idea

Chapter XVI

Mode of Socialisation:
Comparing Effects of Informal and Formal Socialisation on Organisational Performance

Abstract

The objective of this chapter is to compare, through an industry survey, the impact of informal and formal modes of socialisation on organisational competitive perfor-mance. The results of the study show a strong and significant positive relationship between informal as well as formal modes of socialisation and creative performance. The results also indicate that informal socialisation had a stronger positive effect on creativity than formal socialisation. These findings confirm the value of socialisation in innovative organisations, and suggest the need for strategies that would provide its encouragement without coercion.

Introduction

Knowledge is considered to be a key factor for achieving the sustained organisational competitive advantage in the new economy. Yet, while the importance of knowledge for organisational success (or survival) is widely acknowledged, there is far less clear understanding about how to manage it towards accomplishing this end. Many past knowledge management projects that focused solely on technology, failed to deliver on its promises. Therefore, organisations are looking for answers about how can we deliver organisational performance and innovation through knowledge management apart from technological solutions. This study addresses the issue by empirically investigating the potential impact of socialisation among employees on organisational creativity.

Socialisation forms a vital component of Nonaka's (1998) knowledge creation model. It is also found in some other process-orientated knowledge management frameworks under different names (e.g., social learning, knowledge sharing, etc.). Socialisation is assumed to enable tacit knowledge to be transferred between individuals through shared experience, space, and time. Examples include spending time, working together, or informal social meetings. More importantly, socialisation drives the creation and growth of personal tacit knowledge base. By seeing other people's perspective and ideas, a new interpretation of what one knows is created.

In theory, socialisation is considered an important value-creating process. However, in practice, it has been overshadowed by knowledge capture and storage, driven largely by advances in information technology. While these processes are certainly important components of the overall knowledge management effort, companies must go beyond acquiring, accumulating, and utilising existing knowledge, and focus on enabling new knowledge creation for innovation. The unifying thread among various theoretical views is the perception that creativity and innovation are the key drivers of the organisational long-term economic success. By moving deliberately towards enabling creativity and by turning individual creativity into innovativeness for everyone, firms may ensure their long-term advancement and business success.

There is a particularly great importance in continuous innovation and knowledge creation in the hypercompetitive industries. (Ilinitch, D'Aveni, & Lewin, 1996). In this time of change, best practices may become worst practices in little time, and today's wisdom may become tomorrow's folly. Only with effective and relentless creation of knowledge can these companies compete at the forefront. A means by which creativity could be fostered and new knowledge encouraged needs to be defined. Therefore, this paper aims to look at whether and how socialisation may drive and induce creative knowledge in a typical knowledge intensive organisation such as IT.

Socialisation, Creativity, and
Organisational Competitive Performance

Socialisation

The following section briefly summarises the discussion on socialisation presented earlier in the book in Chapters XIII and XV. First, we defined socialisation as the process of communication and interaction between people. Then, we presented different existing perspectives on the issue including knowledge exchange (Devlin, 1999), persuasive argumentation (Heath & Gonzales, 1995), group decision making (Marakas, 1999), sense making (Weick, 1995), and knowledge creation spiral (Nonaka, 1998; Nonaka & Konno, 1998) approaches.

We also looked at some of the suggested benefits of socialisation in terms of taking new information about the focal object or situation into one's context (Devlin, 1999), shifting one's initial position on a given issue from collection of novel persuasive arguments (Heath & Gonzales, 1995), synergic effects of collaborative activities (Marakas, 1999), the creation of shared meaning (Weick, 1995), relationships and trust building (Nonaka & Konno, 1998). Finally, we recognised two different forms of socialisation (virtual and face-to-face) as both being effective ways to transfer knowledge.

According to Handzic and Zhou (2005), regardless of what form of interaction is used, regular cross-team meetings can foster the sharing of lessons learnt or innovation. Storytelling is considered a valuable technique that may be used to describe complex issues, explain events, present perspectives, and communicate experiences. Strategic conversations are suggested to provide a valuable means for idea generation. They can contribute particularly to planning, by connecting and integrating diverse perspectives of the organisation and its environment.

Creativity and Innovation

The literature offers diverse conceptual definitions of creativity. Tomas (1999) defines it in terms of the generation of original ideas. In contrast, Shalley and Perry-Smith (2001) argue that it is not enough to only be original. Also, appropriateness is vital in order to distinguish creative ideas from surreal ideas that may be unique, but have unlawful or highly unrealistic implications. Furthermore, a restricted definition of the concept focuses solely on rare revolutionary and paradigm shifting ideas, while a looser definition includes useful evolutionary contributions that refine and apply existing paradigms (Shneiderman, 2000).

There are also differences among researchers with respect to the way in which creative ideas are generated. Three major perspectives offered by Shneiderman (2000) include inspirationalist, structuralist, and situationalist views. Inspirationalist approach emphasises dramatic breakthrough and intuitive aspects of creative idea generation. Structuralist perspective emphasises the importance of previous work and methodological techniques to explore possible solutions. Situationalist view emphasises the social context as a key part of the creative idea generation process. Another classification of various theories recognises psychoanalytical, behavioral, and process orientation perspectives on creativity (Marakas, 1999). Psychoanalytical perspective maintains that creative idea generation is a preconscious mental activity, behavioural perspective argues that it is a natural response to stimuli, and the process orientation view sees it as a thought process that can be improved through instruction and practice.

Innovation is intertwined with creativity, and the two are often used with only hazy distinctions. Often, both are merely processes through which knowledge is developed and transformed into business value (Gurteen, 1998). A useful definition is that of creativity as the generation and emergence of new ideas. It is thinking outside the box, coming up with novel ideas through divergent, tangential thinking. Conversely, innovation is turning ideas into products, services, and processes (Couger, 1995). Innovation involves refining the ideas begot from creativity, and then transforming them into useful solutions. Innovation requires convergent thought in applying new concepts to certain problems and situation. Practically, the term innovation represents creativity in action.

The main facets of innovation, proposed by influential economist Joseph Schumpeter at the beginning of the century, are still perhaps the best reference for defining innovation (Gallouj, 1998). This was refined and extended by Johannessen et al. (Johannessen, Olsen, & Lumpkin, 2001) to give six means of innovation. They are new products, new services, new methods of production, new market openings, new sources of supply, and new ways of organisation. Of these six, services, methods of production, and ways of organisation are most pertinent to the current research, as we wish to study the incremental creativity and innovation. New products, market openings, and supply sources are more the realm of strategic innovation and creativity.

Organisational Competitive Performance

It is often said that implementing the creation of new ideas is the key for many companies' survival in the rapidly changing world (Nonaka, Toyama, & Konno, 2000). Within this framework, creativity and innovation supplant traditional means as the leverage for oganisational performance. Not only does creativity enable building new innovations, it is also needed, since most business problems cannot be fully defined; the entire problem is unknown and yet needs to be solved. While a hunch could be appropriate, the true process is more complex. Rather, an inexplicable mental model is formed in the mind and the problem solved in that context, with all its uncertainties. Such problems are frequent, and solving them requires a great deal of systematic exhaustive lateral thinking.

While the link between creativity, innovation, and performance should seem intuitive, its acceptance has been questioned in some circles. Diehl and Stroebe (1991) reported significant productivity losses in so-called idea-generating groups. On the contrary, Osborn (1957) suggests that brainstorming may double the amount of ideas generated, while Bossink (2002) found it to be detrimental to the overall level of innovation in their study. Such conflicting evidence should be noted and taken into consideration when one examines the value of creativity. While creativity seems to be unconditionally desirable, it is not always so (Nakamura, 2000). Some of the reasons for this include creativity may risk existing products and investment in products. For every breakthrough and new innovative goods, there are multitudes that become obsolete. Other issues with creativity include difficulty in measuring it and the inherent risk associated with enacting on innovation. So, while creativity is assumed to be a positive asset for modern organisations, this idea is not entirely undisputed.

Empirical Study

Study Objectives

The aim of this chapter is to find effective ways to induce and facilitate creativity, focusing particularly on evolutionary creativity, as it is more applicable across all levels of the organisation. From extensive literature in differing fields, there is ample anecdotal evidence that socialisation has a positive effect on creativity. However, very little formal research has been conducted to challenge or affirm this assumption. Yet, theory suggests that socialisation within the originating "ba" provides a rich and meaningful platform for face-to-face "natural" interaction and creativity. According to Nonaka (1998), knowledge is created in socialisation through interaction of different views, competencies, and experiences. Our intention is to test these assumptions empirically.

Subjects and Procedure

The subjects for the study were members of the Australian IT community described previously in Chapter XV. IT was chosen because it is a knowledge intensive industry. It is also a relatively immature industry with a comparatively low entry cost (compared to other manufacturing based industries), leading to a heightened level of competition. Thus, innovation and creative insights can have a tremendous and immediate impact. Simply, the IT industry is where knowledge and creativity play an important role in everyday work, and where a significant amount of teamwork and interpersonal interactions are required. The nature of the tasks in IT means that work is rarely entirely individual in nature.

The exploratory-survey-based approach was employed as most appropriate, given the nature of independent variables examined. Socialisation and creativity, by their nature, do not flourish under controlled and restrictive environments, such as those in laboratory studies. Modified survey forms from Chapter XV were electronically distributed directly to the recipients, who were randomly selected within the stated sampling groups. Survey distributors were used as a go-between to follow up survey completion. A follow-up e-mail was also sent to remind recipients that the survey should be completed, in order to maximise the response rates. Data collection ceased 3 weeks after the surveys were sent. Out of 170 surveys distributed by e-mail, 96 were returned, a response rate of about 57%. This compares well to other e-mail based surveys that, in the late 1990s, had an average response rate of around 30% (Sheehan, 2001). Three surveys were not correctly completed and were excluded from further analysis.

Research Design and Variables

As before in Chapter XV, survey instruments for measuring socialisation and creativity constructs were based on prior literature (Anakwe & Greenhaus, 1999; Bennet, 2001). However, for the purpose of this study, socialisation was operationalised by three variables: "personal tendency towards socialisation," "informal socialisation," and "formal socialisation."

Once again, variable "informal socialisation" tests the level of socialising and casual interaction. It represents the most innate form of socialisation that occurs naturally. In contrast, formal socialisation refers to the amount of socialisation that occurs as part of an organised event by the workplace. Accordingly, this variable attempts to capture the amount of socialisation that occurs as part of company organised events. Closer investigation of the items for personal tendency reveals that the common thread amongst these items is that they focus more on the individual attitudes towards the workplace rather than socialisation behaviour in the workplace itself.

Creativity has been operationalised by the general amount of creativity and innovation shown at group level. The measure was developed by drawing on factors stated in literature (Amabile, Conti, Coon, Lazenby, & Herron, 1996), along with adaptations from some of the sample scales. Creativity has been itemised as a self-reporting scale of the level creativity within the workplace. That is the extent to which the individual perceives creativity exists in, and innovation is introduced into the workplace. List of specific survey items for measuring all four variables of interest is given in the appendix to this chapter.

Data Analysis

Participants responded to survey questions by indicating the extent of their agreement with sets of given items on a five-point Likert scale (5-strongly agree and 1-strongly disagree). The survey responses collected were combined into one file, and the means for each variable calculated from the response to each of the items. Strenuous validation and reliability testing on each of the scales followed, and refactoring of scales and subscales occurred where necessary. The reliability of the responses to all instrument items was assessed by means of Cronbach alpha coefficients. The personal tendency instrument obtained a coefficient of 0.73, informal socialisation 0.77, formal socialisation 0.72, and creativity 0.77. Scores above 0.6 are considered to be adequate (Nunnelly, 1978). Correlation and regression testing were performed to answer each of the research questions.

Results

A descriptive analysis of responses for socialisation and creativity was performed first to identify any prevailing patterns. The overall mean score for informal socialisation was 3.89 out of 5 (std.dev=0.60, min=2.40, max=4.80); for formal socialisation 3.32 (std.dev=0.72, min=1.60, max=4.40); and for personal tendency towards socialisation 3.86 (std.dev= 0.63, min=1.60, max=4.80). The overall mean score for creativity was 3.36 (std.dev=0.64, min=1.20, max=4.80). This amounts to the majority of the mean scores lying somewhere between the high end of "neutral" and "agree."

To test the hypothesised relationship between socialisation and creativity, the Pearson correlation coefficients were computed next. All three socialisation variables showed significant correlations with creativity ($p<0.005$). The results indicate a large positive correlation between creativity and informal socialisation ($r=0.63$), and moderate positive correlations between creativity and personal tendency towards socialisation ($r=0.43$) and formal socialisation ($r=0.44$).

In view of significant correlations between the variables, further tests were performed to identify the main factors affecting creativity. This analysis was performed using a regression model. The regression results indicate that the independent variables jointly explained nearly half variance in the dependent variable (R-square=0.45, F=23.778, p<0.001). Examining the individual independent variables, in turn, revealed some interesting results. Both informal and formal socialisation were found to have significant effects on creativity. However, the effect of informal socialisation was much stronger (beta=0.51, t=5.55, p=0.000) than that of formal socialisation (beta=0.19, t= 2.059, p=0.042). There was no significant direct effect found of personal tendency towards socialisation on creativity (beta=0.10, t=1.068 p=0.288).

In summary, the results of this study have shown that: (1) IT professionals have fairly favourable attitudes towards socialisation; (2) they engage in both informal and formal modes of socialisation; (3) there is a significant positive relationship between socialisation and creativity; and that (4) creativity is more strongly associated with informal socialisation than with formal socialisation.

Discussion

In this chapter, we have explored relative contributions of informal and formal modes of socialisation to creative performance in the context of a knowledge intensive IT industry. As predicted by Nonaka's (1998) SECI model, the study found that socialisation is indeed an important factor in influencing creative performance. This is especially evidenced by a large and highly significant relationship found between informal socialisation and creativity. That the informal socialisation alone explained over 39% of creativity's variance is a particularly significant and important finding in a KM landscape that is rich in theory and rhetoric, but scarce in empirical evidence. There is also significant support for formal socialisation. Formal socialisation explained about 6% of the variance in creativity. Personal attitudes towards socialisation had no significant direct effect on the level of creativity in the workplace. The exact nature of this factor will need to be further explored.

The strong and significant finding relating to informal socialisation and creativity is indicative of why management would be so interested in maximising the level of effective socialisation. The idea itself is not revolutionary. The ancient Greek philosophers tended to gather around town squares to socialise and contemplate. However, informal "water-cooler" socialisation in the workplace has long been ignored as an important value-creating process for a company (Yavuz & Heidelman, 1999).

This "forgotten" idea, that informal socialisation, the processes of building personal relationships and empathy, forms the basis of creativity and knowledge creation, has been strongly supported by the empirical results of this study. Employees who share the vision and empathise with the ideas are naturally intrinsically motivated: they do what they love and love what they do. Such employees inevitably show more creativity (Amabile, 1997). In promoting a deeper intrinsic interest and desire in an idea, the full benefits of creativity will be realised.

A plausible explanation for formal socialisation's relatively poor showing may be found in that creativity blossoms in an open, almost chaotic climate, and that coercion can often serve to constrict innovation rather than promote it. Yet, knowledge management dictates that we attempt to harness the power of socialisation by finding methods to encourage an increase in socialisation. This form of socialisation was termed formal socialisation in that it artificially manufactured situations where employees had an opportunity to socialise. In a way, it is formally creating an environment fit for informal relationships to develop. The results of this study indicate that formal socialisation does contribute significantly to creativity, as shown by the regression model. Thus, formal socialisation does indeed, to a point, influences the levels of creativity in the workplace, as predicted by our theoretical model. This provides support for the notion that formal socialisation works, albeit at a much lower level of effectiveness that informal.

However, caution must be exercised when interpreting these findings due to a number of limiting factors. These include limitations inherent in a quantitative study, the use of a relatively undeveloped measuring instrument, inability to establish causality, limited demographics, and a relatively small sample size. While this study was able to establish a relatively clear picture of relationships between phenomena, future qualitative research needs to be conducted to explore the exact reasons behind it. In addition, our regression model indicates that while socialisation forms a significant part in explaining and influencing creativity, it is by no means the only factor. The relatively large R-square value, of around 45% for the regression model, confirms that there is certainly a highly significant relationship. What it does not do, however, is provide an explanation for the remaining 55% of unexplained variance. It is this 55% of creativity that needs to be examined in future research.

One of the key questions that needs to be asked is whether the poor effectiveness of formal socialisation was directly due to the higher level of coercion associated with formal socialisation. A study into the relationship between levels of coercion with formal socialisation and creativity would be of great interest to management. In KM, one of the key ideas that gets around is the importance of culture. This idea, like most concepts in KM, is not at all well defined, and yet it is often touted as one of the most vital factors in successful and continuous knowledge creation and creativity (Davenport, De Long, & Breers, 1998; Yavuz & Heidelman, 1999). Management support and encouragement (Davenport & Prusak, 1998), as well as freedom and availability of time for creativity (Nonaka & Konno, 1998), are seen as playing an important role in knowledge culture. Future research is required in order to determine the exact nature of this knowledge culture, and to formulate instruments that will reliably measure it.

Conclusion

This chapter has demonstrated that the chaotic, unstructured nature of socialisation is critical for promoting creativity. However, such spontaneous and informal socialisation can only occur if the environment is right. Informal events provide environment conducive to generation and transfer of high-value tacit knowledge, as well as spark for fresh ideas and responsiveness to changing environment. However, it would be a mistake for organisations to think that they can *make* socialisation happen. In the end, socialisation is up to the individuals' own free will. Therefore, organisations must strike a balance between giving too little encouragement to socialisation and enforcing socialisation. They can only strive to provide the best environment for enabling and fostering informal socialisation and thus, creativity.

References

Amabile, T. M. (1997). Motivating creativity in organisations: On doing what you love and loving what you do. *California Management Review, 40*(1).

Amabile, T. M., Conti, R., Coon, H., Lazenby, J., & Herron, M. (1996). Assessing the work environment for creativity. *Academy of Management Journal, 39*(5).

Anakwe, U. P., & Greehaus, J. H. (1999). Socialisation of employees: Content perspective. *Journal of Managerial Issues, 11*(3).

Bennet, R. (2001). Ba as the determinant of sales force effectiveness: An empirical assessment of the applicability of the Nonaka-Takeuchi model to the management of the selling function. *Marketing Intelligence and Planning, 19*(3).

Bossink, B. A. (2002). Innovative quality management practices in the Dutch construction company. *International Journal of Quality and Reliability Management, 19*(2).

Couger, J. D. (1995). *Creative problem solving and opportunity finding.* Danvers, MA: Boyd and Fraser Publishing Co.

Craig-Lees, M. (2001). Sense making: Trojan horse? Pandora's box? *Psychology and Marketing, 18*(5).

Davenport, T. H., De Long, D. W., & Breers, M. C. (1998, winter). Successful knowledge management projects. *Sloan Management Review,* 43-57.

Davenport, T. H., & Prusak, L. (1998). *Working knowledge.* Boston: Harvard Business School Press.

Devlin, K. (1999). *Infosense: Turning information into knowledge.* New York: W.H. Freeman and Company.

Diehl, M., & Stroebe, W. (1991). Productivity loss in idea generating groups: Tracking down the blocking effect. *Journal of Personality and Social Psychology, 61*(3).

Gallouj, F. (1998). Innovation in reverse. *European Journal of Innovation Management, 1*(3).

Gurteen, D. (1998). Knowledge, creativity and innovation. *Journal of Knowledge Management, 2*(1).

Handzic, M., & Zhou, A. Z. (2005). *Knowledge management: An integrative approach.* Oxford, UK: Chandos Publishing.

Heath, C., & Gonzalez, R. (1995). Interaction with others increases decision confidence but not decision quality: Evidence against information collection views of interactive decision making. *Organisational Behaviour and Human Decision Processes, 61*(3), 305-326.

Ilinitch, A. Y., D'Aveni, R. A., & Lewin, A. Y. (1996). New organisational forms and strategies for managing in hyper competitive environments. *Organisation Science.*

Johannessen, J-A., Olsen, B., & Lumpkin, G. T. (2001). Innovation as newness: What is new, how new and new to whom? *European Journal of Innovation Management, 4*(1).

Marakas, G. M. (1999). *Decision support systems in the 21st century.* Englewood Cliffs, NJ: Prentice Hall Inc.

Nakamura, L. I. (2000, July/August). Economics and the new economy; The invisible hand meets creative destruction. *Business Review—Federal Reserve Bank of Philadelphia.*

Nonaka, I. (1998). The knowledge-creating company. In *Harvard Business Review on Knowledge Management.* Boston: Harvard Business School Press.

Nonaka, I., & Konno, N. (1998). The concept of ba: Building a foundation for knowledge creation. *California Management Review, 40*(3), 40-54.

Nonaka, I., Toyama, R., & Konno, N. (2000). SECI, ba and leadership: A unified model of dynamic knowledge creation. *Long Range Planning, 33.*

Nunnelly, J. C. (1978). *Psychometric theory* (2nd ed.). New York: McGraw Hill.

Osborn, A. F. (1957). *Applied imagination.* New York: Scribner.

Shalley, C. E., & Perry-Smith, J. E. (2001). Effects of social-psychological factors on creative performance: The role of informational and controlling expected evaluation and modelling experience. *Organisational Behaviour and Human Decision Processes, 84*(1), 1-22.

Sheehan, K. B. (2001). E-mail survey response rates: A review. *Journal of Computer-mediated Communication, 6*(2).

Shneiderman, B. (2000). Creating creativity: User interfaces for supporting innovation. *ACM Transactions on Computer-Human Interaction, 7*(1), 114-138.

Solomon, P. (1997). Discovering information behaviour in sense making. *Journal of The American Society for Information Science, 48*(12).

Tomas, S. (1999). Creative problem-solving: An approach to generating ideas. *Hospital Material Management Quarterly, 20*(4), 33-45.

Weick, K. (1995). *Sensemaking in organisations.* Thousand Oaks, CA: Sage.

Woodside, A. G. (2001). Editorial: Sense making in marketing organisations and consumer psychology; Theory and practice. *Psychology and Marketing, 18*(5).

Yavuz, E. M., & Heidelman, D. (1999). Knowledge management: The office water cooler of the 21st century. *Medical Marketing and Media, 34*(4).

Appendix: List of Survey Items for Variables of Interest

Informal socialisation items:

People around the office feel very comfortable asking their peers questions about work informally

People in our office usually keeps to themselves unless they need to (reversed)

Generally, how do you feel about the level of socialisation that goes on within your workplace?

There is a large amount of informal face to face exchange of ideas and know-how among the employees at work

People in our office often chat about things other than work (e.g. social life, sports etc.)

Organised socialisation items:

There are organised activities at work where employees are encouraged to socialise and chat informally

Informal events (e.g. company lunches, drinks) are organised where people are encouraged to exchange their ideas about work

Events are organised where employees are encouraged to relax and mingle informally

There are formal occasions where employees can talk openly about any new ideas or share their experiences with others

Tendency towards socialisation items:

There isn't anyone at work I really enjoy chatting with

I share my work- related expertise with others openly

I am able to share my views and opinions with others without concern to rank and seniority. I talk with my coworkers as equals.

I enjoy socialising with my colleagues outside work

We often use social encounters and ad hoc get togethers, such as lunches, to talk about things happening around the workplace and our work experiences

continued on following page

Creativity items:

My workplace encourages me to think creatively

In my work, we're always on the lookout for innovative ideas and new ways to do things

People in our office are set in their ways of thinking and doing things (reversed)

In my office, new ideas and methodologies get introduced periodically

Generally, how would you rate the level of creativity that occurs within your workplace?

Chapter XVII

Organisational Culture:
Determining Knowledge-Sharing Attitudes

Abstract

The aim of the case study reported in this chapter was to provide a cultural audit of a university school as a typical knowledge-based organisation. The subjects were 24 academic staff members who participated in the study on a voluntary basis. The study found multiple cultures coexisting within the school. However, a fragmented type of cultur,e characterised by the lack of social interaction and commonly shared goals among academics, dominated. Contrary to popular belief within the knowledge management field, the study found that none of this diminished the school's competitive position. These findings suggest that there may not be one generic type of culture that ensures organisational success in knowledge society. Rather, success may be contingent upon how well culture fits the business environment in which it competes.

Introduction

There is a widespread agreement that knowledge will become a major factor of organisational success or even survival in the new-age economy. It has been described as the principal fuel and the currency that will drive the economy (Devlin, 1999), a key resource of tomorrow's organisations in the most competitive society we have yet known (Drucker, 1993), and a hidden gold embodied in the minds and hands of organisational participants (Stewart, 1997). In the new economy, companies will increasingly differentiate themselves on the basis of what they know, and how successful they are in making that knowledge productive. Knowledge management is an emergent response to the need to accelerate both the creation of knowledge and its application to physical resources in the battle for competitive advantage or survival. The central task of those concerned with knowledge management is to determine ways to better cultivate, nurture, and exploit knowledge at different levels and in different contexts. Arguably, knowledge management can create sustainable competitive advantage for organisations.

A global model of knowledge management (Arthur Andersen, 1998a) suggests four organisational initiatives-leadership, culture, technology, and measurement-as major enablers to facilitate knowledge management processes and foster the development of new knowledge. A recent literature review (Baxter & Chua, 1999) revealed western theorists' central preoccupation with technology, particularly codified repositories and information processing, as enablers of "explicit" objective and systematic knowledge. On the other hand, eastern theorists seem to have realised that knowledge creation is highly dependent upon corporate culture. Their focus is on "tacit" knowledge that people derive from their experiences and through sharing (Nonaka, 1998; Nonaka & Takeuchi, 1995). However, as we have repeated many times throughout this book, there is increasing recognition among western organisations that a large proportion of knowledge needed by their businesses is not captured (e.g., on hard drives and filing cabinets), but tacit (i.e., kept in the heads of people). Figures range anywhere between 40% and 90%, depending on the information source (Arthur Andersen, 1998b; Hewson, 1999).

It is argued that people's behaviour and values contribute most to the circulation of tacit knowledge in organisations. Yet, little has been known of the ways in which tacit knowledge is actually shared, conditions under which this sharing occurs, or the impact it has on performance. Therefore, it is not surprising that there is a currently growing appreciation and interest in the issues of culture in knowledge management among researchers and practitioners alike. The main purpose of the current study is to provide some insights into values and behaviours that define a culture of a knowledge-intensive organisation. More specifically, the study will (1) conduct a cultural audit of a university school to identify its current organisational values, and

(2) determine congruence between current organisational culture, and normative values and behaviours, as suggested by knowledge management theorists.

Organisational Culture

Classical studies of organisational culture can be divided into two distinct camps. The scientific camp promotes quantitative approaches, information processing paradigm, and the science of strategy. On the other hand, the humanistic camp recognises the importance of the sharing of values among employees and the creation of a corporate culture that determines how a company thinks and behaves. It is argued that shared experiences lead to shared values; culture, in this sense, is a learned product of group experience. Schein (1985) defines culture as a pattern of basic assumptions invented, discovered, or developed by a given group as it learns to cope with its problems of external adaptation and internal integration. These assumptions have worked well enough to be considered valid and therefore, to be taught to new members as the correct way to perceive, think, and feel in relation to those problems. Pfeffer (1981) stresses the importance of beliefs; he considers organisations as systems of shared meanings and beliefs in which critical administrative activity involves the construction and maintenance of belief systems that assure continued compliance, commitment, and positive effect on the part of participants.

More recently, Nonaka and Takeuchi (1995) criticised these theories for having failed to recognise the importance of knowledge in organisations and their potential to change and create. These two theorists argued that the organisation that wishes to cope dynamically with the changing environment, needs to be one that creates knowledge, not merely processes it. The organisational members must not be passive, but active agents of innovation. They suggest that new knowledge will always begin with the individual, and that making personal knowledge available to others is the central activity of the knowledge-creating company. Within this context, the central task of knowledge management is to create an architecture to facilitate the circulation of personal know-how to potential users. According to Garvin (1998), the first step in building a learning organisation is to foster an environment conducive to individual learning, that is, to allow experimentation and time to gain experience and then, to open up boundaries and stimulate the exchange of ideas.

A more general spiral knowledge model (Nonaka & Takeuchi, 1995) assumes that the process of sharing will result in the organisational amplification and exponential growth of working knowledge. The knowledge spiral characterises both the conversion of personal knowledge into a form of collective intelligence, and the subsequent appropriation of that objectified knowledge by others for their own work.

This happens through processes of socialisation, externalisation, internalization, and combination. Socialisation refers to the ways in which tacit knowledge is transferred from one organisational participant to another through shared experiences and empathy. Externalisation describes attempts at articulating personal knowledge for the benefit of others. Internalisation illustrates the acquisition of personal knowledge through learning by doing. Combination refers to the coupling of previously disparate aspects of organisational knowledge by an individual to create new ways of understanding.

Boisot (1998) recognises that much of the knowledge previously thought to be universal is often specific to a culture, and draws back on deeply rooted and value-laden assumptions of human organisational and institutional functions. He argues that culture remains the means by which nongeneric information is transmitted either within a given generation of agents, or from one generation to the next. The extent to which knowledge is structured and shared defines a culture. Some cultures prefer to deal in knowledge that is well codified, abstract, and unambiguous, others thrive on ambiguity and vagueness. The latter often becomes a source of personal power for those who have access to the knowledge relative to those who do not. Some organisations encourage the pursuit of learning through sharing of one's stock of knowledge assets, others through hoarding it. Boisot believes that the structuring of knowledge through acts of codification and abstraction helps knowledge diffusion.

A number of knowledge-management projects involving the establishment of an environment conducive to more effective knowledge creation, transfer, and use were studied by Davenport, De Long, and Beers (1998). These projects tried to build awareness and cultural receptivity to knowledge, as well as establishing initiatives that attempt to change behaviour relating to knowledge, and to improve the knowledge management process. The main findings indicated that a knowledge friendly culture is difficult to create if it does not already exist. It has components such as people with positive orientation to knowledge, intellectually curious, willing, and free to explore, and encouraged in their knowledge creation and use; people who are not inhibited in sharing knowledge, alienated or resentful of the company, and who do not fear that sharing knowledge will cost them their jobs.

The notion that culture is community, an outcome of how people relate to one another, is asserted by Goffee and Jones (1999). Community is built on shared interests and mutual obligations and thrives on cooperation. It can be characterised by two types of human relations: friendliness among the members of a community and its ability to pursue shared objectives. These determine four types of culture: fragmented, networked, mercenary, and communal. Some of the benefits of friendliness are an enjoyable work environment, which helps morale and *esprit de corps,* creativity fostered through teamwork and sharing of information, openness to new ideas, freedom of expression, acceptance of out-of-the-box thinking, and working beyond the formal requirements of a job. Some of the drawbacks may involve a reluctance to disagree or criticise, a tendency to compromise, and the development of cliques. Some of the benefits of shared objectives are a high degree of strategic focus, swift responses to competitive threats, an intolerance of poor performance, a strong sense of trust that can translate into commitment, and loyalty to the organisation's goals and purpose. Among drawbacks, cooperation may not occur if the individual benefits are not clear, or when roles and responsibilities are strictly divided. The authors do not advocate any one type of culture type over another, but instead urge the need to know how to assess one's organisational culture and determine whether it fits the competitive situation.

Recognising the importance of culture in building knowledge management communities, the main objective of the current study is to conduct a cultural audit of a university school, and to assess whether its culture affects its current competitive position. In order to identify a culture, it is necessary to assess a number of aspects of human relationships. The present study, based on Handzic, Parkin, and Van Toorn (2001), will focus particularly on social interaction and community shared values, as these two aspects have been suggested by past literature as most important and generic defining factors.

Empirical Study

Research Design and Variables

A case study approach was chosen as the preferred research method for the current investigation, as it examines a phenomenon of interest in a natural setting. In addition, its main purpose is to describe the things the way they are and draw meaning from social contexts, rather than to investigate cause-and-effect relationships. Therefore, it is considered a suitable approach for the current research, which involves audit of the corporate culture of a specific real-world organisation. A case-study methodology is often associated with research about human affairs (Yin, 1998). The proponents of this approach also argue that the results of a case study can provide a greater level of depth and understanding of many aspects of a social phenomenon than is possible using other methods (Lee, 1989). However, some authors warn that it requires careful planning and attention to detail in order to establish validity (Miles & Huberman, 1994).

Two aspects of corporate culture investigated in this study were *communication* and *collaboration*. Communication was defined in terms of voluntary interaction among organisational members. It was measured in terms of the following: "People here try to make friends and to keep their relationships strong," "People here get along very well," "People in our school often socialise outside the office," "People here really like one another," "When people leave our school, we stay in touch," "People here do favours for others because they like one another," "People here often confide in one another about personal matters," and "Overall, there is a high level of social interaction in our school."

Collaboration was defined in terms of the organisation's ability to pursue shared goals. Particular items included "Our school understands and shares the same business objectives," "Work gets done effectively and productively by our school," "Our school takes action to address poor performance," "Our school's collective will to achieve is high," "When opportunities for competitive advantages arise, our school moves quickly to capitalise on them," "We share the same strategic goals," "We know who our competition is," and "Overall, there is a high sense of community here." Subjects' responses were captured on a 7-point Likert scale, with disagree/agree as anchor points. Low/high communication or collaboration was indicated by scores less/greater than 4, respectively. A score of 4 indicated an undecided position.

The measuring instrument used in this study was based on the instrument previously tested and used in the literature (Goffee & Jones, 1999). Modifications to the wording were made to reflect specifics of the organisation studied, and two new items (overall social interaction and sense of community) were added. The actual survey form is attached in the appendix to this chapter.

Subjects and Procedure

The university school studied offers undergraduate and graduate programs of study, operates a research center and seminars, produces scholarly articles, and is a highly renowned institution. Participants in the study were academic staff with full-time employment who were with the school for more than 6 months and had no intention of leaving it within the next 6 months. To minimise potential threats to validity, questionnaires were distributed to all academics who satisfied the specified criteria, their answers were anonymous, and given without researchers' presence. Participation was voluntary; 24 out of 29 distributed questionnaires were completed and returned; this return rate of 83% ensures that data are representative.

Results

Descriptive analysis of data was performed using a number of techniques, as suggested by Miles and Huberman (1994), to identify patterns and themes, clusters, and

Figure 17.1. Participants' perceptions of communication and collaboration

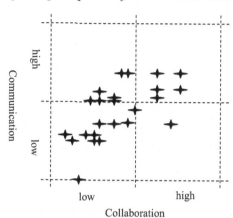

ensure plausibility of findings. Firstly, in order to identify a central tendency in participants' perceptions, the average scores of their responses to relevant questionnaire items were calculated. The mean score obtained for communication was 3.67. The mean score for collaboration was 3.45. Further analysis was performed to identify the most frequently reported scores. These were 2.50 and 2.75 for communication and communality, respectively. Additional analysis found that half of the scores for communication had values below 3.87, and below 3.19 for collaboration. Scores less than 4 indicated that the subjects tended to perceive the level of communication and collaboration in their organisation as being low.

Further analysis of the data was performed by relating individual participants' assessments of two dimensions, communication and collaboration, in order to determine a potential dominant type of culture. Responses were categorised into low/low (fragmented), high/low (networked), low/high (mercenary), and high/high (communal) type of culture, depending on average scores for communication and collaboration dimensions respectively. From the results shown in Figure 17.1, it can be seen that 10 responses clearly fell into fragmented, 4 into networked, 1 into mercenary and 5 into communal categories. The remaining 4 responses were undecided. These results indicate that the majority of participants tended to perceive their organisation as a fragmented culture. Such finding is consistent with the earlier reported perceived tendency towards low communication and low collaboration.

Discussion

Main Findings

The main findings of the current research indicate that the university school investigated here was a predominantly fragmented culture, characterised by the general lack of social interaction, as well as the lack of commonly shared goals among its academic staff. This was demonstrated by low scores obtained for participants' perceptions of both communication and collaboration.

In particular, the study found that participants tended to hold rather negative perceptions of communication. This was demonstrated by average and median response scores below 4 (out of 7), and was also evidenced by the most frequently given response score being well below 4. Such results clearly indicate a low level of social interaction existing among academic staff members in the school. This finding is further supported by notes of one of the researchers, who observed academics for one week during the midsession period. These observations indicated that people mostly worked on their own, they tended to keep their individual office doors shut, or in many cases worked from home. In addition, only a few academics attended a research seminar given by a former colleague during that week. However, small groups of people did occasionally meet for a morning tea or coffee session.

One potential reason for a low level of social interaction found in the school may be that most academics are highly specialised and do their work alone, or with scholars from other institutions who share similar interests (Goffee & Jones, 1999). Indeed, the school teaches 41 different undergraduate and 25 graduate subjects, and has 81 different active research projects. Arguably, that highly specialised researchers and teachers may not necessarily need input from other staff members. They may feel highly confident in both their teaching and research abilities, and may not be inclined to seek advice from others.

The study also found a general lack of shared goals among academics in the school. This was demonstrated by low average, median, and mode scores (all below 4 out of 7) found in participants' perceptions of collaboration. These negative perceptions seem to reflect a low level of consciousness of organisational membership among academic staff. According to Goffee and Jones (1999), this is not surprising. Academics usually have no affinity for the institution that employs them because standards and controls are set outside individual institutions by international professional associations. Furthermore, the career prospects of an academic are more likely to be determined by their research output rather than participation in the shaping of institutional goals and strategies.

A fragmented culture with low communication and collaboration found in the university school studied here is in great contrast to the normative characteristics of a knowledge-enabling culture prescribed by knowledge management literature (Davenport, 1998; Nonaka & Takeuchi, 1995). High levels of social interaction and commonality of goals are regarded by the knowledge management literature as the most important facets of a knowledge creating organisation, and its ability to perform competitively in a new knowledge society (Handzic & Agahari, 2004). Yet, our study found that the lack of social interaction and commonly shared goals did not diminish the competitive position of the university school examined. It is a highly renowned institution, with an excellent research and teaching reputation.

One of the greatest fears in organisations lacking social interaction and common goals is the worry of employees loosing focus or urgency about their work (Goffee & Jones, 1999). However, highly autonomous academics may be motivated rather than alienated by the freedoms of the fragmented organisation, and may guide themselves to ever-higher levels of knowledge and performance. It is, therefore, not surprising that in the context of the university school studied, its fragmented culture was not detrimental to its success. Furthermore, there are reports of similar success in other professional organisations that employ highly trained individuals who have idiosyncratic work styles. This suggests that there is no one generic prescribed model of corporate culture that ensures success, rather, it depends on the context.

Limitations and Directions for Future Research

It is important to note that the current research was limited in its purpose to analysing current culture of the university school in terms of two general aspects of human relationships, communication and collaboration. The study did not address the issue of people's satisfaction with their organisational culture. Yet, successful organisations need both satisfied employees and strong performance. The study also did not attempt to address the question of change from one type of culture to another type of culture. Yet, organisations need to be aware of the dynamic nature of the fit between organisational culture and business environment. Future research may look at some of these issues. Further research is also necessary to systematically address these issues in different tasks and contexts, and among different knowledge workers, if a better understanding of the area is to be achieved.

Conclusion

The aim of the empirical study from this chapter was to provide a cultural audit of a university school as a typical knowledge-based organisation. The study revealed a dominant fragmented type of culture characterised by the lack of social interaction and commonly shared values and goals among academic staff. The study also found that this appears not to have diminished the school's competitive position. Contrary to the prescriptions of knowledge management literature, these findings suggest that there is no one generic type of culture that ensures success. The success of a particular culture may be contingent upon its fit to the business environment within which it operates.

References

Arthur Andersen. (1998a). *The knowledge management practices book.* Arthur Andersen, The Global Best Practices Research Team.

Arthur Andersen. (1998b). *BC knowledge management.* Arthur Andersen, Arthur Andersen Office of Training and Education.

Baxter, J., & Chua, W. F. (1999). Now and the future. *Australian Accounting Review, 9*(3), 3-14.

Boisot, M. H. (1998). *Knowledge assets: Securing competitive advantage in the information economy.* New York: Oxford University Press.

Davenport, T. H, De Long, D. W., & Beers, M. C. (1998). Successful knowledge management projects. *Sloan Management Review, 39*(2), 43-57.

Devlin, K. (1999). *Infosense: Turning information into knowledge.* New York: W.H. Freeman and Company.

Drucker, P. F. (1993). *Post-capitalist society.* New York: Harper Business.

Garvin, D. A. (1998). Building a learning organisation. In *Harvard Business Review on knowledge management.* Boston: Harvard Business School Press.

Goffee, R., & Jones, G. (1999). What holds the modern company together? In *Harvard Business Review on managing people.* Boston: Harvard Business School Press.

Handzic, M., & Agahari, D. (2004). Knowledge sharing culture: A case study. *Journal of Information & Knowledge Management, 3*(2), 135-142.

Handzic, M., Parkin, P., & Van Toorn, C. (2001, September 25-28). Knowledge management: Do we do what we preach? In K. Renaud et al. (Eds.), *Proceedings of the Annual Conference of the South African Institute of Computer Scientists and Information Technologists (SAICSIT 2001),* Pretoria, South Africa (pp. 191-196).

Hewson, D. (1999, November). Start talking and get to work. *Business Life*, 72-76.

Lee, A. (1989). A scientific methodology for MIS case studies, *MIS Quarterly*, *12*(3), 33-50.

Miles, M. B., & Huberman, M. A. (1994). *Qualitative data analysis.* London: Sage.

Nonaka, I. (1998). The knowledge-creating company. In *Harvard Business Review on knowledge management.* Boston: Harvard Business School Press.

Nonaka, I., & Takeuchi, H. (1995). *The knowledge creating company: How Japanese companies create the dynamics of innovation.* New York: Oxford University Press.

Pfeffer, J. (1981). Management as symbolic action. In L. L Cummings, & B.M. Staw (Eds.), *Research in organisational behaviour 3* (pp. 1-52).

Schein, E. H. (1985). *Organisational culture and leadership.* San Francisco: Jossey-Bass.

Stewart, T. A. (1997). *Intellectual capital: The new wealth of organisations.* New York:Doubleday.

Yin, R. (1988). *Case study research: Design and methods.* London: Sage.

Appendix

The University of New South Wales

School of Information Systems, Technology and Management

S1, 2000

Organisational Culture Survey

Instructions: This questionnaire is a part of a research study of organisational cultures as knowledge management enablers/facilitators. Please answer the following questions by circling the response (on a scale 1 to 7) that best expresses your views of the following cultural aspects in your school.

continued on following page

	Questions	Disagree						Agree
1.	People here try to make friends and to keep their relationships strong	1	2	3	4	5	6	7
2.	People here get along very well	1	2	3	4	5	6	7
3.	People in our school often socialise outside the office	1	2	3	4	5	6	7
4.	People here really like one another	1	2	3	4	5	6	7
5.	When people leave our school, we stay in touch	1	2	3	4	5	6	7
6.	People here do favours for others because they like one another	1	2	3	4	5	6	7
7.	People here often confide in one another about personal matters	1	2	3	4	5	6	7
8.	Overall, there is a high level of social interaction in our school	1	2	3	4	5	6	7
9.	Our school understands and shares the same business objectives	1	2	3	4	5	6	7
10.	Work gets done effectively and productively by our school	1	2	3	4	5	6	7
11.	Our school takes action to address poor performance	1	2	3	4	5	6	7
12.	Our school's collective will to achieve is high	1	2	3	4	5	6	7
13.	When opportunities for competitive advantage arise, our school moves quickly to capitalise on them	1	2	3	4	5	6	7
14.	We share the same strategic goals	1	2	3	4	5	6	7
15.	We know who our competition is	1	2	3	4	5	6	7
16.	Overall, there is a high sense of community here	1	2	3	4	5	6	7

Chapter XVIII

Incentives and Rewards:
Motivating Knowledge Sharing

Abstract

This chapter analyses the influence of incentives and rewards on knowledge sharing behaviour. A case study was undertaken to compare knowledge-sharing behaviour among graduate students in a global MBA program under different grading conditions. The study found no difference in the amount and nature of students' contributions to the discussion board between graded, mixed, and nongraded conditions. These findings suggest that intrinsic rewards may have equally powerful effect as extrinsic ones on knowledge-sharing behaviour.

Introduction

Motivating people to share their knowledge with others represents a major challenge in knowledge management. Modern knowledge intensive organisations are trying to address this challenge by linking the knowledge-sharing activities of employees to some incentive and reward systems. The literature suggests that externally or internally induced motivation may have a beneficial effect on knowledge sharing. In general, high level of motivation is expected to lead to greater willingness of people to share what they know with their peers.

In the knowledge-based view of the firm (Spender, 1996; Teece, 2000), knowledge is considered as the main driver of a firm's competitive advantage. The sharing of knowledge across individual and organizational boundaries is considered important for preventing knowledge gaps that are likely to produce less-than-desirable work. Among main motives for knowledge sharing, Muller et al. (Muller, Spiliopoulou, & Lenz, 2005) identifies altruism, conditional cooperation, strategic reciprocity, reputation, social norms, group identity, and payoff.

Bock, Zmud, Kim, and Lee (2005) classify motivating drivers into economic (anticipated extrinsic rewards), sociopsychological (anticipated reciprocal relationships and sense of self-worth), and sociological (fairness, innovativeness, and affiliation). The idea of an incentive system is to align individual benefits of knowledge sharing with corporate goals. Evangelou and Kracapilidis (2005) propose a framework of incentives of both positive and negative reinforcement that act as catalysts to the knowledge-sharing procedure.

Davenport, De Long, and Beers (1998) argue that motivation to contribute knowledge is an intangible critical success factor for any KM project. Hauschild et al. (Hauschild, Licht, & Stein, 2001) found that less successful companies tend to take a top-down approach: pushing knowledge to where it is needed. More successful companies, by contrast, reward employees for seeking, sharing, and creating knowledge. However, even rewarding knowledge sharing explicitly may work only partially as evident from the McKinsey case study (Ghosh, 2004), where carefully planned incentive programs to motivate knowledge sharing through increased visibility, trust, and justified rewards still create issues.

The key lesson from this analysis is that motivation to share is a difficult issue to address, as it relates to changing people's perception and behaviour. It is closely tied to the cultural norm of an organisation. According to Handzic and Zhou (2005), this issue is not well addressed at present. This is reflected in the current KM practice, where less management attention is paid to rewards and incentives for knowledge sharing than to employee training, KM systems development, organisational structure, and organisational culture (Zhou & Fink, 2003).

According to Muller et al. (2005), the design of the suitable incentive systems is difficult in circumstances when companies begin to distribute across countries and cultures. The general lack of empirical research on the issue adds further to the difficulty of the task, as there is no appropriate guidance available on what works and under which circumstances. The purpose of this chapter is: (1) to analyse different incentive and reward systems derived from theory and prior research that may motivate people to share knowledge; and (2) to empirically test their effect on knowledge sharing behaviour.

Incentives and Rewards

Recognising that knowledge workers need to be motivated to share knowledge, this section reviews various existing incentive and reward systems, both extrinsic and intrinsic, that may be used to stimulate their knowledge-sharing behaviour. Handzic and Zhou (2005) note that incentives and rewards for knowledge sharing can take several forms. They can be monetary or nonmonetary, formal or informal, and long-term or short-term. Which approach(s) to use will depend on the circumstances and requires careful consideration.

Smith and McKeen (2003) note that some companies have begun to reflect contributions to knowledge and participation in a community in an individual's compensations. Other companies make sure that people are motivated to contribute by letting them know that it is okay to take time to be part of the community, and that it is okay to make mistakes. In comparison, formal monetary rewards are not necessarily more powerful than informal, nonmonetary rewards.

Bonuses, compensation, and promotions that are often a part of the formal rewards system in organisations do not work well in every circumstance. Contrary to what may be expected, inappropriate use of such incentives could discourage knowledge sharing and lead to other counterproductive practices (Hauschild et al., 2001). Tying annual bonuses solely to frontline employees' sales volume, for example, may spark unhealthy competition. Moreover, the growth of sales volume in the short-term may be achieved at the expense of customer satisfaction, which can be harmful to the future prospect of the firm.

Nonfinancial rewards, such as recognition of expertise (e.g., a title of subject matter expert [SME]), extra days' leave, a thank-you note or e-mail, an opportunity for training, or a present, can also help foster motivation, desire, and contribution. Other potential incentives include coveted office space, an opportunity to travel or to receive more challenging assignments (Hauschild et al., 2001). The list of incentives suggested by Rylatt (2003) also includes having fun, whether it is having birthday cakes, bringing in baby photographs, or having a game of softball; allowing people to change their working hours or duties; acquiring an award trophy or mentioning people's work in a report or newsletter; inviting someone to an important meeting, or special conference; and letting someone have a car spot for a while.

Incentives can be long-term or short-term. If organisations choose short-term incentives, they should be, in the opinion of Davenport et al. (1998), highly visible to attract good public attention. However, given the fact that people tend to hide knowledge for their own advantage, organisations should focus on long-term motivational approaches, and make the extent of knowledge contribution part of the evaluation and compensation structure (Davenport et al., 1998).

According to Muller et al. (2005), the effect of monetary incentives on total knowledge sharing is twofold: firstly, the relative benefits, compared to the costs of knowledge sharing, are enhanced (relative price effect), and secondly, the intrinsic motivation of knowledge sharing is lowered (crowding-out effect). The total effect can be positive if the relative price effect is stronger than the crowding-out effect. But it is also possible that the total effect of incentives is negative. The authors suggest that in cultures with higher individualism, voluntary knowledge sharing is harder to achieve, and other auxiliary activities, like incentive systems, are recommended. In cultures with higher collectivism, knowledge sharing can be enhanced if knowledge sharing is made prominent and the reward of knowledge sharing is higher reputation and status.

When changes need to be made to the established rewards system, an incremental approach would be more workable than a radical one. Rumizen (2002) advises not to make substantial changes, as it could cause undesirable effects. When a change is being implemented, employees should be given time to learn and adapt.

Empirical Study

Study Objectives

Recognising the importance of incentive systems in motivating knowledge sharing, the main objective of the current research, based on Handzic and Lagumdzija (2006), is to study the behaviour of global MBA students as typical representatives of knowledge workers. The goal is to provide a deeper insight into the role of extrinsic and intrinsic incentives and rewards in increasing or lessening individuals' tendencies to engage in knowledge-sharing behaviours.

Research Design and Variables

A case-study approach was chosen as the preferred research method for the current study aimed at examining actual knowledge-sharing behaviour of a specific group of real-world knowledge workers. As already mentioned in Chapter XVII, the case-study methodology is often associated with research about human affairs in social contexts (Yin, 1998). The main advantages of the case-study approach lie in its descriptive nature (it describes the things the way they are) and natural setting (it draws meanings from social contexts). These are believed to provide a greater level of depth and understanding of many aspects of a social phenomenon than is possible using other methods (Lee, 1989). The main disadvantage of the case-study approach is that it requires careful planning and attention to detail in order to establish validity (Miles & Huberman, 1994).

Two aspects of knowledge sharing investigated in this study were amount and nature. Amount of knowledge sharing was measured in terms of average number of messages posted on the discussion board per person. Nature of knowledge sharing was evaluated in terms of two contribution types. This could be either one's new posting to the discussion board or feedback to someone else's posting.

Subjects and Procedure

Subjects for the current study were 29 MBA students enrolled in the Information Technology course at Universitas 21 Global. This institution represents an association of 16 universities from around the world and Thomson Learning. It was established with an aim to provide innovative online management education for global leaders (http://www.u21global.com).

As part of their course, the students participated in peer discussions on various course topics by contributing their ideas, opinions, and comments to the discussion board over a period of 3 months. Knowledge sharing during the initial course period (about 1 month) was voluntary and not graded. During the middle course period, sharing was partly mandatory and graded and partly voluntary. For the purpose of graded knowledge sharing, students were required to contribute three times one main discussion board posting on a given topic and three comments to other students' postings. Total worth of graded discussions was 30% (3 times 10%) of the overall mark. Finally, knowledge sharing among students using discussion board was mandatory as part of their graded team project and worth 20%.

Results and Discussion

Quantitative and qualitative analysis of participants' contributions to discussion board was performed and results presented in Figure 18.1 and 18.2. Different techniques were used, as suggested by Miles and Huberman (1994) to better identify patterns, themes, and clusters, and ensure plausibility of findings.

With respect to quantitative approach, a descriptive analysis of participants' contributions to discussion board was performed. In order to identify a central tendency in participants' knowledge-sharing behaviour, the average number of messages per person was calculated under three grading incentive conditions (ungraded, mixed, graded). The results shown in Figure 18.1 indicate no significant difference between extrinsic and intrinsic incentive effects on subjects' knowledge-sharing behaviour. The mean scores obtained were 9.55 for ungraded, 10.07, 11.55, 10.76(avg=10.79) for mixed, and 9.35 for graded condition. Scores above 4 in mixed grading conditions indicated that the subjects tended to share much more of their knowledge than required to get their grades.

These findings suggest that both extrinsic and extrinsic incentives were similarly powerful drivers of knowledge-sharing attitudes and behaviour among participants. It appears that the participants balanced the benefit and cost of engaging in knowledge sharing by expending similar amount of time and effort to obtain good grades on one hand, and to position themselves favourably within their virtual community of practice on the other hand

Such findings are contrary to other recently reported ones. More specifically, Bock et al. (2005) found that extrinsic rewards exerted negative effect on individuals'

Figure 18.1 Number of contributions per person by incentive systems

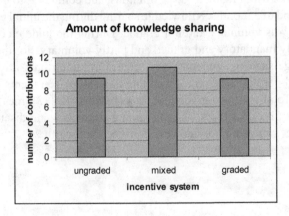

Figure 18.2 Nature of knowledge contributions

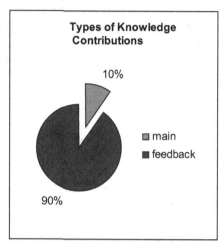

knowledge-sharing attitudes among Korean managers. The difference may be potentially attributed to the culture factor. Participants in this study came from a variety of countries and cultures. In contrast, in Korean culture, characterised by high collectivism, knowledge sharing can be enhanced by intrinsic motives (e.g., higher reputation and status) rather than extrinsic ones (Muller et al., 2005).

Further qualitative analysis of the data was performed by classifying individual participants' contributions into two categories: main or feedback. From the results shown in Figure 18.2, it can be seen that 90% of all contributions fell into the feedback category. The remaining 10% were main type. These results indicate that the overwhelming majority of participants tended to respond to other people's ideas rather than contribute their own. With respect to the quality of feedback, both tendencies, agreements, and disagreements with given points of view were found to be equally prominent. The excerpt of the content of actual discussions on the topic of mobile devices and wireless networks is provided in the Appendix to this chapter.

Study Limitations and Directions for Future

It is important to note that the current research was limited in a number of aspects. Further studies in other contexts are necessary to verify current findings and further deepen our understanding of the role of incentive systems in motivating/inhibiting knowledge sharing. While the case-study design gives a realistic picture of the behaviour in a real system, it does not allow us to control possibly critical variables, as would be the case in an experimental environment. Muller et al. (2005) suggest that using alternative empirical designs would be useful to measure the values of each employee directly using the survey method. Moreover, the direct change in relative value of incentives would be a useful guide to further test the incentive effect for knowledge sharing.

Conclusion

This chapter has presented results of a case study examining the relative influence of extrinsic and intrinsic incentives on knowledge-sharing behaviour in the real-world context of a global MBA education. The case study produced both quantitative and qualitative results that provided deeper insights into the issue compared to alternative experimental studies. In summary, the study found that both extrinsic and intrinsic incentives were equally powerful motivating forces that drove participants to engage in knowledge sharing. However, commenting on other people's work was more prominent behaviour than contributing one's own ideas.

References

Bock, G. W., Zmud, R. W., Kim, Y. G., & Lee, J. N. (2005). Behavioral intention formation in knowledge sharing: Examining the roles of extrinsic motivators, social-psychological forces, and organizational climate. *MIS Quarterly, 29*(1), 87-111.

Davenport, T. H, De Long, D. W., & Beers, M. C. (1998). Successful knowledge management projects. *Sloan Management Review, 39*(2), 43-57.

Evangelou, C., & Kracapilidis, N. (2005). On the interaction between humans and knowledge management systems: A framework of knowledge sharing catalysts. *Knowledge Management Research & Practice, 4*(3), 253-261.

Ghosh, T. (2004, May). *Creating incentives for knowledge sharing* (Working paper). MIT, Sloan School of Management.

Handzic, M., & Lagumdzija, A. (2006, September). Motivational influences on knowledge sharing. In *Proceedings of the European Conference on Knowledge Management (ECKM2006)*, Budapest, Hungary.

Handzic, M., & Zhou, A. Z. (2005). *Knowledge management: An integrative approach.* Oxford, UK: Chandos Publishing.

Hauschild, S., Licht, T., & Stein, W. (2001). Creating a knowledge culture. *McKinsey Quarterly, 1,* 74-81.

Lee, A. (1989). A scientific methodology for MIS case studies. *MIS Quarterly, 12*(3), 33-50.

Miles, M. B., & Huberman, M. A. (1994). *Qualitative data analysis.* London: Sage.

Muller, R. M., Spiliopoulou, M., & Lenz, H. J. (2005). The influence of incentives and culture on knowledge sharing. In *Proceedings of the 38th Hawaii International Conference on System Sciences*, HI.

Rylatt, A. (2003). *Winning the knowledge game.* Sydney, Australia: McGraw-Hill.

Rumizen, M. C. (2002). The complete idiot's guide to knowledge management. Madison, WI: CWL Publishing Enterprises.

Smith, H. A., & McKeen, J. D (2003). Creating and facilitation communities of practice. In C. W. Holsapple (Ed.), *Handbook on knowledge management* (pp. 393-408). Berlin: Springer.

Spender, J. C. (1996). Making knowledge the basis of a dynamic theory of the firm. *Strategic Management Journal, 17*(2), 45-82.

Teece, D. J. (2000). *Managing intellectual capital.* Oxford, UK: Oxford University Press.

Yin, R. (1988). *Case study research: Design and methods.* London: Sage.

Zhou, A., & Fink, D. (2003). Knowledge management and intellectual capital: An empirical examination of current practice in Australia. *Knowledge Management Research and Practice, 1*(2), 86-94.

Appendix

The following text is an excerpt from the participants' discussion on the impact of mobile and wireless technologies.

Person A to all participants

Dear all,

All my friends and colleagues have mobile phones. PDA is also getting more popular with the technology development improving on the functions, size and cost.

Wireless LANs is also getting very common in Malaysia since coffee beans, starbucks and other cafes/ restaurants/ pubs offering free WIFI access for their customers. My company which has only 2 lawyers and 1 permanent clerk has not used wireless LANS, but we chosen cabled LANS. It would have been a very different decision made if we have a large organisation with many people where the cabling can get complicated. However, my parents' office is on wireless LANS due to my tech savvy my brother and the complication of fixing cables.

I do think these devices and technologies have increased productivity and efficiency. They allow me to stay in touch with my office/ clients at any point of time, especially when I'm travelling overseas. For example, I was out of the office on last Friday and one major client wanted us to update a status on their e-system and it was impossible for me to rush back to office to do so at that point of time. So I just need to go to any area with wireless LANS signal and get it done.

By the way I do use wireless LANS at home also, for studies mainly. I chose wireless than cable due to the convenience of me able to use my laptop in my room, living room or anywhere i want to without restricted my mobility to the modem. Moreover, wireless enable more than one user at the same time and my brother can enjoy the benefit of the wireless LANS in his room when necessary. This decision was made due to no extra cost needed for maintaining wireless LANS except having to buy a wireless modem in the initial stage, which is not expansive now.

Just my thoughts

Person B to Person A

Hi,

What a coincidence, the current MBA studies is also the reason why I bought a wireless router. In fact, the wireless router helped increased the usage of my notebook. I can now study anywhere within the house (while keeping an eye on my boy) while my wife surfs the net using the desktop. In that sense, productivity and mobility increased.

Of course, with my boy older now, he starts to meddle with my keyboard even before I managed to login to U21.

Person C to Person A

It is a good idea to get wireless at home. I have a cable broadband and a lot of times when I want to study my son is playing on the PC. Using a wireless will allow both of us to be on the internet

Person D to Person A

Dear

Cost benefit analysis of implementing a new technology is important for businesses before embarking on IT projects. This is amply illustrated in your discussion where your organization clearly realized that with the current employee strength full benefits may not be leveraged through a wireless LAN.

Adoption of technology also depends on the values and personality of key decision makers. A tech savvy business head such as your brother act as catalysts for adopting newer technology.

Mobile devices are a boon to professional such as lawyers and consultants. Apart from managing the calendar and appointments, mobile devices enable them to retrieve information and handle proposals / client queries in an efficient and timely manner.

However mobile phones make the employees / individuals available for work almost 24/ 7 which has increased the stress levels and also reduced communication in the family.

I make it a point not to access emails on holidays and refuse to take work related calls on my mobile.

Are there any studies in Malaysia on the effect of mobile devices on individuals' life style and work life balance?

Cheers

Person A to Person D

Dear

Yes mobile phones have brought along high stress level in Malaysia, in making individuals available for 24/7. I think this depends very much of the culture of the place. For example, it would be different in Europe where people there appreciate privacy and are not likely to disturb other for work during off office hours, unlike Asian employer or customer mentality that all time of the staff or supplier belong to them. So generally, it is hard to have individual life style and work life balance in Malaysia especially as an employee.

Person E to Person A

Hi,

I agree with you that stress level of employees, due to the availability of mobile devices, very much depends on the culture of the region / country. You also rightly mentioned that it is very difficult to avoid high stress levels in Asia countries due to the difficulty in seperating out the individual life amd work life. This is definitely a cultural issue.

Thanks and Regards

Person E to Person D

Hello,

your post mentions two most important issues related to the development of the latest mobile devices and related technologies : The positive side of the development is faster customer / client service, faster handling of queries etc. The other side of the coin is to make the employees work for 24x7 and the corresponding increase in stress level and lesser time for the family / personal life. The most important part is to strike a balance between these two contrasting demands. There is a direct and positive co-relation between the level of service provided to the customers / clients and the stress level an employee suffers.

As you mentioned, you can avoid accessing e-mails on holidays. What about mobile calls ? And especially if the call is from your boss / superior ? In my opinion, it is very difficult to avoid such calls. It requires a great deal of understanding and discipline between boss and subbordinate in order to avoid such circumstances.

Regards

Chapter XIX

Specialist Training:
Cultivating Knowledge
Management Professionals

Abstract

The growing importance of knowledge and innovation in the marketplace brings with it a need for the better management of professional knowledge for knowledge workers in the New Economy. This chapter illustrates some major steps undertaken at the University of New South Wales, Australia, towards building an educational system for KM professionals that can meet the requirements of the knowledge economy. The chapter describes new multidisciplinary curriculum initiatives and instructional learning developments considered or implemented at the school of information systems, technology and management.

Introduction

Responsibility for knowledge can be shared among all employees within an organisation in order to build a structure conducive to learning. Alternatively, having supportive organisational structure for KM may involve establishing a set of special KM roles and positions within the organisation. An organisation may seek to appoint a particular individual to be responsible for KM at the senior executive level, or as managers and facilitators at team levels. These individuals may assist in smoothing knowledge flows and enhancing the quality of knowledge objects.

A recent report presented by Essex (2003) reveals that one in four large global firms appoint executives with titles of "chief knowledge officer" (CKO), "chief learning officer" (CLO), or "director of intellectual capital" (DIC). According to Handzic and Zhou (2005), a CKO is typically charged with gathering knowledge from a firm's geographically, functionally, and intellectually dispersed divisions and orchestrating its use wherever it is needed. Usually, the person works at capturing and leveraging structured knowledge, using information technology to drive the process. A CLO, on the other hand, is more overtly concerned with training and education, and human resources, as opposed to information systems, as a key enabler. The job is usually described as "creating and supporting an environment in which learning and applying what we learn is a daily priority." A DIC tends to focus more on converting and/or extracting knowledge into revenues and profits.

Handzic (2003) identifies four categories of KM-related titles and roles found in the literature. These include: (1) knowledge scientists, who show others what would be possible if they were willing to try; (2) knowledge managers, whose prime concern is with knowledge needs of the organisation; (3) knowledge engineers with various specialisations, who act as advisors to knowledge managers on what can be done given the current "state of the art"; and (4) knowledge workers who produce and reproduce knowledge in every element of the economy.

The snapshot of knowledge managers' major characteristics and activities reported by McKeen and Staples (2000) suggests that they are well-educated and experienced individuals whose primary goal is to guide their organisations towards managing knowledge for maximum benefit, and who see changing people's behaviour as the key challenge. The profile of a typical knowledge manager includes the following individual characteristics: highly educated; already a seasoned organizational performer and chosen for the KM position based on proven performance; a "researcher" who seeks new knowledge and likes to learn; attracted to "being at the forefront of something new and exciting"; motivated more by a challenge than a formal power; receives intrinsic rewards from helping others, some altruism and evangelism; a risk-taker, sometimes a maverick; and sees knowledge management as a way to "make a mark within the organization."

With respect to roles, typically the KM role reports directly to the CEO, from four levels down; has modest budget, small staff, few entitlements; job description is "roll your own" variety, 50% chances of a written job description; role has existed just over 2 years; current KM was the first ever appointed in the organization; job was created by/for the current KM; original purpose was to "leverage the intellectual capital across the organization"; education, awareness, and promotion of KM philosophy is major preoccupation; changing the organization remains the key challenge; and KM role typically follows a "middle-out" strategy down and implement up.

Handzic (2003) suggests that knowledge management professionals should have the following set of competencies and skills to be able to play their roles: promote and sell the concept and practice of knowledge management in an organisation by communicating its importance with different stakeholder groups; evaluate the existing organisational knowledge and identify barriers to its effective transfer and utilisation; develop initiatives to introduce and improve processes of creating, transferring, and utilising knowledge in work processes of an organisation; propose interventions to create an infrastructure that encourages and facilitates knowledge processes within an organisation; formulate a comprehensive KM strategy and direct its implementation in an organisation.

Many universities, professional societies, training centres, and communities offer specialised graduate and undergraduate courses, seminars, workshops, and informal learning opportunities. However, it should be noted here that the KM professionals are a relatively new phenomenon, and there is still no clear consensus about what roles they should play in an organisation and what competencies and skills they need to have to play these roles. The purpose of this chapter is to describe new knowledge management curriculum and instructional/learning developments underway at the University of New South Wales, Australia.

Converging Disciplines

The changing economic landscape, particularly the growing importance of innovations for economic growth and competitive advantage in the New Economy, suggests the need for better management of professional knowledge of future knowledge workers in the field of KM. New-age workers are expected to be skilled at creating, acquiring, and transferring knowledge and modifying their behaviour accordingly (Garvin, 1998). They are anticipated to be capable of continually expanding their capacity to create desired results, nurture new thinking patterns, set free collective aspirations, and learn how to learn together (Senge, 1990). It is also suggested that inventing new knowledge should be a modern worker's way of behaving or being (Nonaka, 1998).

Organisations' increasing demand for new skills and capabilities for future KM professionals necessitates a corresponding response from the education sector. In general, these demands have not been adequately addressed (Seufert & Seufert, 1999). Major criticisms are directed at content that does not reflect the cross-disciplinary nature of the field, has no base in reality, and does not cultivate creativity and problem-solving skills and instructional methods that largely impart knowledge rather than allow constructing it through experience. Handzic and Scifleet (2002) describe one success story.

During 1999 the School of Information Systems and the School of Library, Archives and Information Studies at the University of New South Wales joined together to form one new school, the School of Information Systems, Technology and Management (SISTM). The success of this merger is evident within the teaching programs of the School, which is now able to offer a program of study to students who can select from a range of Information Systems and Information Management courses. At Graduate level the School offers a Masters of Commerce in both Information Systems and Information Management. At Undergraduate level it is possible to undertake a dual major in both Information Systems and Information Management.

With a "traditional" focus on Management Information Systems (MIS) and formal computer-based services that meet organizational and operational needs, the strategic significance of Information Systems to business has seen Information Systems aligned with faculties of Business, Commerce, and Economics. Librarianship and information science, with its focus on the management of material artifacts, has traditionally been aligned with the Social Sciences and Arts faculties (Buckland, 1999).

The international landscape shifted considerably in the late 1990s when Schools of both Information Systems and the Information Sciences began to change the focus of their curriculums to reflect requirements driven by the Internet, networked telecommunications, and the new paradigm of knowledge management (Davis, Feinstein, Gorgone, Longenecker, & Valacich, 2001). At the School of Information Systems, Technology and Management, accounting for change in the New Economy has resulted in the development of new programmes and new courses that reflect a convergence in the way we think about, and teach, digital technology, information content, and business management. The example of one course, *INFS5927 Knowledge Management Systems and Technology,* is presented in the Appendix to the chapter.

Knowledge Management Curriculum Development

During 2000, a special working party, consisting of representatives from the School of Information Systems, Technology and Management and interested parties from other relevant university schools, developed a new stream of multidisciplinary graduate programmes of study. These programmes are articulated to provide a cross-disciplinary perspective on Knowledge Management, E-Business Management, and Services Management. The following section presents specific details of the Knowledge Management programme as outlined in the proposal documents.

The special working party report (Special Postgraduate Coursework Programs: Knowledge Management, 2000) provides the following justification for introducing programmes of study in knowledge management. First, the report views *knowledge management* an an emergent response to a "third wave," digital, or *knowledge economy* that is replacing the industrial society that has prevailed for the last 200 years or so. Second, the report endorses Drucker's (1993) argument that "in a knowledge economy the only thing that increasingly will matter in national as well as international economics is management's performance in making knowledge productive."

Furthermore, it recognises that organisations in the knowledge economy increasingly will inhabit environments that are *chaotic;* where the link between cause and effect becomes difficult to discern, small changes can be amplified beyond comprehension, and the future eludes prediction. The report notes that in this environment, organisations live with an inherent ambiguity, whilst competing on the edge of stability and instability. Only two things are believed to be certain for such organisations: their own decomposition as product/service life cycles rapidly change, and the impossibility of focusing organisational futures around known strategic portfolios. The report argues that survival depends on ceaseless innovation and a capability to find opportunities for the exercise of new strategies.

The report also argues that, in the knowledge economy, the intellect or knowledge of people will be the primary resource that is accumulated, developed, and enhanced in the battle for competitive advantage. It predicts that success will accrue to organisations that can offer ongoing, enriching service to individual customers, who perceive these offerings not as products but as solutions to their particular problems or needs; establish themselves as integral parts of diverse but relevant value chains that permit the leveraging of resource use, whilst capitalising on their own distinctive capabilities; establish flexible, responsive, proactive, but directed, organisational processes that thrive on change and uncertainty, as means of exploiting market and competitive opportunities routinely and profitably; capitalise on knowledge resources available inside and outside the organisation through the effective use of technology, diverse cultures, and modes of management that are visionary, change oriented, and inclusive; and mobilise a "strategic intelligence" that is sufficient to sustain organisational identity and capabilities, whilst negotiating the ongoing, radical change driven by new service offerings.

Finally, the report describes knowledge management as an organisational phenomenon that involves appreciating differences in types of knowledge and ways of knowing, and their personal, public, and cultural manifestations; understanding the underlying economics of knowledge development and use, including the effects of rapid dissemination and the possibility of increasing returns on knowledge resources; accessing forms of legal right and remedy that protect proprietary or user advantages in knowledge resources; appreciating the nature of "knowledge work" and the needs and expectations of "knowledge workers"; appreciating relationships between knowledge, learning, and innovation in, and by, organisations; designing and negotiating systems for recognising and valuing the knowledge creation and utilisation capabilities of organisations; designing knowledge management architectures, systems, and processes in organisations; impacting processes by which knowledge is mobilised, conserved, leveraged, and enhanced within organisations; negotiating knowledge creation, diffusion and use within and across organisations and cultures, and in relationships with customers, suppliers, and other stakeholders; strategically managing knowledge in generating new service offerings and enhanced organisational capabilities.

Accordingly, a series of Special Programs in Knowledge Management are proposed and designed to: provide multidisciplinary perspectives on knowledge management as an emergent organisational phenomenon; provide an orientation to working and managing in contexts where knowledge is a central capability and a driver of organisational success; and provide choice in adapting study programs to academic or work backgrounds and career aspirations or needs.

Innovative Teaching and Learning

One of the major criticisms directed at current management education is that a large amount of knowledge is imparted to the learner. Another noticeable weakness lies in the neglect of process-oriented learning, that is, making the learning and thought process visible in order to develop the learners' metacognition (Joyce & Weil, 1986). There is a call for better balance between the imparting of knowledge to the learner and the learner's own construction of it. A suggestion is made that the quantity of material to be learnt by telling should be reduced to a minimum and that the lesson time should, instead, be devoted to the cultivation of such qualities as problem solving, decision making, and creativity through self-directed and collaborative learning. The complexities of learning and the large number of interacting factors that affect individual and group learning present many challenges. The following sections provide an overview of the latest innovative approaches proposed and considered for the use at the UNSW's School of Information Systems, Technology and Management in a series of discussion documents.

Technology-Mediated Teaching and Learning

The *Discussion Paper on Technology-Mediated Teaching and Learning* (2001) states that the design of quality learning draws on the full range of digital and analogue media for its purposes. Currently, the Internet and other networked technologies attract the most interest. The document looks to technology to provide mechanisms and media to support learning strategies in three main modes: Adjunct - in which the technology supplements a course of study offered principally face-to-face; Mixed—in which technology partly replaces elements of traditional class interaction; and Online—in which all the content and processes of interaction are supported by technology.

The document identifies the following as desirable ways in which online technology is used for the three modes of learning described. *Access to a well-structured knowledge base:* Using universal Internet standards, the student can access quality learning materials, on demand, that are superior to those available or manageable in face-to-face settings; *Active engagement with content:* On the Internet, this is supported through the setting of tasks that may be published to the group or privately to the teacher via e-mail or a student Web site. Other active engagement may be achieved through the development of preprogrammed interactive components or simulations that are made accessible through computer labs, face-to-face classrooms, or online; *Interaction with the teacher:* Online discussion and dialogue may be held both synchronously through "chat" sessions, or more commonly through asynchronous discussions and bulletin boards. In a fully online course, this is the principal channel of communication within the group, but also in mixed and adjunct modes, it can facilitate interaction over and above that possible within the constraints of a face-to-face class. *Opportunities for interaction with other learners:* The online discussion group also enables student-to-student interaction that may be informal and initiated by the learners or a formal group task set by the teacher; *Individual reflection on learning:* Online learning incorporates explicit instances for reflection and reporting on cognition. Teachers also require ways to look back on the learning process, and adjust strategies and activities to redress misconceptions; *Feedback and formative assessment:* Online groups offer an achievable and retrievable record of class interactions as a forum for formative feedback. Individual and confidential feedback may be provided via private threads or e-mail.

Furthemore, the document recommends that these processes within the School should be enabled through *support for development* and adequate *infrastructure. For teachers*, the recommended support is in the form of guidelines regarding minimum standards for course development, design, and delivery; processes and criteria by which learning materials are to be reviewed; workshops and individual support in educational design in response to the specific needs of courses offered within a discipline; technical assistance for staff in content design and interactive media production; assistance in the transition from classroom to online learning processes, and in the development of adjunct materials through the modeling of best practice; provision of feedback, in the form of reports from the learning system, on issues arising from student use of mediated learning material; opportunities to share and discuss practice within the School through the formation of a learning community. *For students*, the recommended support is in the form of specific information about the mediated learning and its use in each course, in addition to the basic *Course Outline* requirements; training and information to equitably access courseware and other UNSW online resources; access to technical assistance throughout the duration of a course/program; prompt and accurate response to inquiries, which will be logged and recorded for later analysis; opportunities to evaluate and comment on the teaching and learning process throughout a course.

The document also suggests that the School needs to provide necessary infrastructure for the mediated teaching and learning purposes. This infrastructure includes a technology plan that includes electronic security measures (i.e., password protection, encryption, back-up) to ensure quality standards and the integrity and validity of information held within the online teaching system; a local intranet, accessible to staff and students to enable high-speed access to e-mail, courseware servers, and teaching spaces; high-capacity local servers, to store and structure repositories of media content for courses; high-speed connection with the external Internet, to enable access to the resources and connectivity of this global resource; modem connections for students to access School courses and course repositories from off campus; access to, and support for, the software necessary to enable discipline discourse for both on and off campus groups; technical support for commonly used computer platforms and software, which is reviewed annually in the light of new technologies; templates for commonly used educational strategies, student and course Web pages to minimise preparation time.

Interactive Teaching and Learning

The promotion of interactive teaching and learning within the School, advocated by the Discussion Paper on Interactive Teaching and Learning (2001), reflects recent research into student learning, serves to build a community of practice that values and accommodates student diversity in learning, and is likely to improve the quality of learning experiences and satisfaction with the outcomes. Both staff and students are supported in various ways to make the most of opportunities for interactive learning and to develop their own skills in interaction. A commitment to moving towards more interactive teaching practices is expected to enhance the quality of learning in the School.

In this discussion paper, learning is recognised not only as a process of cognitive development for the individual, but also a social process of engagement with others within the learning environment. Recent constructivist theories of learning place the individual as an active participant in her/his environment, rather than a passive recipient of stimuli. Learning is seen as a process in which the student constructs new knowledge, skills, and understandings in response to her/his environment, continually integrating new experiences and information into existing cognitive structures, and ultimately transferring that knowledge to new situations. The emphasis is on the *processes of learning*, rather than curriculum content. Principles of so-called deep learning also encourage active engagement with both content and other learners, along with opportunities to reflect on, and consolidate, new knowledge into an existing knowledge base. The document supports Vygotsky's description of the ideal as a "zone of proximal development" in which the individual learner can continually expand knowledge, skills, and talents within a supportive framework or scaffold provided by the teacher and institution. Eventually, the ideal graduate becomes an independent learner who can maintain the process of knowledge construction outside of the safety of the institution.

Furthermore, the document suggests three main reasons to teach interactively. First, interactive teaching offers some insight into what students actually know. This is its *summative* function, as it leads to testing and measuring student knowledge and understanding through questions, tests, and exams. Second, interactive teaching is *formative*. The teacher seeks to direct students' cognitive processing along particular paths through conversations or dialogue. The resulting cognitive experience of the students will move them towards accepted conceptions of the topic within the discipline. Third, interactive teaching is *motivational*. A teacher has a responsibility to keep students interested, and this is more easily done when the student is actively involved. When teachers ask students to work in small groups on a case study or problem, the resulting discussion not only serves to build new knowledge, it also serves to motivate students. The anticipation of feedback from their peers or the teacher is a strong incentive. Interactive teaching methods can address each of these issues. Through well-designed learning processes, new material can be integrated into a student's existing set of knowledge constructs in a way that provides for a deeper level of understanding to occur.

The document notes that the following five skill sets of teachers are seen to be associated with effective interactive learning by students: using and developing professional knowledge and values; communicating, interacting, and working with students and others; planning and managing the teaching and learning process; monitoring and assessing student progress and learning outcomes; and reflecting, evaluating, and planning for continuous improvement. In order to promote, maintain, or develop these skill sets by its academic staff, the School provides: opportunities for staff to discuss and evaluate interactive teaching; regular dissemination of current developments related to interactive teaching of disciplines of the School; technical resources, teaching spaces, and infrastructure necessary for the conduct of a variety of desirable modes of active and interactive learning; staff development activities, such as workshops, seminars, and individual coaching to build these skill sets; time release for the planning and coordination of interactive teaching strategies across Courses and Programs.

In addition, the document recognises that students also need specific competencies, guidance, and support if they are to maximise their opportunities to learn interactively. Such opportunities are enhanced by explicit statements by the School of expectations for student participation in learning. These statements should be communicated in advance of study through orientation and induction programs and ideally, should become a sign of the learning culture of the School; skills in written, and spoken communication sufficient for active learning by individuals and positive contributions to the learning of others; a level of metacognition by students regarding their own learning styles and preferences, and an appreciation of the role that culture and upbringing play in determining cognitive frameworks and learning; self-management skills in identifying goals, setting priorities, and independently managing time and resources towards meeting the expectations of a course; sufficient levels of technological literacy to access the learning materials and processes offered by staff. Support mechanisms, both educational and social, to address skills deficits or other impediments to participation and learning; mechanisms by which students can provide evaluative feedback to staff in order to improve the design of learning processes.

Cross-Cultural Teaching and Learning

The *Discussion Paper on Cross-Cultural Teaching and Learning* (2001) reflects the commitment of staff and students to the development of effective cross-cultural learning in the school. This document is part of an ongoing discourse about the kinds of students we have enrolled in our School and the ways in which we wish to approach their education.

The document defines culture broadly as a set of values and beliefs shared by a group of people. Membership of such groups may be determined by birth, by choice, or by life circumstances. Cultural values and beliefs may be anchored by ethnicity, gender, religion, nationality, and language. Students and staff in the School of School of Information Systems, Technology and Management have a range of cultural backgrounds and affiliations. In particular, the cultural diversity of students is striking. This diversity poses a number of critical issues for teaching and learning in the School.

In order to help both teachers and students become more culturally aware of themselves and others, and to manage cultural diversity in the School, the document proposes the following eight principles:

1. **Be consistent:** We need to start by creating an environment in which the rules of interaction are apparent. Rather than trying to second-guess the competing expectations or prejudices of all, create a new "culture of the classroom" as a model for managing diversity and use this to mirror the global workplace. People respond to clear direction, especially in socially and culturally sensitive contexts or in processes in which they are unsure. A teacher may spend some time during the introductory weeks of a course negotiating what is expected and acceptable to the group regarding interaction, group work, questions, and respect. Staff and students should be confident that the general expectations are consistent across programs and reflect those of the professional world.

2. **Provide information:** Wherever possible, be aware that miscommunication is the greatest impediment to learning, and seek to provide information to all in accessible ways. Course content and assessment details, for instance, can be communicated in the Course Outline, on a Web site, in class, and in individual consultations. Especially in the beginning, take the time to ensure that students have time to become familiar with the class culture and its expectations, and provide information in multiple forms.

3. **Encourage communication:** As communication is the essential process whereby learning occurs, foster opportunities for students to express themselves. This will involve the use of questioning, discussion, debate class presentations, and open invitations to contribute personal experience to case studies. In class, allow "wait time" in all interactions to encourage some individuals to overcome their desire to avoid participation. Ask if students know of other ways of approaching issues. Confirm and validate contributions with recognition and thanks. Give notice of a request for participation; do not spring a surprise on an unprepared student.

4. **Avoid stereotyping:** Stereotyping is how novice learners first sort and process different phenomena. They create large, easily managed categories that make sense of unfamiliar information. However, as expertise grows, learners modify these categories to differentiate the detail found in individuals. Eventually, we become intellectually aware of individuals' differences and can appreciate the dangers of generalisation. If stereotypes are used, for instance, in case studies, recognise this and explain why. Look beyond immediate physical and language differences to seek understandings of intention.

5. **Avoid ethnocentrism:** Appreciate that there are many views of the world. Avoid deficit models in which we suggest that other cultures simply lack some qualities that we value. Asian students consistently display higher scores on deep approaches and lower scores on surface approaches to learning despite the conception that they want to "rote" learn content. Promote equitable participation by all, rather than dominance by a few.

6. **Involve others in your development:** To see ourselves as others do is difficult. Check your perceptions with colleagues, and invite peer review of your style of teaching and interaction. Ask others to help monitor your language and interpersonal dynamics. Ask peers to suggest and share techniques for motivating classroom interaction.

7. **Be an example:** Model inclusive language and behaviour where possible. Carry this through to the handouts, notes, and OHTs used in class. Also, admit to uncertainties and ask others to suggest strategies in difficult situations. Seek to use global examples and analogies when illustrating a point. Avoid jargon or colloquialisms and model active listening.

8. **Structure group work to manage diversity:** Make the team dynamic and its management a part of the assessment. Allow members to contribute in writing as well as verbally. Provide planning sessions to allocate responsibilities and follow up with support. Make sure each member can access the information necessary for their component of the task; some overseas students do not have the same networks and resources as local students. Do not force representational membership of groups, allow students with a common culture to work together.

Conclusion

KM professionals are a relatively new phenomenon, and there is still no clear consensus about what roles they should play in an organisation and what competencies and skills they need to have to play these roles. This chapter illustrated some major steps made by the University of New South Wales, Australia, towards building an educational system for KM professionals that can meet the requirements of the knowledge economy. In particular, the chapter described new multidisciplinary curriculum and instructional/learning developments considered and implemented at the School of Information Systems, Technology and Management.

References

Buckland, M. (1999, April 14). *Library services in theory and context* (2nd ed.). Retrieved from http://sunsite.berkeley.edu/Literature/Library/Services/

Davis, G. B. Feinstein, D. L., Gorgone, J. T., Longenecker, H. E. Jr., & Valacich, J. S. (2001). IS2002: An update on information systems model curriculum. In *Proceedings of the 16th Annual Conference of the International Academy for Information Management* (pp. 389-399).

Discussion paper on cross-cultural teaching and learning. (2001). Draft discussion paper, Faculty of Commerce and Economics, University of New South Wales.

Discussion paper on interactive teaching and learning. (2001). Draft discussion paper. Faculty of Commerce and Economics, University of New South Wales.

Discussion paper on technology-mediated teaching and learning. (2001). Draft discussion paper. Faculty of Commerce and Economics, University of New South Wales.

Drucker, P. F. (1993). *Post-capitalist society.* New York: Harper Business.

Essex, D. (2003). Knowledge management programs pay big dividend. *ITworld. com.* Retrieved from www.itworld.com/App/236/ITW1795/

Garvin, D. A. (1998). Building a learning organisation. In *Harvard Business Review on knowledge management.* Boston: Harvard Business School Press.

Handzic, M. (2003). *The challenge of educating KM professionals.* Paper presented ate the meeting of the nswKM forum, Sydney, Australia.

Handzic, M., & Scifleet, P. (2002, December). Impact of new economy on IS education: A case of UNSW. In *Proceedings of the International Conference on Informatics Education and Research (ICIER 2002)*, Barcelona.

Handzic, M., & Zhou, A. Z. (2005). *Knowledge management: An integrative approach.* Oxford, UK: Chandos Publishing,

Joyce, B., & Weil, M. (1986). *Models of teaching.* Englewood-Cliffs, NJ: Prentice-Hall.

McKeen, J. D., & Staples, D. S. (2003). Knowledge managers: Who they are and what they do. In C. W. Holsapple (Ed.), *Handbook on knowledge management* (Vol. 1, pp. 21-41). Berlin: Springer.

Nonaka, I. (1998). The cnowledge-creating company. In *Harvard Business Review on knowledge management.* Boston: Harvard Business School Press.

Proposed Special Programs in Services Management. (2001). Working party report. Faculty of Commerce and Economics, University of New South Wales.

Senge, P. (1990). *The fifth discipline*. New York: Doubleday.

Seufert, S., & Seufert, A. (1999). Collaborative learning environments for management education. In *Proceedings of the 13th Annual Conference of the International Academy for Information Management* (pp. 279-284).

Special Postgraduate Coursework Programs: E-Business Management. (2000). Working party report. Faculty of Commerce and Economics, University of New South Wales.

Special Postgraduate Coursework Programs: Knowledge Management. (2000). Working party report. Faculty of Commerce and Economics, University of New South Wales.

Appendix

The University of New South Wales

School of Information Systems, Technology and Management

INFS5927 Knowledge Management Systems and Technology

Course Outline

Session 2, 2004

Objective

The objective of this course is to provide the student with an understanding of the business of managing the generation, formulation, dissemination, retention, storage, measurement, application, distribution, archival and disposal of corporate knowledge. It considers various systems and technology supporting knowledge management. It also addresses knowledge discovery in databases and corporate data warehouses, by identifying understandable patterns in data.

Text

Hasan H. and Handzic M. (eds) (2003) Australian Studies in Knowledge Management, UOW Press

References

Holsapple C.W. (ed) (2003) Handbook on Knowledge Management, Springer

(Other relevant references will be provided during the semester in relation to specific topics)

Class Arrangements

The subject will comprise a combined 3-hour lecture/tutorial/seminar/laboratory session per week. Sessions are held at the following times:

Wednesday 14:00 – 16:00	ME 304
Wednesday 16:00 – 17:00	Quad Lab1

Assessment

Tutorial work and participation	10%	
Homework – case study	10%	(due week 4)
Research Essay	40%	(due week 8)
Project assignment (group)	40%	(due week 12)

Complete details of the assessments and requirements will be provided in due time. In order to pass the subject, a satisfactory performance (normally 45% of the maximum assessment mark) is required in each component of the assessment. Late submissions will incur a penalty of 10% of the maximum mark per day. An extension in the time of submission will only be granted under exceptional circumstances by the lecturer-in-charge. In all cases documented evidence must be provided.

Staff

The main contact persons for any further information, assistance or complaint regarding the course are:

Dr. Meliha Handzic, Room: QUAD 2082A, Tel: 9385–4935, E-mail: m.handzic@ unsw.edu.au

Ghassan Beydoun, Room: QUAD 2085, Tel: 9385–5517, E-mail: g.beydoun@unsw. edu.au

Course Web site

The course Web site http://www.kmrg.unsw.edu.au/teaching will be used for distribution of readings and announcements. Please check it regularly.

Schedule

Week starting	Lecture Topic	Text Reading
1 26/7	Introduction	*NIL*
2 2/8	Perspectives on knowledge management	H&H Ch 1
3 9/8	Drivers of knowledge management	H&H Ch 2
4 16/8	Knowledge creation and innovation	H&H Ch 3-4
5 23/8	Knowledge sharing and socialisation	H&H Ch 5
6 30/8	Socio-Cultural Influences on KM	H&H Ch 9
7 6/9	Industry report (*guest lecture*)	H&H Ch 8
8 13/9	Computer-Based KM Systems	H&H Ch 10
9 20/9	Knowledge capture and organisation	H&H Ch 6
27/9	RECESS	
10 4/10	Knowledge discovery and visualisation	H&H Ch 7
11 11/10	Knowledge Measurement	H&H, Ch 11
12 18/10	KM Practices from Business and Government	H&H, Ch 12-14
13 25/10	KM Strategy	H&H Ch 15
14 1/11	KM future, course review and evaluation	H&H Ch 16

Academic Misconduct

Students are reminded that the University regards academic misconduct as a very serious matter. Students found guilty of academic misconduct are usually excluded from the University for 2 years. However, because of the circumstances in individual cases the period of exclusion can range from one session to permanent exclusion from the University.

The following are some of the actions which have resulted in students being guilty of academic misconduct in recent years:

1.   Taking unauthorised materials into an examination
2.   Submitting work for assessment knowing it to be the work of another person
3.   Improperly obtaining prior knowledge of an examination paper and using that knowledge in the examination
4.   Failing to acknowledge the source of material in an assignment

Please also refer to school policies http://sistm.web.unsw.edu.au/student/schoolpolicies. html

Section IV

Issues and Challenges for Knowledge Management Practice and Research

Chapter XX

Theory vs. Practice:
Finding Out if We Do
What We Preach

Abstract

One area of omission in knowledge-intensive studies is within higher education and research organisations where there is the virtuous circle of teaching, research, and consulting professional work. Using a model adapted from Handzic (2001) and a survey modified from Arthur Andersen (1998) this chapter explores perceived importance (in theory) and perceived implementation (in practice) of knowledge management in two large university schools. The discrepancy between faculty members' perceptions forced us to confront our own biases. Guidance was sought from ethnographic accounts that allow the researchers to state personal feelings in a confessional accompaniment to the formal findings.

Introduction

The literature in management and organisation indicates a widespread recognition of the association of knowledge and organisational success. Despite early awareness of the construct (Drucker, 1967) and comprehensive overviews (Despres & Chauvel, 2000; Earl, 2001), there remains little overall advance in understanding the construct itself (Drucker, 1993; Stewart, 1997). Specific applications of knowledge to work have been explored by industry practitioners (e.g., Collison & Parcell, 2001 at BP; Mann et al., 1991 in power utilities), management commentators (O'Dell & Grayson, 1998) and researchers (e.g., Carneiro, 2000; Newell et al., 2003). This produces the distinction that knowledge is associated with skills (e.g., Macintosh & Stader, 1999) or making judgements and decisions in particular circumstances (Carr, 1999), so it is not surprising that differences exist among scholars as to what constitutes useful knowledge and the ways in which it is created. Some theorists show more interest in codified repositories and information processing as enablers of "explicit" objective and systematic knowledge (Budzik & Hammond, 1999; Carr, 1999; Den Hartog & Huzinga, 1997 in Huysman & de Wit, 2002; Klösgen, 1996). Others focus on the "tacit" knowledge that people derive from their experiences and from social interaction with others (Malhotra, 2000; Nonaka & Takeuchi, 1995). The shift in emphasis from sharing knowledge to making productive use of knowledge is reflected in the shift from individual focus to that of communities (Wenger, McDermott, & Snyder, 2002).

As organisations become more knowledge based, their success will increasingly depend on knowledge workers becoming successful at contributing to effective decision making and creating innovation. It is, therefore, not surprising that there is a growing recognition amongst researchers and practitioners alike for the need to better understand what knowledge is, the value of knowledge, and how it should be managed. In some cases this is formalised as knowledge management (KM), and in other cases as the learning organisation (DiBella, Nevis, & Goiuld, 1996) or organisational memory (Weick, 1979). Both are recent responses to the need to better understand and manage knowledge for success or survival. The central task of those concerned with knowledge management is to determine best ways to cultivate, nurture, and exploit knowledge at individual and organisational levels. In other words, it needs to ensure to get the right knowledge to right people just in time (Snowden, 2002), and help people share and put knowledge into action in ways that strive to improve organisational performance (Dixon, 2000; O'Dell & Grayson, 1998).

A distinctive application of KM is applying knowledge to knowledge itself. Knowledge intensive firms focus on the commercialisation of knowledge (e.g., Gibbons, Limoges, Nowotny, Schwartzman, Scott, & Trow, 1999; Starbuck, 1992), innovation and creativity (e.g., Brown & Duguid, 2000; Gerlach & Lincoln, 2000), or the work of experts (e.g., Albert & Bradley, 1997). Consulting firms are a particular example of KM practitioners (Savary, 1999). One area of omission in knowledge intensive studies is within higher education/research, where there is the virtuous circle of teaching, research, and consulting professional work. The author and her colleagues undertook the following study with the objective to examine the issue in a particular academic environment from the twin perspective of the individuals and expert in KM (Oliver, Handzic, & VanToorn, 2003).

Adapted Knowledge Management Framework

An adapted integrated model of knowledge management is presented in Figure 20.1. This illustrates the essential components of knowledge management and their interrelationships. The model (adapted from Handzic, 2001) proposes two major types of organisational factors (namely leadership and culture) and technology (e.g., information and communication tools) that may act as an enabler or constraint on knowledge processes (e.g., creation, transfer, utilisation) and foster the development of organisational knowledge. The model also incorporates a feedback loop to suggest the need for continuous knowledge measurement and potential adjustment of strategies over time.

Leadership refers to an individual (or a group) who takes ownership of KM initiatives in the organization. Leaders are responsible for setting the KM vision and subsequently, establishing strategic priorities, altering skills of management, facilitating suitable culture, and gaining commitment from senior executives, so as to move the company in the direction of that vision (Davenport & Prusak, 1998). It is argued

Figure 20.1. An adapted KM framework

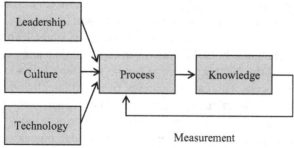

here that without proper leadership setting the pace, the KM endeavour may be in vain. Leadership is an important characteristic of the KM structures and, therefore, affects their adequacy.

Culture refers to the deep structure of organizations that is rooted in the values, beliefs, and assumptions held by organizational members. According to Bryant and Haynes (2001), a supportive culture values learning, encourages reflection and thinking, does not blame people for mistakes, encourages knowledge sharing, values both innovation and second-hand solutions, embodies high levels of trust, and recognizes explicit and tacit knowledge.

Handzic and Zhou (2005) explain that technology enablers cover a wide range of information and communication technologies and systems that provide a platform for knowledge support in a more meaningful way. For example, warehousing enhances organisational memory; knowledge maps improve access to knowledge resources; search engines locate internal and external knowledge; groupware delivers the right knowledge to the right people at the right time; data-mining tools extract new knowledge; workflow systems facilitate knowledge integration; Internet serves multiple purposes and processes.

To succeed in managing organisational key knowledge assets, organisations need to address the issue of measurement. In terms of what constitutes knowledge assets, different authors have different views. According to Handzic and Zhou (2005), they can be classified into human capital (e.g., employee know-how, expertise, and experience); organisational internal capital (e.g., management, organisational structure, attitudes, information systems, culture, manuals, and procedures); and customer or external capital (e.g., brands, reputation, customer and supplier relationships). With respect to measurement approach, monetary school of thought attempts to extend current accounting practice and apply monetary measures to value knowledge assets. In contrast, holistic school of thought provides nonfinancial customer, process, learning, and growth perspectives. For each perspective, key success factors are developed and translated into critical indicators.

Finally, the framework distinguishes three generic types of knowledge processes: those that generate new knowledge, those that transfer the existing knowledge, and those that apply possessed knowledge to produce new knowledge. These are categorized by grouping similar processes at different stages of knowledge existence. For example, knowledge can be generated by creative ideas, study, learning by doing, or by recognizing potentially useful patterns in captured data and expressing them in understandable form. Next, knowledge can be transferred by social process or by technological process. This can be achieved by social interaction of people who meet face-to–face, or via articulated knowledge into explicit form through KMS. Knowledge can be applied by some processes to produce new forms. For example, this can be done by processing and combining knowledge possessed into an integrated judgmental response.

Empirical Study

Study Objectives

Although there have been many individual case studies of various knowledge management initiatives in organisations (e.g., Collison & Parcell, 2001; Fruin, 1997; Galliers, 2002; Gerlach & Lincoln, 2000), there is little empirical evidence regarding the actual penetration and impact of knowledge management (Kluge, Stein, & Licht, 2001; Machlup, 1962; Porat, 1977). The studies available emphasised the introduction of KM programmes and therefore, considered factors such as facilitators of, and barriers to, success. Therefore, there was scope for a study that examined perceptions (Likert, 1967) from both the individual and organisation points of view.

The aim of the study was to investigate five aspects of knowledge management including leadership, culture, technology, process, and measurement. In light of the foregoing commentary, the first stage of this study is to outline the organisational environment and specific factors to assess the approach and extent to which two semiautonomous university schools manage their organisational knowledge.

Organisational Description

Two university schools studied are highly renowned teaching and research institutions in the field of information systems, technology, and management (ISTM), and computer science and engineering (CSE). They offer both undergraduate and postgraduate programs of study. They operate a joint research centre, plan and conduct a series of research seminars, and produce scholarly articles.

Wiig (1995) and Liebowitz (2000) discuss the use of surveys to explore a professional's thoughts about managing knowledge and solicit perspectives on the adequacy and efficiency of KM. The survey instrument employed in this study was based on a previously available instrument (Arthur Andersen, 1998). A copy of the survey instrument used is available in the appendix to this chapter. It provides the benefits of consistency, balance in coverage, and capture of individual attitudes. Modifications were made to the wording to reflect specifics of the organisation being studied and to achieve consistency in framing among questions (Oppenheim, 1992; Schulman and Presser, 1996). The survey design allows the respondent to rate the importance of particular KM practices and, in a parallel set of questions, the perceived extent to which they are implemented. Prior to administration, the survey items were assigned to the four aspects in two independent interrater exercises. Reliability is in excess of 0.9. Participants in the study were academic staff with full-time (continuing and contract) employment.

To minimise potential threats to validity, questionnaires were distributed to all academics who satisfied the specified criteria, and a brief explanation was provided. Responses were anonymous and participation was voluntary. Distributed questionnaires were completed without the researchers being present. High level of response and the profile across positions ensures that the sample is representative of the population.

While the formal survey sought specific responses, the researchers also considered their own organisational environment. The researchers recognised the potential for bias in the study in view of their role and responsibilities within the school. Guidance was sought from well-regarded ethnographic accounts (Geertz, 1974; Trauth, 1997; Van Maanen, 1988). Their ethnographic approaches present the problem of presenting a convincing result (Crapanzo, 1986). As the current research involves an audit of the corporate culture of a specific real-world organisation, it becomes necessary to consider the results themselves and their meaning in the social context to the researcher. Proponents of this approach also argue that the results can provide a greater level of depth and understanding of self-image (Pratt, 1986). As the design generates insufficient data to investigate cause-and-effect relationships, it requires careful planning and attention in order to establish validity (Cook, 2000). In short, the survey required a personal perspective account, as well as a positivist count in reviewing the results.

Results

A descriptive analysis of data was performed, as suggested by Tukey (1977), to identify prevailing patterns and ensure plausibility of findings. In order to identify a central tendency in participants' perceptions, the average scores of their responses to relevant questionnaire items were calculated. These scores are presented in Table 20.1, the scale for questionnaire items being 1-7 (7 being the maximum and 1 being the minimum).

With respect to the perceived importance of the five knowledge management practices studied, the mean scores obtained ranged from 4.66 to 5.68. Participants from ISTM and CSE rated a mean score of 5.28 and 5.31 for leadership, 5.36 and 5.68 for culture, 4.84 and 5.24 for technology, 4.66 and 4.05 for process, and 4.75 and 5.25 for measurement practices. With a seven-point scale, scores greater than 4 indicated that participants tended to perceive all five practices as being quite important, but the most important of all was the culture.

With respect to the perceived implementation of these practices, the mean scores obtained were 3.08 and 3.61 for leadership, 3.24 and 4.33 for culture, 3.38 and

Table 20.1. Summary results of knowledge management practices survey

Knowledge Management Practice	Perceived Importance Mean Score		Perceived Implementation Mean Score	
	ISTM	CSE	ISTM	CSE
Leadership	5.28	5.31	3.08	3.61
Culture	5.36	5.68	3.24	4.33
Technology	4.84	5.24	3.38	3.60
Process	4.66	5.05	2.39	2.93
Measurement	4.75	5.25	2.11	3.01
	5.32	**5.31**	**3.16**	**3.50**

3.60 for technology, 2.39 and 2.39 for process, and 2.11 and 3.01 for measurement practices. Scores less than 4 indicated that participants perceived the level of implementation of these knowledge-management practices in their respective schools as being rather low, particularly with respect to knowledge process and measurement practices. The only exception was the CSE culture with a score of 4.33.

Discussion

Main Findings

The key finding from the survey of knowledge-management practices in the school studied is the variance between the perceived importance and implementation. This was demonstrated by low scores obtained for participants' perceptions of the implementation of knowledge processes and their sociotechnological enablers, as compared to their perceptions of their respective importance. Each of the factors in the model is now considered.

The results show that academics appreciated the prime importance of school culture and what it means in term of the encouragement of knowledge development. Typically, a supportive culture values learning, encourages reflection and thinking, and encourages knowledge sharing (Bryant & Haynes, 2001). In addition, in knowledge cultures there is flexibility and a desire to innovate and drive the learning process, and an environment where employees take responsibility for their own learning. However, the results show that the value of importance over-scored implementation.

Our analysis of people's perceptions regarding these aspects of KM appear to suggest that the actual culture was acceptable to CSE academics, as they were fairly happy with the current trend. In contrast, low scores for ISTM academics indicate that they felt that there was no good and strong culture within their school to support effective knowledge development.

The participants perceived strong leadership as another very important knowledge-management practice. Examples of knowledge-supportive leadership typically include recognition of the cental importance of managing knowledge to organistional strategy, encouraging learning to support existing and create new competencies, developing human resource plans and reward schemes based on the contribution to the development of organisational knowledge. The high level of awareness of leadership importance found in this study is an encouraging finding. However, the low implementation results indicate current management disinterest in KM. This suggests there may be a need for a new type of leader to guide education/research institutions towards managing and using their knowledge resources for maximum benefit. Handzic and Zhou (2005) suggest that the distinguishing characteristics of leadership is that of being a catalyst through inspiring, mentoring, setting examples, listening, and engendering trust and respect. This requires individuals with a diverse range of knowledge, skills, and abilities, including interpersonal, communication and change management, business and technical expertise, and ability to build relationships.

With respect to technology, the findings indicate that it was also considered as quite important KM practice, although more so among CSE than ISTM academics. It is generally believed that technological infrastructure has the potential to enable or facilitate knowledge processes by providing a platform for knowledge capture or sharing. Some examples where technology can be successfuly used to facilitate knowledge processes include linking all members of the firm to one another and to all relevant external parties, creating an institutional memory that is accessible to the entire organisation, linking the organistion with its customers and partners, supporting collaboration amongst employees, fostering human-centered, real-time, integrated, and smart systems. Findings of this study indicate that there may be a need for further investment in technological infrastructure in order to fully facilitate knowledge-management processes.

In addition, the study highlighted a low level of implementation of knowledge processes. Facilitated or not, organisational knowledge is enhanced through a series of interrelated processes of knowledge creation, transfer and utilisation. Organisations that implement these processes may exhibit some of the following characteristics: systematic identification of knowledge gaps and well-defined processes to address and close them, the development of sophisticated and ethical intelligence-gathering mechanisms, and the involvement of all workforce members in looking for ideas.

Formalising the process of capturing and transferring knowledge, including documentation and lessons learnt, valuing and transferring tacit knowledge across the organisation through encouraging experimentation and socialisation. Our findings indicate that academics recognise the importance of these processes quite well, as shown by their high response scores. However, once again, these findings indicate a low level of implementation of many of these processes.

Finally, findings indicate that participants tended to view their schools' knowledge measurement practices as being in the formative stages of development. Our proposed framework clearly suggests, the need for continuous knowledge measurement in order to monitor and adjust an organisation's knowledge management strategy over time. Implementing good knowledge measurement practices is usually evidenced in finding ways to link knowledge management to results, developing specific sets of indicators to manage knowledge, including a balanced set of soft and hard, financial and nonfinancial indicators, as well as by allocating resources towards efforts that measurably increase organisational knowledge base. The results of the study indicate that these areas need to be addressed by the school.

Insiders' Reaction

In considering how to offer perspective on these findings, a group of academics from ISTM turned to a confessional mode and considered their own position in relation to the survey (Oliver et al., 2003). This approach parallels that suggested and practised by Schultze (2000). This section offers a brief summary appraising authors' motivations, practices, and reactions to the findings.

After returning to early western conceptions of knowledge, Snowden (1999) concludes that trust, naiveté, and curiosity are key words in knowledge management. This unlikely combination provided the authors with useful insights. As KM researchers and practitioners themselves, the authors were concerned that there was a lack of recognition of the contribution of KM in education, given government expectations for innovation and competitiveness in a global market (Carneiro, 2000; Cronin & Davenport, 2001; Kidwell, Van der Linde, & Johnson, 2001).

Unlike other countries, the Australian government commitment to the knowledge economy can be described as mild, given the latest knowledge economy policy documentation at www.fed.gov.au has a deadline for submission dated 2001. Thus, any organisational commitment to KM will default to policies and champions within the governing body. This double absence is clearly distressing to the authors, as they are acutely aware that members of the school tacitly hold considerable institutional knowledge (Stein, 1995). The authors had a number of experiences where they wasted time on administrative matters, or made suboptimal decisions through lacking access to that knowledge.

Recognising the evidence of management disinterest in KM gave impetus for considering external linkages to obtain sustenance and support for KM. Rather than waiting for KM to be adopted officially, the informal tactics were practised centred on using small internal communities of practice, supplemented by linkages to external networks. This latter approach may not necessarily provide examples of best practice, however, it confirms an ever-present awareness of both deficiencies and potentialities while stimulating the members to provide teaching and research within the ability of their resourcing.

Conclusion

The empirical findings presented in this chapter provide an insight into the penetration of knowledge-management practices into a typical knowledge-intensive organisation, such as university school. In particular, our findings demonstrate a high level of awareness of importance with a low level of actual implementation. This suggests that the schools studied are in the early formative stages of embracing knowledge-management practices.

From the results presented in this paper, one may conclude that KM is an important aspect of organisational management success that needs to be carefully considered. The high level of awareness of its importance found in this study is an encouraging finding. If planned and implemented carefully, in alignment with organisational objectives and core competencies, it may enable the release of the organisational knowledge resources that will bring ultimate success.

In terms of the implementation of knowledge-management practices, our findings indicate that a major challenge exists in this area. The results of the study identify organisations in the formative stages of this process. The low level of implementation, found with respect to the several types of knowledge-management practices investigated, are the major indicators of this being an emerging area. Findings also indicate and highlight areas where issues need to be further addressed within the schools being studied. Further research is proposed to explore these issues including a follow-up survey to ascertain any change in perception, without there having been any change in the management.

When considering the nature of the organisations being studied, the findings indicate that a major challenge exists for the university schools. Whilst operating in an ever-changing world and environment, the challenge will be to find and implement the most appropriate mix of knowledge management practices in alignment with the schools' goals and strategies. This challenge must be embraced and faced head-on in order to ensure the schools' continued success.

References

Albert, S., & Bradley, K. (1997). *Managing knowledge: Experts, agencies and organizations.* Cambridge: Cambridge University Press.

Arthur Andersen. (1998, January). *The knowledge management practices book.* Australia: Arthur Andersen.

Bassi, L. J., & van Buren, M. E. (2000). New measures for a new era. In D. Morey, M. Maybury, & B. Thuraisingham (Eds.), *Knowledge management: Classic and contemporary works* (pp. 355-373). Cambridge, Massachusetts: MIT Press.

Brown, J. S., & Duguid, P. (2000). *The social life of information.* Boston, Massachusetts: Harvard Business School Press.

Bryant, J., & Haynes, G. (2001). *Managing knowledge for competitive advantage.* Paper presented at the IEE Seminar.

Budzik, J., & Hammond, K. (1999, October 31-November 4). A system for the capture, organisation and re-use of expertise. In L. Woods (Ed.), *ASIS '99 Proceedings of the 62nd annual meeting. Knowledge creation, organisation and use*, Washington DC. Medford, NJ: Information today.

Carneiro, A. (2000). How does knowledge management influence innovation and competitiveness. *Journal of Knowledge Management, 4*(2), 87-98.

Carr, N. G. (1999). A new way to process knowledge. *Harvard Business Review*, September-October, 24-25.

Collison, C., & Parcell, G. (2001). *Learning to fly: Practical lessons from one of the world's leading knowledge companies.* Oxford: Capstone.

Cook, T. D. (2000). Toward a practical theory of external validity. In L. Bickman (Ed.), *Validity and social experimentation: Donald Campbell's legacy, volume 1* (pp3-43). Thousand Oaks, CA: Sage Publications.

Crapazano, V. (1986). Hermes dilemma: The masking of subversion in ethnographic description. In J. Clifford, & G. E. W. Marcus (Eds.), *Writing culture: The poetics and politics of ethnography* (pp. 51-76). Berkeley: University of California.

Cronin, E., & Davenport, E. (2001). Knowledge management in higher education. In G. Bernbom (Ed), *Information alchemy: The art and science of knowledge management* (pp. 25-42). San Francisco: Jossey-Bass.

Davenport, T. H., & Prusak, L. (1998). *Working knowledge.* Boston: Harvard Business School Press.

Despres, C., & Chauvel, D. (2000). A thematic analysis of the thinking in knowledge management. In C. Despres, & D. Chauvel (Eds.), *Knowledge horizons: The present and the promise of knowledge management* (pp. 55-86). London: Butterworth-Heinemann.

DiBella, A. J., Nevis, E. C., & Goiuld, J. M. (1996). Organizational learning style as a core capability. In B. Moingeon, & A. Edmondson (Eds.), *Organizational learning and competitive advantage* (pp. 38-55). London: Sage Publications.

Dixon, N. M. (2000). *Common knowledge: How companies thrive by sharing what they know.* Boston, MA: Harvard Business School Press.

Drucker, P. F. (1967). *The effective executive.* London: William Heinemann.

Drucker, P. F. (1993). *Post-capitalist society.* New York: Harper Business.

Earl, M. J. (2001). Knowledge management strategies: Towards a taxonomy. *Journal of Management Information Systems, 18*(5), 218-233.

Fruin, W. M. (1997). *Knowledge works: Managing intellectual capital at Toshiba.* Oxford: Oxford University Press.

Geertz, C. (1974). From the native's point of view. *Bulletin of the American Academy of Arts and Sciences, 28,* 27-45.

Gerlach, M. L., & Lincoln, J. R. (2000). Economic organization and innovation in Japan: Network spin-offs and the creation of enterprise. In G. von Krog, I. Nonaka, & T. Nishiguchi (Eds.), *Knowledge creation: A source of value* (pp. 151-196). London: Macmillan Press.

Gibbons, M., Limoges, C., Nowotny, H., Schwartzman, S., Scott, P., & Trow P. M.(1999). *New production of knowledge.* London: Sage Publications.

Handzic, M. (2001, November 8-9). Knowledge management: A research framework. In *Proceedings of the 2nd European Conference on Knowledge Management (ECKM 2001),* Bled, Slovenia.

Handzic, M., & Zhou, A. Z. (2005). *Knowledge management: An integrative approach.* Oxford, UK: Chandos Publishing.

Huysman, M., & de Wit, D. (2002). *Knowledge sharing in practice.* Dordrecht: Kluwer.

Kidwell, J., Van der Linde, K. M., & Johnson (2001). Applying corporate knowledge management practices in higher education. In G. Bernbom (Ed.), *Information alchemy: The art and science of knowledge management* (pp. 1-24). San Francisco: Jossey-Bass.

Klösgen (1996). Knowledge discovery in databases terminology. In U. M. Fayyad, G. Piatesky-Schapiro, P. Smyth, & R. Uthurusamy (Eds.), *Advances in knowledge discovery and data mining* (pp. 573-592). Menlo Park, CA: AAAI Press/MIT Press.

Kludge, J., Stein, W., & Licht, T. (2001). *Knowledge unplugged: The McKinsey and Company global survey on knowledge management.* London: Palgrave.

Liebowitz, J. (2000). *Building organisational intelligence: A knowledge management primer.* New York: CRC Press.

Likert, R. (1967). The method of constructing an attitude scale. In M. Fishbein (Ed.) *Readings in attitude theory and measurement* (pp. 90-95). New York: John Wiley.

Machlup, F. (1962). *The production and distribution of knowledge in the United States.* Princeton: Princeton University Press.

Macintosh, A., & Stader, J. (1999). Knowing who knows what—Skills and capability ontologies. In *International symposium on the management of industrial and corporate knowledge. ISMICK99 Pre-proceedings.* Rotterdam: School of management of Erasmus University of Rotterdam.

Malhotra, Y. (2000). From information management to knowledge management: Beyond the hi-tech hidebound systems. In T. K. Srikantaiah, & M. E. Koenig (Eds.), *Knowledge management for the information professional* (pp. 37-61).

Mann, M. M., Rudman, R. M., Jenckes, T. A., & McNurlin, B. C. (1997). EPRI-NET: Leveraging knowledge in the electric utility industry. In L. Prusak (Ed.), *Knowledge in organizations* (pp. 73-97). London: Butterworth-Heinemann.

Newell, S, Huang, J. C., Galliers, R., & Pan, S. L. (2002). Implementing enterprise resource planning and knowledge management systems in tandem: Fostering efficiency and innovation complementarity. *Information and Organization, 13*(1), 25-52.

Nonaka, I., & Takeuchi, H. (1995). *The knowledge creating company: How Japanese companies create the dynamics of innovation.* New York: Oxford University Press.

O'Dell, C., & Grayson, C. J. (1998). *If only we knew what we know.* New York: Free Press.

Oliver, G., Handzic, M., & VanToorn, C. (2003, September 18-19). Knowledge management in academia: The shoemaker's paradox, In *Proceedings of the European Conference on Knowledge Management (ECKM 2003),* Oxford, UK.

Oppenheim, A. N. (1992). *Questionnaire design, interviewing and attitude measurement,* London: New edition, Pinter.

Porat, M. (1977, May). *The information economy: Definition and measurement* (OT Special Publication 77-12(1)). Washington DC: US Department of Commerce.

Pratt, M. L. (1986). Fieldwork in common places. In J. Clifford, & G. E. W. Marcus (Eds.), *Writing culture: The poetics and politics of ethnography* (pp. 27-50). Berkeley: University of California.

Savary, M. (1999). Knowledge management and competition in the consulting industry. *California Management Review, 41*(2), 95-107.

Schultze, U. (2000). A confessional account of an ethnography about knowledge work. *MIS Quarterly, 24*(1), March, 3-41.

Schuman, H., & Presser, S. (1996). *Questions and answers in attitude surveys: Experiments on question form, wording and context.* Thousand Oaks, CA: Sage Publications.

Snowden, D. (1999). A framework for creating a sustainable programme. In S. Rock (Ed.), *Knowledge management: A real guide* (pp. 7-17). London: Caspian Publishing and IBM.

Snowden, D. (2002). Complex acts of knowing: Paradox and descriptive self-awareness. *Journal of knowledge management, 6*(2), 100-111.

Starbuck, (1997). Knowledge by knowledge intensive firms. In L. Prusak (Ed.), *Knowledge in organizations* (pp. 147-175). London: Butterworth-Heinemann.

Stein, E. W. (1995). Organisational memory: Review of concepts and recommendations for management. *International Journal of Information Management, 15*(1), 17-32.

Stern, D. (1996). Human resource development in the knowledge-based economy: Roles of firms, schools and governments. In D. Neef (Ed.), *The knowledge economy* (pp. 249-265). London: Butterworth-Heinemann.

Stewart, T. A. (1997). *Intellectual capital: The new wealth of organisations.* New York: Doubleday.

Trauth, E. M. (1997). Achieving the research goal with qualitative methods: Lessons learned along the way. In A. S. Lee, J. Liebenau, & J. I. DeGross (Eds.), *Information systems and qualitative research* (pp. 225-245). London: Chapman and Hall.

Tukey, J. W. (1977). *Exploratory data analysis.* Reading, MA: Addison-Wesley.

Van Maanen, J. (1988). *Tales from the field: On writing ethnography.* Chicago: University of Chicago Press.

Weick, K. E. (1979). *The social psychology of organizing* (2nd ed.). Reading, MA: Addison-Wesley.

Wenger, E., McDermott, R., & Snyder, W. M. (2002). *Cultivating communities of practice.* Boston: Harvard Business School Press.

Wiig, K. M. (1995). *Knowledge management: The central management focus for intelligent-acting organisations.* Arlington, TX: Schema Press.

Appendix

Survey of Knowledge Management Practices in Education: Academics Perspective

Please indicate your views regarding knowledge management practices in your school by circling the number that best reflects the importance of each practice to you and the level of implementation of the practice within your school.

	Knowledge Management Practice	Importance Low High	Implementation Low High
1.	Managing knowledge is central to the school strategy	1 2 3 4 5 6 7	1 2 3 4 5 6 7
2.	The school uses learning to support the existing core competencies and create new ones.	1 2 3 4 5 6 7	1 2 3 4 5 6 7
3.	Individuals are hired and evaluated for their contributions to the school knowledge.	1 2 3 4 5 6 7	1 2 3 4 5 6 7
4.	The school encourages and facilitates knowledge sharing	1 2 3 4 5 6 7	1 2 3 4 5 6 7
5.	A climate of openness and trust permeates the school.	1 2 3 4 5 6 7	1 2 3 4 5 6 7
6.	Student value creation is a major objective of knowledge management	1 2 3 4 5 6 7	1 2 3 4 5 6 7
7.	Flexibility and a desire to innovate drive the learning process.	1 2 3 4 5 6 7	1 2 3 4 5 6 7
8.	Academics take responsibility for their own learning	1 2 3 4 5 6 7	1 2 3 4 5 6 7
9.	Technology links all members of the school to one another and to all relevant external public.	1 2 3 4 5 6 7	1 2 3 4 5 6 7
10.	Technology creates an institutional memory that is accessible to the entire school.	1 2 3 4 5 6 7	1 2 3 4 5 6 7
11.	Technology brings the school closer to its students	1 2 3 4 5 6 7	1 2 3 4 5 6 7
12.	The school fosters development of human-centred information technology	1 2 3 4 5 6 7	1 2 3 4 5 6 7
13.	Technology that supports collaboration is rapidly placed in the hands of academics.	1 2 3 4 5 6 7	1 2 3 4 5 6 7
14.	Information systems are real-time, integrated and smart.	1 2 3 4 5 6 7	1 2 3 4 5 6 7
15.	The school has invented ways to link knowledge management to results.	1 2 3 4 5 6 7	1 2 3 4 5 6 7
16.	The school has developed a specific set of indicators to manage knowledge.	1 2 3 4 5 6 7	1 2 3 4 5 6 7
17.	The school's set of measures balances hard and soft indicators.	1 2 3 4 5 6 7	1 2 3 4 5 6 7

continued on following page

18.	The school allocates resources toward efforts that measurably indicate its knowledge base.	1 2 3 4 5 6 7	1 2 3 4 5 6 7
19.	Knowledge gaps are systematically identified and well-defined processes are used to close them.	1 2 3 4 5 6 7	1 2 3 4 5 6 7
20.	A sophisticated and ethical intelligence-gathering mechanism has been developed	1 2 3 4 5 6 7	1 2 3 4 5 6 7
21.	All academics of the organisation are involved in looking for ideas in (non) traditional places.	1 2 3 4 5 6 7	1 2 3 4 5 6 7
22.	The organisation has formalised the process of transferring lessons learned.	1 2 3 4 5 6 7	1 2 3 4 5 6 7
23.	Tacit knowledge of academics is valued and transferred across the organisation.	1 2 3 4 5 6 7	1 2 3 4 5 6 7

Chapter XXI

Codification or Personalisation:
Choosing the Right Knowledge
Management Strategy

Abstract

This chapter reports the results of an empirical examination of the effectiveness of two knowledge management strategies (codification and personalisation) in improving decision-making performance in a simulated forecasting task. Codification was manipulated with and without a procedural knowledge map, and personalisation in terms of an interactive and noninteractive decision environment. Results indicate that only codification had a significant effect on performance. Subjects with a procedural knowledge map demonstrated less frequent use of decision heuristics, and generated more accurate forecasts compared to those without such a map. Subjects from an interactive decision environment performed similarly to those working on their own.

Introduction

The growing interest in knowledge management has been fuelled by three major development trends: globalisation, with the increasing intensity of competition; digitalisation, enabled by advances in information and communication technology; and the rise of knowledge-based organisations together with changing organisational structures, new worker profiles, preferences, and predispositions. As organisations move towards becoming knowledge based, their business success will increasingly depend on how successful knowledge workers are at developing and applying knowledge productively and efficiently.

Knowledge management (KM) is seen as a key factor in realising and sustaining organisational success from improved efficiency and innovation. The basic assumption of KM is that organisations that manage organisational and individual knowledge better will deal more successfully with the challenges of the new business environment. More specifically, knowledge management is considered as central to process and product improvement, to executive decision making, and to organisational adaptation and renewal (Earl, 2001).

The central task of those concerned with organisational knowledge management is to determine ways to better cultivate, nurture, and exploit knowledge at different levels and in different contexts. However, there are serious differences among researchers in what constitutes useful knowledge and the ways in which it should be managed. Various descriptive and prescriptive KM models and frameworks have been appearing in the academic literature of many disciplines for some time and recently, there have been a sequence of articles attempting to summarise and categorise these (for review, see Handzic & Hasan, 2003).

According to Tsui (2003), the two most dominant approaches to deploying KM initiatives in organisations are codification and personalisation, introduced by Hansen et al. (Hansen, Nohria, & Tierney, 1999). The proponents of codification approach show a central preoccupation with explicit knowledge. They favour greater emphasis on the use of technology, especially organisational databases and discovery tools. On the other hand, the proponents of personalisation seem to be more interested in tacit knowledge and sharing. They focus more on people and cultural issues in the attempt to establish knowledge communities. Locating and connecting people of common interest is the prime goal here.

It is not unusual for organisations to adopt a combination of the two approaches in deploying KM initiatives. Some authors argue that such a holistic approach to KM is the only possible way to realise the full power of knowledge (Davenport & Prusak, 1998). Others, like Hansen et al. (1999), emphasise that trying to pursue the "wrong" approach, or both at the same time, can waste time and money and even undermine business success. They propose that the codification approach is more suited for situations where work tasks are similar and existing knowledge assets can be reused. In contrast, they suggest that the personalisation approach is more suited for situations where the tasks are fairly unique and knowledge largely tacit. Empirical evidence to support these propositions is largely missing.

To gain a greater understanding of the effectiveness of different KM strategies, this study attempts to address the issue by empirically investigating the impact of personalisation and codification approaches in the context of decision making. Managerial decision making can be viewed as a knowledge-intensive activity. In response to the demands of their work, decision makers often obtain explicit knowledge from the stores of business intelligence available in organisations, and gain tacit knowledge through personal interactions with peers. It is implicitly assumed that the availability of knowledge stores, and the opportunity for peer interaction, should lead to an increase in their working knowledge, this resulting in improved decision performance. However, little is known about the actual success of these initiatives and the returns resulting from them. Therefore, it is of particular interest to this study to examine whether and how two different KM strategies (codification and personalisation) affect decision makers' working knowledge, and what impact this may have on the quality of their subsequent decisions.

Review of Knowledge Management Strategies

Codification

Knowledge has been widely recognised as a critical organisational resource for competitive advantage in the new economy. One of the important objectives of knowledge management is to capture, codify, organise, and store relevant knowledge for later use by organisational members. Hansen et al. (1999) call this a codification approach to managing knowledge. The assumption is that the availability of a KM system, such as a codified knowledge repository, should lead to increased organisational knowledge, and result in improved performance (Hahn & Subramani, 2000). Various technologies, including databases, textbases, data warehouses, and data marts, may be useful in building organisational knowledge repositories.

Currently, there is ample evidence to show that organisations do implement these technologies as part of their best KM practices (A. A., 1998). However, there is little empirical evidence regarding the impact of these knowledge repositories on organisational performance (Alavi & Leidner, 2001). Some researchers point out that our ability to accumulate and store knowledge artefacts has by far surpassed our ability to process them, and warn of the danger that vast institutional memories may easily become tombs rather than wellsprings of knowledge (Fayyad & Uthurusamy, 2001).

As cognitive overload increasingly chokes the effective utilisation of codified knowledge in organisations, scholars are pointing to some promising new knowledge technologies. Knowledge maps, or k-maps, are seen as a particularly feasible method of coordinating, simplifying, highlighting, and navigating through complex silos of knowledge artefacts (Wexler, 2001). Knowledge maps point to knowledge but they do not contain it. They are guides, not repositories (Davenport & Prusak, 1998). One of the main purposes of k-maps is to locate important knowledge in an organisation and show users where to find it. (Kim, Suh, & Hwang, 2003). Effective k-maps should point not only to people, but to document and databases as well. K-maps should also locate actionable information, identify domain experts, and facilitate organisation-wide learning (Eppler, 2003). They should also trace the acquisition and loss of knowledge, as well as map knowledge flows throughout the organisation (Grey, 1999).

A review of literature reveals a number of different types of k-maps. Eppler (2003) recognises five types: knowledge application, knowledge structure, knowledge source, knowledge asset, and knowledge development maps. Wexler (2001) identifies concept, competency, strategy, causal, and cognitive maps. Plumley (2003) suggests that knowledge maps are either procedural, conceptual, competency, or social network based. Essentially, concept, structure, asset, and cognitive maps provide a framework for capturing and organising domain knowledge around topical areas. Competency and source maps act as yellow pages, or directories, that enable people to find needed expertise within an organisation. Finally, procedural or application maps present business processes with related knowledge sources. Any type of knowledge that drives these processes or results from execution of these processes can be mapped. For example, this could include tacit knowledge in people, explicit knowledge in databases, customer, or process knowledge (Plumley, 2003).

Procedural k-maps may offer various benefits. They help to improve the visibility of knowledge by showing which type of knowledge has to be applied at a certain process stage or in a specific business situation. On top of this, these maps also provide pointers to locate that specific knowledge (Eppler, 2003). Procedural k-maps also help to improve the usability of knowledge by forcing participants to identify key knowledge areas that are critical to their business tasks. Finally, the analysis of this knowledge map triggers ideas for sharing and leveraging knowledge most suited to the organisation and the business context (Plumley, 2003).

The main objective of this study is to empirically test these assumptions. In particular, the study will examine whether and how the availability of a procedural knowledge map may help decision makers to improve performance in a judgemental forecasting task.

Personalisation

In the personalisation knowledge management approach, knowledge is tied to the person who develops it and shares through person-to-person interaction (Hansen et al., 1999). The spiral model of knowledge creation (Nonaka, 1998; Nonaka & Takeuchi, 1995) suggests the crucial importance of socialisation in developing and transferring tacit knowledge in an organisation. The spiral model proposes that knowledge creation starts with socialisation, which is the process of converting new tacit knowledge through shared experiences in day-to-day social interaction. Socialisation within the originating "ba" (Nonaka & Konno, 1998) provides a rich and meaningful platform for face-to-face natural interaction. Sometimes labelled as colocated communication, this enables a medium in which multiple senses and means (e.g., tone, eyes, body) can be used to convey knowledge. A chat between employees may well foster the development of trust and provide a foundation for vital creative working.

A comprehensive survey of best KM practices (A. A., 1998) reveals that most organisations implement some kind of KM initiative to connect people and enable their interaction and collaboration. However, there are differences among researchers regarding the value of virtual (technology-mediated) interaction in comparison with real (face-to-face) interaction in knowledge management. Some researchers warn that technologies lack the emotional richness and depth of real, live, in-person interaction (Santosus, 2001), and are unable to fully develop relationships and an understanding of complex situations (Bender & Fish, 2000). Others argue that communication mediated by technology is no less effective than face-to-face communication (Warkentin, Sayeed, & Hightower, 1997). More and more cybercommunities are also beginning to challenge traditional ideas about communities' needs for a physical presence.

There are also differences among the researchers regarding the nature of socialisation. Perhaps the most intuitive function of socialisation is to transfer knowledge between people. The exchange model of social process suggests that people interact primarily for the purpose of information collection. The situation-theoretic approach to interaction (Devlin, 1999) assumes that, for most conversations, the aim of each participant is to take new information about the focal object or situation into his or her context. The persuasive arguments perspective (Heath & Gonzales, 1995) assumes that an individual's position on any given issue will be a function of the number and persuasiveness of available arguments. It assumes that individuals come up with a few arguments of their own, but during interaction they collect novel arguments and may shift their initial opinions.

The group work approach recognises the collaborative nature of the interaction act and suggests the potential synergy associated with collaborative activity (Marakas, 1999). However, much of the earlier research into group interactions questions the relative virtues of collaborative over individual performance due to the groupthink phenomenon. According to some theorists (Janis, 1982), members of the cohesive long-term groups strive for unanimity, and do not realistically appraise alternative courses of action. This results in unfavourable outcomes.

Decision-making involves a significant amount of social interaction. Individuals often seek to consult with others before deciding what jobs to take, what cars to buy, or what changes to make in their personal life. Managerial decision makers also follow similar interactive procedures when making business decisions. They collect information and opinions from their subordinates, peers, and superiors, but make final decisions alone. Because they make their final decisions individually, decision makers can use or ignore the information they collect during social interaction. It is argued that situations, where individual decision makers interact in a social environment but make their own decisions, should be free from groupthink-style outcomes. In such situations, interaction is assumed to allow individuals to more accurately assess their information and analysis, and improve individual decision performance.

Given the high emphasis placed on socialisation by KM theory, and few inconclusive findings reported by prior empirical studies (for review, see Handzic & Low, 2001), the main objective of this study is to examine whether and how an interactive decision environment may influence decision makers' performance in a judgemental forecasting task.

Empirical Study

Experimental Task

A forecasting task simulation was created for the purpose of studying the effect of codification and personalisation strategies to aid knowledge gain and support decision making. It was implemented in Microsoft Visual Basic language. The procedural knowledge map was developed and incorporated into the simulation in order to give users a clearer and more understandable knowledge visualisation that could lead to higher quality decisions. Users assumed the role of the Production Manager for the Dream Cream dairy company in Sydney. One of their responsibilities was to make decisions on daily production of ice creams sold from the company's outlet at Bondi Beach. Users were required to make accurate sales estimates for ice cream to be sold the following day. Users completed the task for 35 consecutive days.

All participants were provided with sequential historic information of the task-relevant variable (product sales) to provide some cues to suggest future behaviour. The task differed with respect to codification and personalisation strategies implementation.

One half of the subjects worked in an interactive decision environment, and were encouraged to share (in pairs) their information and opinions with others while making decisions, but were not required to reach a consensual decision. The other half made decisions on their own, without any interaction with others. One half of the participants performed a decision problem with a support of a procedural knowledge map, and another half performed the same task without such an aid.

Financial remuneration was based on users' performance. Users incurred costs depending on the accuracy of daily estimates. Therefore, minimisation of cost, or in other words, maximisation of accuracy was the goal of the task. Over and under estimation errors were equally costly. At the beginning of the experiment, task descriptions were provided to inform subjects about the task scenario and requirements. The given text differed with respect to the knowledge map provided and the form of interaction allowed. In addition, throughout the experiment, instructions and feedback were provided to each participant to analyse earlier performance and to adjust future strategies.

Experimental Design and Variables

A laboratory experiment with random assignment to treatment groups was used, as it allowed for greater experimental control and made possible drawing of stronger inferences about causal relationships between variables. The experiment had a 2×2 factorial design with two independent factors: (1) *codification strategy* (with or without procedural knowledge map*)*, and (2) *personalisation strategy* (interactive or noninteractive decision environment).

Codification strategy was manipulated in terms of the procedural knowledge map availability. The manipulation was achieved by developing two different versions of the experimental instrument. In one version, users were provided only with a simulated repository of knowledge artefacts, and in the other version, a procedural knowledge map was added to it in the form of a set of guidelines. These guidelines described critical steps in the decision process based on decomposition of time series pattern into trend, seasonality, noise, and cycle subpatterns (Makridakis & Wheelwright, 1989). More information about the decomposition method is given in Chapter VII of this book. Personalisation strategy was manipulated in terms of the nature of decision environment. The manipulation was achieved by completely constraining, or maximally encouraging (through dialogue), sharing of ideas and information before making ones own decisions.

Decision performance was evaluated in terms of *cost* operationalised by absolute error (AE) and expressed in dollar terms, and *accuracy* operationalised by symmetric absolute percentage error (SAPE). AE was calculated for each trial as an absolute difference between subjects' forecasts and actual sales values. SAPE was calculated by dividing AE by an average of actual and forecast values, and multiplying by 100% (for details and justification, see Makridakis, 1993). Subjects' decision behaviour was evaluated in terms of self-reported dominant *forecasting method*. Individual subjects' *confidence* in the quality of decisions and *satisfaction* with their KM support were collected for control purposes and to supplement the measures of actual performance. These were rated on seven-point Likert scales, with 1 as least and 7 as most end points.

Time-Series Generation

For the purpose of the study, the product sales time series was artificially generated as a seasonal series with an upward trend, in order to take into account days of the week and the holiday time influences. The error term was added to account for irregular or random events. The intention was to create a decision task that is "knowable" but "complicated." According to Kurtz and Snowden (2003), such tasks require sensing of incoming data, analysis of that data using a method that seeks to identify the patterns, and response in accordance with interpretation of that analysis or in accordance with expert advice. In the current study, the optimal response required subjects to detect and decompose the time series into trend, season, and noise elements, and take these into account when making future predictions. Kurtz and Snowden suggest that a simple error in an assumption can lead to a false conclusion and result in poor performance. Thus, the detection of peak seasonal demands often can mean the difference between effective and ineffective decision.

Subjects and Procedure

Forty-eight graduate students enrolled in the Master of Commerce course "Knowledge Management Systems and Technology" at UNSW took part in the experiment. They participated on a voluntary basis, and received no monetary incentives. Some previous studies indicated that graduate students are appropriate subjects for this type of research (Ashton & Kramer, 1980; Remus, 1996; Whitecotton, 1996).

The experimental session was conducted in a microcomputer laboratory. On arrival, subjects were randomly assigned to one of the two treatment groups by choosing a microcomputer from a number of units set for the experiment. Before commencing the task, subjects were briefed about the purpose of the experiment, and read case study descriptions incorporated in the research instrument. They then performed the task. The session lasted about 1 hour.

Research Instrument

The research instrument used to facilitate the current study was adapted from Handzic (1996). The software was written in Microsoft Visual Basic. It included a task simulator, a decision support component, and a data collection component. The sample screen layout of research instrument is shown in Figure 21.1.

The instrument simulated a "complicated" forecasting task in a repetitive decision environment. The same program versions were used for interactive and noninteractive treatment groups. Entry of the final decision was enabled through clicking with the mouse on the special entry line and OK button for confirmation. Each prediction was displayed on the screen as a dot located above or below the corresponding actual sales. In this way the subjects were able to quickly estimate the direction and magnitude of their errors.

Several features have been implemented in the simulation software to aid users in learning the sales pattern and making their predictions as accurate as possible. These features were based on two concepts: time series analysis and graphical visualisation. Time series of sales events for 20 days were initially provided in order to guide the decision-making process. They were presented in the form of line curves in one consolidated graph. With the line graph of past sales, the users had a reasonable amount of knowledge to make fairly accurate future decisions. However, in a knowledge-based economy, "fairly good" is not enough. Therefore,

Figure 21.1. Screen layout of research instrument with procedural k-map

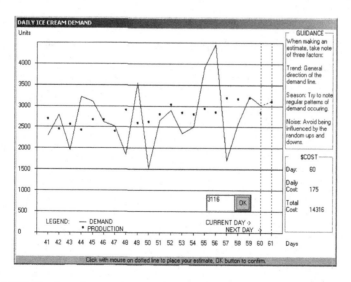

an extra KM feature was provided in one software version (see Figure 21.1) to help users extract as much useful knowledge as possible from raw content. To do so, the procedural knowledge map was employed. It consisted of a set of guidelines and pointers to key knowledge required to perform the task. It was assumed that these components jointly provided users with a very good idea of how to discover and use the predictive sales pattern in data. Alternatively, users could discuss the issue with peers and learn from each other.

Finally, the instrument enabled unobtrusive recording of the observed behaviour and performance. In addition, the instrument captured the subjective assessments of various task, behaviour, and performance aspects of interest. The ratings were made by selecting the most appropriate options from a simple questionnaire included in the simulation software. These records were saved in separate files for each subject and treatment for later analysis.

Results

Descriptive results (means or frequencies) for accuracy, method, confidence, and satisfaction variables by experimental groups are presented in Table 21.1. The collected data were further analysed by a series of parametric (Two-way ANOVA) and nonparametric (Mann-Whitney) statistical tests. The analyses found some significant results.

As expected, the results indicate significant positive effects of codification on cost, accuracy, method, and confidence, but not satisfaction. The mean AE of the subjects

Table 21.1. Descriptive results for dependent variables by experimental groups

Dependent Variable	Without K-map		With K-map		N
	Noninteractive	*Interactive*	*Noninteractive*	*Interactive*	
Cost (AE)	761.73	735.10	698.45	692.61	1680
Accuracy (SAPE)	7.8%	7.5%	7.0%	6.9%	1680
Method (Simple/Complex)	8/4	7/5	3/9	5/7	48
Confidence (Score)	2.9	2.7	3.5	3.8	48
Satisfaction (Score)	5.2	4.9	4.2	4.9	48

with the k-map was significantly smaller compared to those without the k-map (695.53 vs. 748.42, F=3.636, p=0.057). Similarly, mean SAPE of the subjects with the k-map was significantly smaller than that of their counterparts without the k-map (6.9% vs. 7.6%, F=5.151, p=0.023). Consistently, the subjects with the k-map tended to feel more confident in their performance than those without the k-map, as shown by their higher mean rank score (28.65 vs. 20.35, U=188.500, p=0.033). Better performance suggested greater knowledge of the decision problem and the subsequent application of a more appropriate forecasting method. Indeed, Mann-Whitney results revealed significant differences in strategies used by the two groups (28.00 vs. 21.00, U=204.000, p=0.045). Subjects with the k-map tended to use, less often, simple heuristics such as random or naive (8 vs. 15), and more often, complex methods such as averaging or trend analysis (16 vs. 9) as their dominant approach. However, codification had no significant impact on satisfaction. Although, to our surprise, subjects tended to like slightly less the system with the k-map than that without the k-map, the difference between their mean rank scores was not statistically significant (22.23 vs. 26.77, U=233.500, p=0.248).

In contrast to codification, the results indicate that personalisation had no significant impact on any of the dependent variables evaluated. With respect to cost and accuracy, interacting subjects tended to perform similarly to those working on their own. The mean AE of the subjects in the interactive environment was not significantly different from that in the noninteractive environment (713.86 vs. 730.09, F=0.343, p=0.558). Similarly, subjects in the interactive environment had similar mean SAPE as those in the noninteractive environment (7.2% vs. 7.4%, F=0.555, p=0.456). Consistent with the cost and accuracy results, subjects in the interactive environment reported similar level of confidence in their performance as those in the noninteractive environment. No significant difference was found between their mean rank scores (24.19 vs. 24.81, U=280.500, p=0.872). This suggested comparable knowledge of the decision problem and the choice of similar methods for the task performance. Indeed, Mann-Whitney test found no significant difference in strategies used by the two groups (24.00 vs. 25.00, U=276.000, p=0.775). The results show that interacting subjects tended to use, as their dominant approach, both simple heuristics (12 vs. 11) and complex methods (12 vs. 13) as often as their noninteracting counterparts. Finally, subjects were equally satisfied with both working environments, as shown by their similar mean rank scores (24.88 vs. 24.13, U=279.000, p=0.849).

Discussion

The main findings of this study make two important contributions to the development of KM theory: (1) support the contention that for the effective use of knowledge, decision makers need to pursue primarily one KM strategy; and (2) identify codification as a more appropriate strategy for solving "complicated" decision problems. More specifically, the study has demonstrated that the procedural knowledge map improved decision accuracy, reduced related cost, heuristics, and enhanced confidence, but not satisfaction. Peer interaction made no difference in decision performance at all.

Codification Effect

Subjects provided with a procedural knowledge map were found to better understand the decision task, apply more appropriate forecasting method and consequently, make more accurate decisions and incur less cost than those performing the task without such a map. Subjects were also found to be more confident in the quality of their decisions. Interestingly, the k-map made no impact on user satisfaction.

The beneficial effect of this knowledge map is consistent with the theoretical expectations suggested by the KM literature (Eppler, 2003; Plumley, 2003; Wexler, 2001). The map used in this study presented critical stages of the decision-making process, and pointed to key knowledge areas required at each stage. Thus, it improved the visibility of knowledge in the time-series data, and helped participants to identify and locate it. The "reuse" economics (Hansen et al., 1999) can also explain the beneficial effect of the codification model found in this study. Once the k-map was developed and made available, it could allow fast and reliable reuse of explicit knowledge across the repetitive experimental trials.

The positive effect of the map can also be attributed to the nature of the task domain at hand. According to Kurtz and Snowden (2003), in ordered task domains, patterns are knowable, and the only issue is whether we can afford the time and resources to move from knowable to known. Applying methodology that seeks to identify the patterns through study of task properties is considered both legitimate and desirable. The procedural k-map in this study provided such a methodology. It facilitated the analysis and led to more appropriate responses in accordance with interpretation of that analysis.

The lack of any impact of k-map on perceived satisfaction is quite interesting. One would hope that the users provided with more sophisticated tool would also have more favourable attitudes towards it. However, according to Straub et al. (Straub, Limayem, & Karahanna-Evaristo, 1995), perceptual and behavioural scores can be radically different. This finding can be potentially attributed to the characteristics of the task context in which the investigation was carried out. The current study provided an iterative task context, with the k-map provided on the screen at all times. Constant reinforcement of the same guidelines could have irritated subjects and thus affected their satisfaction. In addition, subjects could have learnt the task over time through experience and from feedback, and would not feel the need for such a reminder after a while.

To test the potential learning effect, additional analysis of the collected data across five blocks of trials was done. The results confirm a significant main and no interaction effect of block on accuracy. As suggested, subjects tended to significantly improve the quality of their decisions over time. This was demonstrated by smaller errors (SAPE) found among these subjects in the later than in the earlier periods of the task (8.5% vs. 7.3% vs. 7.3% vs. 7.6% vs. 5.6%, F=7.817, p=0.000).

Personalisation Effect

With respect to personalisation, the current study found no significant impact on performance. Subjects provided with an opportunity for peer interaction were found to use similar forecasting methods and consequently, make similar quality decisions and incur similar costs as those performing the task on their own. The opportunity for peer interaction also made no difference in subjects' confidence and satisfaction.

The lack of beneficial effect of personalisation found is contrary to Nonaka's knowledge creation theory (Nonaka, 1998), which emphasises the critical importance of the process of socialisation for knowledge development. Rather, it agrees with the proposition that the impact of interaction on decision making is highly contingent upon the nature of the task. Previous empirical research found no significant effect of interaction in simple tasks, and significant positive impact in complex tasks (Handzic & Low, 2001). These results are in accord with the proposition that personalisation is more appropriate for unordered decision domains with more complex, uncertain, or novel problems, and codification for simpler, knowable, or repetitive tasks (Hansen et al., 1999; Kurtz & Snowden, 2003). However, the task used in this study was, by definition, neither simple nor complex, but complicated. As such, it was knowable, and subjects could theoretically learn from each other, but failed to do so.

One potential reason for the lack of personalisation effect on performance could be the level of expertise about the problem brought by the participants to the interactive act. For example, participants bringing similar levels of expertise to the interaction act are likely to enhance only confidence, but not accuracy of their decisions (Heath & Gonzales, 1995). However, our findings show that about one half of subjects in the current study had a good understanding of the task, as evidenced in their methods. So, there was an opportunity for those with less knowledge to learn from those with more knowledge through dialogue (Devlin, 1999).

The fact that this did not happen suggests the lack of trust in peer advice. A chat between peers is assumed to foster the development of trust, and provides a foundation for creative working. The persuasive arguments perspective (Heath & Gonzales, 1995) further assumes that an individual's position on any given issue may shift as a result of interaction with others due to the collection of persuasive arguments. However, conflict, status, and number of participants in the interactive act all may have an adverse effect on performance The current study tried to avoid these by limiting interaction to groups of two (Panko & Kinney, 1992; Schwartz, 1995), and by giving participants equal and dual judge-advisor roles. Despite all of this, the current study shows that participants placed greater reliance on technology than people when solving complicated problems.

Other Issues

With respect to overall performance, the study revealed relatively poor performance across all treatments. The poor overall accuracy and confidence resulting from simple heuristics could be potentially attributed to the lack of monetary incentives. Other similar studies (Handzic, 1997; Sniezek & Buckley, 1995) provided their students with substantial monetary rewards for their performance. It is possible that without monetary incentives, the subjects did not try as hard as possible to use the full potential of their KM solutions to improve decisions. By not giving extrinsic incentives, this study attempted to prevent knowledge "hoarding," and promote cooperation rather than competition among the participants. It was also assumed that graduates chosen from the pool of students attending an advanced master's level course should be motivated to do their best on the task by the intrinsic interest in the subject matter.

Alternatively, poor overall performance could be attributed to the characteristics of the task information and the task performers. The computerised knowledge repository available to participants in the current study with or without the procedural k-map was not sufficient to perform well on the task. The participants also needed analytical information such as an evaluation of the trend, season, and noise components, as well as the relevant know-how to integrate this information into a decision response. This crucial information was assumed to be a part of individual tacit knowledge. However, nonexpert participants were not likely to have high levels of the required tacit knowledge to perform well on the task without prior training or experience. An encouraging finding is that performance did improve over time.

In summary, the current study provides a number of interesting findings that may have some important implications for organisational KM strategies. First, they suggest that decision makers faced with complicated decision tasks may greatly benefit from codification strategy. Procedural k-maps may enhance critical knowledge visibility and usability, and thus alleviate the negative effects of task difficulty and subsequent use of decision heuristics. This, in turn, may result in improved decision accuracy and lead to desired business outcomes. Second, these findings suggest that pursuing personalisation instead of, or in addition to codification, may not be beneficial to decision performance. Overall, the current study findings provide important empirical support for Hansen et al.'s (1999) theory.

However, some caution is necessary regarding the generalisability of these findings due to a number of limiting factors. One of the limitations refers to the use of a laboratory experiment that may compromise external validity of research. Another limitation relates to artificial generation of time series that may not reflect the true nature of real business. The subjects chosen for the study were students and not real-life decision makers. The fact that they were mature graduates may mitigate the potential differences. No incentives were offered to the subjects for their effort in the study. Consequently, they could find the study tiring and unimportant and would not try as hard as possible. Most decisions in real business settings have significant consequences. Further study is necessary, which would address these limitations and extend current research to other tasks and contexts.

Conclusion

This chapter was able to show the ability of a procedural knowledge map to improve understanding and enhance performance of a forecasting task. From our research findings, one may conclude that codification KM strategy can effectively enhance decision makers' working knowledge and performance in the context of a complicated decision task. An alternative or additional personalisation strategy did not provide any benefit in such a task context. However, the study is not without limitations. Different techniques may have advantages and disadvantages under different situations and thus, careful consideration of different combinations of techniques is necessary. Further empirical research is recommended that would address some of these issues.

References

A. A. (1998, January). *The knowledge management practices book*. Australia: Arthur Andersen.

Alavi, M., & Leidner, D. E. (2001). Knowledge management and knowledge management systems: Conceptual foundations and research issues. *MIS Quarterly*, *25*(1), 107-136.

Ashton, R. H., & Kramer, S. S. (1980). Students as surrogates in behavioural accounting research: Some evidence. *Journal of Accounting Research*, *18*(1), 1-15.

Bender, S., & Fish, A. (2000). The transfer of knowledge and the retention of expertise: The continuing need for global assignments. *Journal of Knowledge Management, 4*(2).

Davenport, T. H., & Prusak, L. (1998). *Working knowledge: How organisations manage what they know*. Boston: Harvard Business School Press.

Devlin, K. (1999). *Infosense: Turning information into knowledge*, New York: W.H. Freeman and Company.

Earl, M. (2001). Knowledge management strategies: Toward a taxonomy. *Journal of Management Information Systems, 18*(1), 215-233.

Eppler, M. (2003). Making knowledge visible through knowledge maps: Concepts, elements, cases. In C. W. Holsapple (Ed.), *Handbook on Knowledge Management* (Vol. 1, pp. 189-205), Berlin: Springer-Verlag.

Fayyad, U., & Uthurusamy, R. (2002). Evolving into data mining solutions for insight. *Communications of the ACM, 45*(8), 28-31.

Grey, D. (1999). *Knowledge mapping: A practical overview.* Retrieved December 20, 2003, from http://www.smithweaversmith.com/knowledg2.htm

Hahn, J., & Subramani, M. R. (2000). A framework of knowledge management systems: Issues and challenges for theory and practice. In *Proceedings of the International Conference on Information Systems (ICIS 2000)* (pp. 387-398), Brisbane, Australia.

Handzic, M. (1996). *Utilisation of contextual information in a judgmental decision making task*. Unpublished PhD thesis, UNSW, Sydney, Australia.

Handzic, M. (1997). Decision performance as a function of information availability: An examination of executive information systems. In H. Rehesaar (Ed.), *Proceedings of the 2nd New South Wales Symposium on Information Technology and Information Systems*, Sydney: UNSW.

Handzic, M., & Hasan, H. (2003). The search for an integrated KM framework. In H. Hasan, & M. Handzic (Eds.), *Australian studies in knowledge management* (pp. 3-34). Wollongong: UOW Press.

Handzic, M., & Low, G. (2002). The impact of social interaction on performance of decision tasks of varying complexity. *OR Insight, 15*(1), 15-22.

Hansen, M. T, Nohria, N., & Tierney, T (1999, March-April). What's your strategy for managing knowledge? *Harvard Business Review*, 106-116.

Heath, C., & Gonzalez, R. (1995). Interaction with others increases decision confidence but not decision quality: Evidence against information collection views of interactive decision making. *Organisational Behaviour and Human Decision Processes, 61*(3), 305-326.

Janis, I. (1982). *Groupthink: Psychological studies of policy decisions and fiascoes.* Boston: Houghton-Miffin.

Kim, S., Suh, E., & Hwang, H. (2003). Building the knowledge map: An industrial case study. *Journal of Knowledge Management, 7*(2), 34-45.

Kurtz, C. F., & Snowden, D. J (2003). The new dynamics of strategy: Sense-making in a complex and complicated world. *IBM Systems Journal, 42*(3), 462-482.

Makridakis, S. (1993). Accuracy measures: Theoretical and practical concerns. *International Journal of Forecasting, 9,* 527-529.

Makridakis, S., & Wheelwright, S. C. (1989). *Forecasting methods for management.* New York: John Wiley & Sons.

Marakas, G. M. (1999). *Decision support systems in the 21st century.* Englewood Cliffs, NJ: Prentice Hall Inc.

Nonaka, I. (1998). The knowledge-creating company. In *Harvard Business Review on Knowledge Management.* Boston: Harvard Business School Press.

Nonaka, I., & Konno, N. (1998). The concept of ba: Building a foundation for knowledge creation. *California Management Review, 40*(3), 40-54.

Nonaka, I., & Takeuchi, H. (1995). *The knowledge creating company: How Japanese companies create the dynamics of innovation.* New York: Oxford University Press.

Panko, R., & Kinney, S. (1992). Dyadic organisation communication: Is the dyad different? In *Proceedings of the 25th Hawaii International Conference on Systems Sciences,* HI (pp. 244-253).

Plumley, D. (2003, March). Process-based knowledge mapping: A practical approach to prioritising knowledge in terms of its relevance to a business or KM objective. *Knowledge Management Magazine.*

Remus, W. (1996). Will behavioural research on managerial decision making generalise to managers? *Managerial and Decision Economics, 17,* 93-101.

Santosus, M. (2001). *KM and human nature.* Retrieved December 18, 2001, from http://www.cio.com/knowledge/edit/k121801_nature.html

Schwartz, D. (1995). The emergence of abstract representation in dyad problem solving. *The Journal of the Learning Sciences, 4*(3), 321-345.

Sniezek, J. A., & Buckley, T. (1995). Cueing and cognitive conflict in judge-advisor decision making. *Organisational Behaviour and Human Decision Processes, 62*(2), 159-174.

Straub, D., Limayem, M., & Karahanna-Evaristo, E. (1995). Measuring system usage: Implications for IS theory testing. *Management Science, 41*(8), 1328-1342.

Tsui, E. (2003). Tracking the role and evolution of commercial knowledge management software. In C. W Holsapple (Ed.), *Handbook on knowledge management* (Vol. 2, pp. 5-27). Berlin: Springer-Verlag.

Warkentin, M. E., Sayeed, L., & Hightower, R. (1997). Virtual teams versus face-to-face teams: An exploratory study of Web-based conference system. *Decision Sciences, 28*(4).

Wexler, M. (2001). The who, what, why of knowledge mapping. *Journal of Knowledge Management, 5*(3), 249-263.

Whitecotton, S. M. (1996). The effects of experience and a decision aid on the slope, scatter, and bias of earnings forecasts. *Organisational Behaviour and Human Decision Processes, 66*(1), 111-121.

Chapter XXII

Visions and Directions:
Balancing Academic and Practitioner Positions on KM

Abstract

This final chapter of the current book outlines key visions and directions for knowledge-management research and practice. The following sections present the results from a small survey of academics and practitioners about the present and future of knowledge management, a synthesised vision and direction for KM future, and the author's own views on how this book can help promote scholarly inquiry in the field.

Introduction

For the last chapter of this book, it was appropriate to consider what expectations were held about the future of KM. In order to help the author with direction setting and signal the kinds of topics and methods that may be particularly important, the author felt it was appropriate to obtain informed views of other academics and practitioners interested in KM. In order to achieve this, the author has decided to carry out the follow-up analysis of data from a small survey conducted by Edwards et al. (Edwards, Handzic, Carlsson, & Nissen, 2003) and compare views of academics and practitioners interested in KM.

However, readers are issued a "health warning" that the survey reported here does not reflect the kind of scale, detail, and rigour that one would normally expect for a research article (Edwards et al., 2003). For example, there are too few responses, there is a bias towards those who actively participate in certain KM activities, and the instrument used has not been validated. Thus, the survey design or results are not offered as an exemplar of rigour. Rather, the interest was to quickly "feel the pulse" of academics and practitioners, especially to help indicate the breadth of backgrounds and issues relevant to KM. Therefore, a relatively informal survey of researchers and professionals with an interest in KM was conducted.

The criterion for "interest in KM" was participation in KM conferences and e-mail lists (two of each). After pilot testing, 158 questionnaires were distributed to different people or e-mail addresses, although it is possible that, in a few cases, two distinct e-mail addresses may have represented the same person. One reminder was also sent by e-mail. Twenty-five usable questionnaires were returned, representing a response rate of 15.8%, which is acceptable by normal survey standards. The initial results of the collected survey data are reported in Edwards et al. (2003).

The results of our follow-up analysis comparing academic and practitioner views are presented in six sections. The first examines the respondents' demographic information. The second presents respondents' views about KM, influential ideas in KM, and influential people in KM. The next three sections examine their views on the most useful forms of support for KM activities; the most important types of KM technologies; and the most important factors in KM initiatives, respectively. The final results section presents respondents' views on the most important challenges facing research and practice in the field of knowledge management. The chapter and the book end with a synthesised vision and direction for KM from the author's perspective.

Survey of Academics and Practitioners

Of the total of 25 survey respondents, 68% were academics and 24% were practitioners. The remaining 8% were both. For the purpose of our analysis, these respondents were considered as parts of both academic and practitioner groups. The main objective of the analysis was to find out if there were any significant differences in the ways academics and practitioners think about the present and the future of knowledge management.

Respondent Profiles

The profile of the respondents in each group of interest (academics and practitioners) was examined in terms of their experience with KM, subject area of academic qualifications, and importance of KM to them as an area of work/interest.

Experience with KM

The survey results for experience with KM show similar distributions for two respondents' groups. Table 22.1 shows a high proportion of both academics and practitioners in the 3- to 4-year group (53% vs. 50%) and fewer respondents in the under 3, and 5-and-over groups. In particular, 16% academics and 13% practitioners had 1 to 2 years of experience with KM, 21% academics and 13% practitioners had between 5 and 10 years of experience, while the remaining 11% academics and 25% practitioners had over 10 years of experience with KM. While these responses suggest that KM is not a recent phenomenon, they also show that it has gained an increased popularity within the last couple of years.

Table 22.1. Respondents' experience in knowledge management

Years	Academics %	Practitioners %
< 3	16	13
3 - 4	53	50
5 - 10	21	13
>10	11	25

Subject Area of Qualifications

The survey results shown in Figure 22.1 indicate similar distributions for subject areas of qualifications for two respondents' groups. The majority of academics, as well as practitioners, had their most recent subject area either in business and economics (37% vs. 50%) or in engineering and information technology (47% vs. 38%). Other subject areas represented include social research, psychology, biology, and education (16% vs. 13%). A high proportion of respondents from business and technology areas suggests that these disciplines place particularly high value on knowledge management. The variety of other disciplines mentioned confirms the multidisciplinary nature of KM.

Importance of KM

Figure 22.2 shows that both survey respondents' groups have similar active interest or work in the area of KM. This is not surprising given the population sampled, but clearly indicates the relevance of the responses to the target audience at which this book is aimed. About two thirds of respondents from both the academic and practitioner group considered KM as their main area of interest or work (63% vs. 68%), while the remaining one third had a significant interest in KM (38% vs. 32%).

Figure 22.1. Subject area of respondents' qualifications

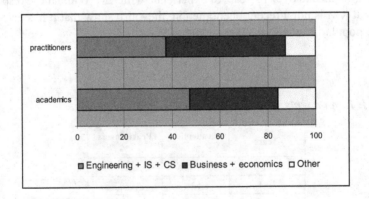

Figure 22.2. Importance of KM as an area of respondents' interest/work

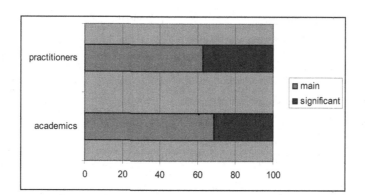

KM Foundations

This section compares the academic and practitioner respondents' opinions about the KM phenomenon, as well as their assessments of the most influential ideas and people in KM.

Opinions About KM

Table 22.2 compares academic and practitioner respondents' opinions about a series of 10 statements, in order to identify their positive and negative attitudes towards KM aspects. Each statement was rated by the respondents on a 5-point Likert scale, where 1=strongly disagree and 5=strongly agree. The table shows mean values for two respondent groups.

When asked about their opinion about knowledge, there was a high level of agreement between academics and practitioners (4.89 vs. 4.75) that "Some knowledge cannot be put into explicit form." This implies a widespread recognition of the *stickiness* of tacit knowledge. However, the groups held significantly different beliefs regarding the prime knowledge location. Academics tended to believe that "Knowledge only exists in the minds of humans" (3.89); practitioners disagreed (2.50). Similarly, academics tended to believe that "Organisational knowledge goes beyond that of its people" (4.00), practitioners did not (2.66). These results suggest that fundamentally different human- and object-orientated conceptualisations of knowledge may dominate academic and practitioner circles respectively.

Table 22.2. Most important ideas in KM

Statements	Academics	Practitioners	Difference
The divide between West & East needs to be bridged	3.84	3.00	ns
There is a split between Western & Eastern approaches	4.26	3.25	p=0.04
Knowledge only exists in the minds of humans	3.89	2.50	p=0.08
Organisational knowledge goes beyond that of its people	4.00	2.63	p=0.04
Most organisations see KM as a technological issue	3.74	3.38	ns
KM should be built around processes, not structure	3.89	4.25	ns
KM needs to be based on sound theory	4.05	3.75	ns
Some knowledge cannot be put into explicit form	4.89	4.75	ns
Organisations cannot use both collaboration & codification	2.00	2.25	ns
Collaboration approaches do not give enough help	3.00	3.13	ns

There was a shared view by academics and practitioners alike that "KM practice needs to be based on sound theory" (4.05 vs. 3.75), and that "KM should be built around processes, not structure" (3.89 vs. 4.25) of an organisation. Contrary to Zyngier et al. (Zyngier, Burstein, & Rodriguez, 2003), both groups of the respondents felt that "Most organisations see KM as a technological issue" (3.74 vs. 3.38). They also agreed, although marginally, with the view that "Collaboration approaches do not give enough help" (3.00 vs. 3.13) in implementation.

Finally, both groups of the respondents recognised that "There is a split between Western and Eastern approaches" to KM (4.26 vs. 3.25), but academics felt this split significantly stronger than practitioners. Interestingly, both groups only marginally felt that "The divide between West and East needs to be bridged" (3.84 vs. 3.00). This implies a fair degree of tolerance for differences in approaches to KM. This view is further reinforced by similarly strong opposition of both academics and practitioners to the idea that "Organisations cannot use both collaboration and codification" KM strategies together (2.00 vs. 2.25).

Influential Ideas in KM

Respondents were asked to give a textual response about the three most important ideas in KM. These ideas were grouped into the six categories: strategy (e.g. competitive advantage); culture (including organisational learning); intellectual and social capital; KM processes and practices; technology; and theories about KM.

The results shown in Table 22.3 reveal that theories about KM and KM processes and practices appeared most often among both academics (36% vs. 19%) and practitioners (33% vs. 44%). However, as might be expected, theories about KM were relatively more important to academics (36% vs. 19%), and KM processes and practices to practitioners (44% vs. 33%). This is perhaps unsurprising, given that there needs to be some sound theory before issues of practice and the application of theory can be really considered. Intellectual and social capital was the third most important category of ideas to academics (19%), while technology was more important to practitioners (11%). Business aspects were ranked fourth by academics and equal fourth with Intellectual and social capital by practitioners (11% vs. 6%). Technology was ranked fifth among academics with 9% responses. Finally, culture took the last, sixth place between both respondent groups (6% vs. 0%).

From the variety of themes reported in our earlier study (Edwards et al., 2003), the most frequently cited as important were an integrated content-narrative-context framework of KM, and the concept of communities of practice. The third most frequently cited idea was the explicit-tacit knowledge taxonomy. It was a little surprising that neither Nonaka and Takeuchi's (1995) SECI spiral model nor the codification-personalisation distinction of Hansen et al. (1998) received any first place rankings.

Table 22.3. Most important ideas in KM

Category of Ideas	Academics %	Practitioners %
Strategy (e.g., competitive advantage)	11	6
Culture (including org. learning)	6	0
Intellectual and social capital	19	6
KM process and practice	19	44
Technology	9	11
Theories about KM	36	33

Table 22.4. Most important authors in KM

Author	Academics %	Practitioners %
Nonaka (single or in team with Takeuchi)	33	13
Davenport (single or in team with Prusak)	20	20
Snowden	4	7
Others	43	60

Influential People in KM

The distribution of responses regarding most influential people in KM, shown in Table 22.4, identifies the same top three names (Nonaka, Davenport, and Snowden) in both respondents' groups. However, Nonaka was singled out as the most influential author by academics, while Davenport was more important to practitioners. Snowden holds a strong third position (when higher ranks are weighted more) in both groups. The remaining responses are divided evenly among more than 20 other authors.

KM Activities and Support

Respondents were asked to fill in what they believed were the most useful forms of support for a set of KM-related activities, under the headings of IT/software support and noncomputer support. The overall results, shown in Figure 22.3, indicate that the two respondent groups differed with respect to usefulness of IT and non-IT forms of support. Specifically, academics indicated non-IT forms of support more frequently as useful than IT forms, while practitioners found them similarly useful.

The detailed percentage responses, presented in Table 22.5, indicate that academics consider non-IT support more useful than IT support for all activities except one. Practitioners indicate IT support as more useful for one activity, and consider both IT and non-IT support equally useful for all others. Two elements of IT support responses worthy of mention include knowledge repositories for knowledge reten-

Figure 22.3. Preferences for different forms of support for various KM activities

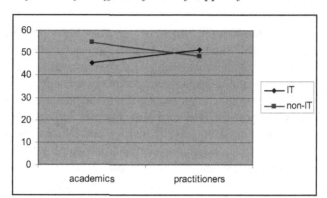

Table 22.5. Preferences for different forms of support for KM activities

Activity	Academics IT/non-IT	Practitioners IT/non-IT
Knowledge creation	44 / 56	50 / 50
Knowledge acquisition	47 / 53	50 / 50
Knowledge sharing	47/ 53	50 / 50
Knowledge retention	53 / 47	50 / 50
Knowledge valuation	27 / 73	50 / 50
Knowledge application	43 / 57	50 / 50
Knowledge discovery	47 / 53	60 / 40
Knowledge integration	47 / 53	50 / 50
Total	45 / 55	52 / 48

tion, and the role of data mining in knowledge discovery. Out of non-IT forms of support, brainstorming was mentioned most frequently in relation to knowledge creation, face-to-face interaction of some kind for knowledge sharing, patents for knowledge valuation, and team working for knowledge integration.

KM Technologies

Respondents were asked to write in "the most important types of technology that can provide support for KM" (up to three). Results, shown in Table 22.6, indicate that communication and collaboration technologies were cited as important more frequently by academics, and databases and document management systems by practitioners. This is consistent with answers given to the previous question on the most useful form of support for KM activities. Internet/intranet/extranet/portals combined were frequently cited, equally, by both groups. When considering other responses of high importance, search/retrieval and data-mining tools were rated among the three highest by academics, but not by practitioners. Overall, the results suggest practitioners' preference for codification and academics' preference for personalisation approaches to KM.

KM Influences

This section examines and compares the respondents' opinions about how KM relates to different aspects of an organisation's work. The respondents rated different factors in terms of the importance that *is usually placed* and *should be placed* on these factors in KM initiatives. Table 22.7 shows no significant differences between academic and practitioner groups in their perceived and desired importance levels. Hence, these responses were pooled for further analysis. The combined results are presented in Figure 22.4.

Table 22.6. Respondents' views of important types of technology to support KM

Type of technology	Academics %	Practitioners %
Internet/intranets/extranets/portal	25	22
Databases/document management systems	17	28
Communication/collaboration	27	17
Search/retrieval/mining	19	6
Other (various)	13	28

Figure 22.4. Comparison of importance placed on different KM factors

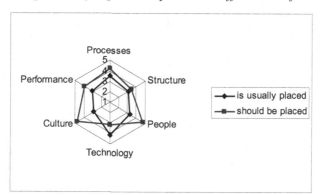

With respect to the importance that *is usually placed* on different aspects of an organisation's work in KM initiatives, the scores shown in Table 22.7 inform us that *technology* is the single most important aspect, with mean value of 4.15. It is followed by business *processes* (3.50), *people* (3.23), *structure* (3.13), and *performance* (3.00). In contrast, *culture* was indicated as being insufficiently considered in KM initiatives (2.80). Overall, these responses reveal a dominant role played by technology in an organisation's KM initiatives.

With respect to the importance that *should be placed* on different aspects of an organisation's work in KM initiatives, the scores in Table 22.7 show that respondents believed that much more importance should be placed on *people* (4.73), *culture* (4.69), *processes* (4.23), and *performance* (3.92), much less on *technology* (3.15), and about the same as is on *structure* (3.43). Overall, these responses reveal a desire to place a greater emphasis on human aspects of an organisation's work in an organisation's KM initiatives.

Interestingly, the overall average scores rose significantly, from 3.30 for the importance that *is usually placed* to 4.03 for the importance that *should be placed* on different aspects of an organisation's work in KM initiatives. This suggests a widespread belief that organisations need to consider KM initiatives more carefully, taking into account a broader range of factors.

Table 22.7. Comparison of importance placed on different factors

KM factor	Is usually placed			Should be placed			Is usually placed	Should be placed	
	A	P	dif	A	P	dif	A+P	A+P	dif
Processes	3.67	3.13	0.167	4.28	4.13	0.657	3.50	4.23	0.006
Structure	3.06	3.29	0.688	3.56	3.14	0.377	3.13	3.43	0.411
People	3.22	3.25	0.963	4.83	4.50	0.283	3.23	4.73	0.000
Technology	4.11	4.25	0.658	3.22	3.00	0.693	4.15	3.15	0.000
Culture	2.78	3.00	0.663	4.72	4.63	0.749	2.80	4.69	0.000
Performance	3.00	3.00	1.000	3.83	4.14	0.467	3.00	3.92	0.017
Total	3.31	3.32	0.958	4.08	3.92	0.432	3.30	4.03	0.000

Note: A—academics, P—practitioners

Challenges for Research and Practice

The following section summarises major challenges for knowledge management research and practice identified from a variety of themes in responses obtained. For further details, readers should refer to Edwards et al. (2003). With respect to research, the challenge mentioned most often (20%) was the need for a consistent and cohesive theory supported by empirical evidence to provide sound and stable foundations for the field. This is one of the main objectives of this book. Other often-indicated challenges were connecting research and practice (8%), and finding and measuring business benefits (8%). Notable issues mentioned by the remaining 64% of the respondents include tacit knowledge, context, and integration of disparate KM elements.

With respect to practice, the challenge mentioned most often (16%) was evaluation and measurement. Among other, more often mentioned, challenges were choosing right KM strategy (8%), creating trust-based organisational culture (8%), and demonstrating value of and motivating people to share knowledge (8%). The remaining 60% responses reflected a wide variety of elements including demystification, gaining acceptance, regaining credibility, and making KM a part of practice and daily processes of an organisation.

Synthesised Vision and Direction for KM

From the questionnaire responses, it is clear that knowledge management covers a very broad and somewhat fragmented field. The people who are interested in, and involved in knowledge management come from different educational backgrounds, and have a wide range of concerns. However, there is a constructive tension in place, between *difference* and *integration* (Chae & Bloodgood, 2004).

The author of this book embraces difference, as evidenced by a wide variety of studies presented in 22 chapters that differ in perspectives on knowledge (explicit and tacit), in levels of analysis (individual, group and organisational), in the concerns of research, and those of practice (e.g., people, culture, structure, technology, processes, and performance). It is our strongly held belief that these differences serve to make the book more fruitful and relevant to a wider community. However, they are embraced in a spirit of integration, of debate, of complementarity, and of building bridges between research and practice.

One specific issue identified from the questionnaire responses is a strong disagreement between academics and practitioners on whether "knowledge only exists in the minds of humans" and whether "organisational knowledge goes beyond that of its people." This suggests that more future research is needed to address the nature of knowledge and articulate its unique aspects as distinct from information and data. Another stream of research could address the question of the most valuable knowledge for competitive advantage. Every organisation houses valuable intellectual material. However, the importance of different human, structural, and relational capital may be highly contingent upon business tasks and processes, as proposed earlier by Hansen, Nohria, and Tierney (1999).

Another important specific issue is identified by respondents' concern for KM activities and forms of support. From the questionnaire responses, it is clearly visible that academics are more concerned with communication and collaboration activities and non-IT forms of support, while practitioners pay more attention to IT-based initiatives, particularly those for storage and organisation of explicit knowledge. This suggests the need for models that will integrate and reconcile the demands of diverse behavioural and technocratic (as well as economic) perspectives on knowledge management. This book seeks common ground between different perspectives, and integrates them into a holistic driver-context-enabler-process-knowledge-outcome framework of KM presented in Chapter I. For more information about this and other integrated approaches to KM, readers are referred to Nonaka and Takeuchi (1995), Liebowitz and Megbolugbe (2003), and Handzic and Zhou (2005).

There is another important specific issue shown by survey respondents' concern about the emphasis that they believe is currently given to technology in KM initiatives, although they still rate technology as an important factor. Resolving the issue of the "right" place and role of IS/IT in KM will require further research on whether and how successfully IS/IT can be integrated into processes of creation, transfer, and utilisation of knowledge in organisations. This book hints at some helpful forms of IT support. For more information on these and other useful IT-based KM initiatives, readers are referred to our earlier book *Knowledge Management: Through the Technology Glass* (Handzic, 2004). What remains to be looked into by future research is how different IT and non-IT knowledge management initiatives may interact to create potential synergy effects.

The most important single KM challenge identified from the questionnaire responses (that binds all issues together) is to produce a coherent and cohesive body of theory, based on empirical evidence (Edwards et al., 2003). This book fills some of the existing theory-practice gap identified by Alavi and Leidner (2001). It includes important empirical research that produces detailed answers to the questions of why a particular KM initiative works, for whom, and in what circumstances. This research is done with the necessary rigour called for by Handzic and Hasan (2003) to ensure objectivity and convince people, whether academic or practitioner, of the usefulness of knowledge management and its study, as well as to warn them of its limitations.

Specific aspects where special emphasis may be needed in future research include: what KM offers above information management, the role of information systems and IT in KM, KM in the extended and perhaps virtual organisation (Edwards et al., 2003). Other useful lines of inquiry may consider: exploring KM initiative-culture fit, determining methods of making users active knowledge contributors, uncovering what knowledge to include in KM systems, and examining KM benefits (Alavi & Leidner, 1999).

Both strategic issues (e.g., competitive advantage, motivation to participate, creativity, and innovation) and operational issues (e.g., knowledge currency, methodologies, technical standards) need to be addressed (King, Marks, & McCoy, 2002). The issues of trade-offs between knowledge sharing within and across organisations, technological and organisational barriers, explicit and tacit knowledge, technology, and people, will continue to be of interest in the future (Becerra-Fernandez, Gonzales, & Sabherwal, 2004). Research on these topics may benefit from a focus on possible links between knowledge and business strategy, on knowledge processes that make knowledge actionable, and on aligning the technical and social elements for knowledge management. This, in turn, will require many researchers and practitioners working together in a holistic and systematic manner. With such an approach, there is a good chance that the field will evolve and mature by producing sound methods and tools. Without this kind of work, there is an imminent danger that the hype surrounding KM will kill off the field and have it dismissed as a fad.

This book is trying to play its part in helping to produce and disseminate the coherent and cohesive body of theory of KM. In doing so, it is offering an integrated KM approach, balance of social and technical aspects, theory and practice, and research rigour. To further advance understanding of knowledge and how it should be managed, much more needs to be done. Some readers may be inspired to undertake research on one of the KM issues and challenges described. Alternatively, they may find that they can apply some of approaches, methods, and tools described in practice.

References

Alavi, M., & Leidner, D. E. (1999, February). Knowledge management systems: Issues, challenges, and benefits. *Communications of AIS, 1*, Article 7.

Alavi, M., & Leidner, D. E. (2001). Knowledge management and knowledge management systems: Conceptual foundations and research issues. *MIS Quarterly, 25*(1), 107-136.

Becerra-Fernandez, I., Gonzales, A., & Sabherwal, R. (2004). *Knowledge management: Challenges, solutions, and technologies.* Upper Saddle River, NJ: Pearson Education, Inc.

Chae, B., & Bloodgood, J. M. (2004, August). Paradoxes in knowledge management: A dialectic perspective, In *Proceedings of the Tenth Americas Conference on Information Systems,* New York (pp. 2284-2294).

Edwards, J., Handzic, M., Carlsson, S., & Nissen, M. (2003). Knowledge management research and practice: Visions and directions. *Knowledge Management Research & Practice, 1*(1), 49-60.

Handzic, M. (2004). *Knowledge management: Through the technology glass.* Singapore: World Scientific Publishing.

Handzic, M., & Hasan, H. (2003). Continuing the knowledge management journey, In H. Hasan, & M. Handzic (Eds.), *Australian Studies in Knowledge Management.* Wollongong: UOW Press.

Hansen, M. T, Nohria, N., & Tierney, T. (1999). What's your strategy for managing knowledge? *Harvard Business Review, 77*(2), 106-116.

Handzic, M., & Zhou, A. Z. (2005). *Knowledge management: An integrative approach.* Oxford, UK: Chandos Publishing.

King, W. R., Marks. P. V., & McCoy, S. (2002, September). The most important issues in knowledge management. *Communications of the ACM,* 95.

Liebowitz, J., & Megbolugbe, I. (2003). A set of frameworks to aid the project manager in conceptualising and implementing knowledge management initiatives. *International Journal of Project Management, 21*, 189-198.

Nonaka, I., & Takeuchi, H. (1995). *The knowledge creating company: How Japanese companies create the dynamics of innovation.* New York and Oxford: Oxford University Press.

Zyngier, S. M., Burstein, F., & Rodriguez, M. L. (2003). Knowledge management strategies in Australia: Analysis of uptake and understanding, In H. Hasan, & M. Handzic (Eds.), *Australian studies in knowledge management.* Wollongong: UOW Press.

About the Author

Meliha Handzic is currently acting dean and associate professor of information systems at Sarajevo School of Science and Technology, a partner of the University of Buckingham, UK, and adjunct faculty at Universitas 21 Global, Singapore. She received her PhD in information systems from the University of New South Wales, Australia, where she taught and led a research group until 2004. Her main research interest lies in the area of knowledge management with a particular focus on processes and sociotechnological enablers of knowledge creation, sharing, retention, and discovery in the context of decision making. Handzic has published four books: *Australian Studies in Knowledge Management, Managing Software Engineering Knowledge, Knowledge Management: Through the Technology Glass, Knowledge Management: An Integrative Approach*, and over 100 articles in international journals and conference proceedings. Presently, she is an active member of several professional societies and groups including AIS, IFIP TC8, and IAIM, regional editor of the journal *Knowledge Management Research & Practice*, and serves on editorial boards, executive, and program committees for several international journals and conferences. Prior to joining academia, Handzic worked for the United Nations Development Programme in Asia and Africa. She also has had a wide-ranging industrial experience in Europe.

Index

C

codification or personalisation 279–296
collective effectiveness 193–207
communities of practice 193–207
  social aspects 195

D

decomposition 86

E

e-learning
  perceptions 112

group level analysis 115
qualitative analysis 114
quantitative analysis 112
portal 107–118
electronic
  brainstorming 47–57
  idea generation 47–57
  system
    description 49
    genex framework 49
  memory 69–83
exercising space 151–163
experiential learning 152

G

groupware 58–68

I

incentives and rewards 233–244
inquiry systems 18–31
  Hegelian inquirer 21
  Kantian inquirer 21
  knowledge workers
    survey of 28
  Leibnizian inquirer 20
  Lockean inquirer 21
  review of 20–22
  Singerian inquirer 22
IT community description 198

K

knowledge
  application 38
    automating 132–150
  availability 69–83
  availablity
    decision making 71
  basic concepts 1–17
  creation 36–37
  credibility 119–131
  discovery
    approaches 98
    data-mining 99
    technologies 98
  gain 18–31
  interpretation 84–95
  management (KM) 1–17
    activities and support 304
    adapted framework 265
    components
      examples of 16
    cultivation professionals 245–262
      cross-cultural teaching and learning
        254
      innovative teaching and learning 250
      interactive teaching and learning 252
    curriculum development 249

  foundations 301
  influences 306
  initiatives 1
  model 33–36
    anatomy of 11
    ba 33–34
    cynefin 35–36
    Handzic k-space 39
  strategy 279–296
    review 281
  technologies 306
miner 96–106
  discovery
    pattern 96–106
sharing 233–244
  attitudes 221–232
  personal interaction 164–178
  social interaction 166
  technologies 60
space 32–46
storage 37
transfer 37

L

learning 1–17
  organisational 5–7

M

management 1–17
memory 1–17
  corporate 3–17
    mechanisms
      socially orientated 7–8
      technology-based 8–10

N

neural network 132–150
  empirical study 137
  literature review 134

O

organisational culture 221–232

Q

quality
  concept of 121
quality monitor system (QMS) 119–131
  empirical study 122

S

social environment 164–178
socialisation
  creativity 210
  formal 208–220
  informal 208–220
  innovation 210
  mode of 208–220
specialist training 245–262

T

task
  complexity 181
  contingencies 179–192
theory vs. practice 263–278

U

user experience 107–118

V

visions and directions 297–312
visualisation system 84–95